DATE DUE

DEMCO, INC. 38-2931

D1058885

The Haygoods
of Columbus

A LOVE STORY

WIL HAYGOOD

The Haygoods
of Columbus

A Love Story

A Peter Davison Book

HOUGHTON MIFFLIN COMPANY

BOSTON • NEW YORK

1997

Copyright © 1997 by Wil Haygood

For information about permission to reproduce selections
from this book, write to Permissions,
Houghton Mifflin Company, 215 Park Avenue South,
New York, New York 10003.

For information about this and other Houghton Mifflin trade
and reference books and multimedia products, visit
The Bookstore at Houghton Mifflin on the World Wide Web
at http://www.hmco.com/trade/.

Library of Congress Cataloging-in-Publication Data
Haygood, Wil.
The Haygoods of Columbus : a love story / Wil Haygood.
p.   cm.
"A Peter Davison book."
ISBN 0-395-67170-1
1. Haygood, Wil — Family. 2. Haygood family.
3. Columbus (Ohio) — Biography.   I. Title.
F499.C753H39 1997
977.1'57043'0922 — dc20   96-36736 [B] CIP

Printed in the United States of America

Book design by Robert Overholtzer

QUM 10 9 8 7 6 5 4 3 2 1

FOR STEVE FLANNIGAN

What thou lovest well remains, the rest is dross
What thou lov'st well shall not be reft from thee
What thou lov'st well is thy true heritage

— EZRA POUND, CANTO LXXXI

1

Any life seems an accumulation of events, fate, some luck. When I was a little boy, in love with nature, with fishing, I'd walk alone the two miles to the Olentangy River dam in my hometown of Columbus, Ohio. I'd dance across slippery rocks, water swirling underneath and the dam gushing near my face, until I reached my favorite spot, which lay right below the center of the dam. I'd stand there on rocks, balancing myself, with rising woods in the distance, and I'd disappear into thought, fast-moving fish, sunlight glinting off the water, the water moving downriver. The dam at my back turned noiseless, the entire world went silent. It was the one place in the city, however, that my grandmother did not wish me to go. Boys sometimes disappeared at that dam, beneath its cold waters, the life drained from them. But I fished happily, kept safe for some mysterious reason, falling now and then but never in water past my waist, and even then rising quickly with a deep secret in my chest: I did not know how to swim.

Not long ago my mother, Elvira, handed me a watch. It's a beautiful timepiece, squared and edged in maroon, dead of time now, just old. It belonged to her father, Jimmy, my grandfather. It is the first thing my mother has ever given me that has led back to her family. My mother has never made a habit of looking back. Jimmy received the watch from his Uncle Doc, my great-great-uncle. I remember Uncle Doc, an old shiny man with grainy eyes full of mystery. He lived alone in a rooming house on Mt. Vernon Avenue, back in the days when a man could live in a rooming house and still hold his head high.

I never knew what my grandfather Jimmy and Uncle Doc did before arriving in Columbus. There were things in my family I guess I was not meant to know. I never knew Jack, my father, never knew him like a son knows a father, even as I came to love that man, his voice heavy and sweet. I never knew why my mother sometimes disappeared. Never for more than two days. Her destination could be near as Mt. Vernon Avenue. Sometimes it was more exotic, all the way up to Detroit, Michigan, three pairs of dangerous high heels in her suitcase, a weekend of partying with relatives. Still, it seemed like an eternity. My tummy would fill up like a cup with loneliness, and I'd cry. For years I didn't know about my brother the pimp, Jack's bastard son, who in due time came rolling thunderously into all of our lives.

The things I knew seemed fine enough. I knew how to find my jar of marbles in the dark. I knew that living on the north side of Columbus in a green house with yellow trim, a back yard with a dirt hill, a raspberry bush to run circles around, I was happy. Sometimes I floated; I swear, it felt like I floated through days, mornings, afternoons. Even now I sometimes wake up on the edge of sleep and try to summon back that time and place, the way the air felt in that midwestern town, the leafy autumn days, human voices butterflying through screen doors, the shuffle of old men's shoes — Jimmy's brothers, my great-uncles. I never thought about why we lived with our grandparents. I certainly never thought about how oddly matched a couple my grandparents seemed. Or why it was my grandmother's voice I heard telling me to stay away from the Olentangy River dam, not my mother's.

My green house: I believed forever meant just that — forever. We'd live in that house forever. But we didn't. In the summer of 1968 my mother moved our family to the east side of Columbus, across town and over the St. Clair Avenue bridge. She disrupted my life and tried to renew her own. I could hardly blame her for doing that. But it was an upheaval, and it seemed not only strange but scary. By the end of that first summer, there were only two things I wanted to do in the whole wide world. I wanted to learn how to bounce a basketball better. And I wanted to get to know Elvira, my mother. She had started that disappearing again.

She was up on Mt. Vernon Avenue mostly. There were nightclubs on that avenue. There were men in straw hats who drove Hudson automobiles. Actually, there was more than that — my mother met my father, Jack Haygood, on that avenue, in front of the Pythian Theatre. The Pythian had acts on its stage from New York City. The Pythian even had a rococo stage. My mother thought she might become a fashion model. A photographer had hung a photograph of her inside his studio on the avenue. She became a waitress instead. It was the kind of avenue where you kept smiling even if your best dream got turned around.

You learned about things on Mt. Vernon Avenue. About things that hummed, that flew: life. I came to learn that it was the one avenue in our town that kept the town honest. It had honesty and — although I didn't know what the word meant at the time — seduction. Things were done under the cover of darkness. My grandmother Emily was fond of saying — and saying it slowly, which gave the words a chill all their own — "The things you do in the dark will come to light." A brother who hung out at the Vernon Club on Mt. Vernon Avenue and talked of going to Hollywood made it to Hollywood. But when I went in search of him years later, I found him on Skid Row in a cardboard box, the sunny look gone from his handsome face. My half-brother, Macaroni, the pimp — how ridiculous that word now sounds — was a Mt. Vernon Avenue legend. That is, until he had to flee. Bounty hunters were looking for him. I had to chase after Macaroni too, found him in California too, settled high on the Marin County hills by San Francisco with a beautiful view of the ocean. It was the west wing cellblock of San Quentin Penitentiary.

By the time my mother handed me my grandfather's watch, I had become a writer, someone always flooded with questions, accustomed to traveling and running down answers. Time haunts and a clock gets rewound; old unanswered mysteries start to pull. Fresh off Mt. Vernon Avenue, I too journeyed. My brothers went west; I went east, to New York City. I didn't drown in that dam, but I found myself staring at the world from a dingy seventeen-dollar-a-night room in New York, shaking with fear.

This is the chronicle of a family's odyssey, about how we got from there to here, and the misfortune — and luck — along the way. It is about the things that came to light. It is about Jimmy and Emily, my grandparents. And there are some things here about my mother's Mt. Vernon Avenue, the blood and rhythm it offered a town, that special way it could draw a long-necked woman out of her waitress uniform and into her girdle, her sequins and lamé. I guess my mother wore a girdle to make her behind look tight. I guess that's what made those high heels so dangerous. Elvira preferred the Idle-a-While, a darkened bar up on the avenue. You might run across some rude characters; it could get a little raunchy. My mother thought the place had class. Pretty music floated from the jukebox. The bartender knew what she drank: she was a bourbon lady, always had been. When she was gone from the lock of my eyes, however, I pouted. I wanted my mother back. I didn't know what was out there in the dark. I wondered why my mother had to go to Mt. Vernon Avenue every Friday and Saturday night, leaving me wide awake to dream myself to sleep with this question on my mind: will she come back?

2

Iт wᴀs ᴀ sᴍᴀʟʟ southern town that had suffered mightily during the Civil War. The Alabama River snaked through it, roiling beneath craggy bluffs. My mother was born, along with a twin brother, in 1932 in a tiny farmhouse in the woods of Selma, Alabama. It was March 18, and the woods would have been chilly. There were two colored hospitals in Selma, but they were considered a luxury. So the twins were delivered at home by a midwife. Both babies were sickly. It was feared that they would not survive. Their grandmother gathered herbs from the woods and fed them raw to the babies. She rocked in a chair, prayed, and watched as they steadily improved, becoming healthy.

Jimmy Burke, my mother's father, was a farmer. He learned farming on his father's farm with his brothers. There were eight Burke sons; Jimmy was the oldest. The sons were all hard men, short in height and good with their fists. They loved their mother deeply but feared John Burke, their father.

John Burke whipped his boys until he drew blood. That was his version of discipline. After a whipping, he'd go silent, his eyes as still as buttons. It was John Burke's fist that Jimmy and his brothers would always hear pounding on the door in the morning; the sun had risen, it was time to work — get up. John Burke was not talkative. He was an unsmiling man who hated to see any one of his sons sitting, whistling, daydreaming. Those who knew him in Selma regarded him as a dependable man and a good farmer, the kind of man who kept a little money in the bank. He rode around Selma in a Model T Ford, a possession for which he was admired. The sons got around in a horse-driven buggy. On their farm the Burkes planted collard greens, okra, tomatoes, peanuts, of course cotton. The twins, Elvira and Ira, hated picking cotton, complained about the sun and the wide fields, which looked as if they could swallow a child up whole. The Burke sons loaded their cotton onto steamships that sat at the docks behind Water Avenue in Selma, then watched the ships chug off down the Alabama River.

Both of my grandfather's parents had seen slavery with their own eyes in and around Alabama's Black Belt. It was called the Black Belt because of its dark, rich soil. Years later, after I had read books, I asked my grandfather about his mother and slavery. He shut down on me like a winter night. I never asked again.

Selma fell to Union troops on April 2, 1865. Looting and burning followed the clash. The town committed itself to rebuilding after the war. By 1925 it looked almost quaint. Those who weren't farming worked with the Southern Railroad. When they could find work, black women worked as domestics.

When there was time, Jimmy hunted with his brothers. They'd hunt mink, little elusive furry creatures that you had to set traps to catch. The traps were set alongside logs out in the swamps. Lacy, one of Jimmy's brothers, proved to be the best mink hunter. Lacy was talkative, had a whiny voice, counted every penny he slipped into his pockets, and could stay in the woods alone for hours. When a mink had been caught in one of his traps, he'd raise the thing up to the light, then he'd grin himself all the way home. Lacy and my grandfather sent their minks parcel post up to the F. C. Taylor Fur Company in St. Louis. They considered the fifteen dollars they received for each pelt more than fair. Sometimes Jimmy and Lacy and the other brothers snared red foxes. F. C. Taylor Company paid only ten dollars for each red fox. Lacy smiled anyway.

The Burke brothers did, however, find time to play. There was a colored minor-league baseball team in Selma. The brothers were crazy about the Selma Cloverleafs. They'd hustle up into the stands and square their short, squat bodies in the seats, grunting, twisting, more controlled than animated. Jimmy and his brothers played the game themselves. Some afternoons, farming chores finished, they'd gather in a wide open field. Jimmy, built low to the ground, preferred the outfield. Bending over, working his jawbone, he would see blades of grass, earth, open sky, and the silhouette of the batter. Jimmy chewed tobacco as if it were food.

It was the Depression, with its wide claws, that wiped out the Burke farm in 1937. The sons scuffled off to find work. John Burke did not have an ounce of sentiment to give. The sons would have to find their own way out of the darkness. Jimmy got a job in the Selma brickyards. He made bricks, shoving them into hot ovens. They'd come out in all kinds of colors. But the job didn't last, and in 1938 he picked his family up, the three children and his wife, and moved the eighty-five miles over to Birmingham.

My grandfather Jimmy met his wife, Emily, on a Saturday afternoon in Selma. He courted her by taking her to socials and to hayrides. His smile was both tricky and infrequent: a man smiling to himself when he managed to smile at all. He did not tell jokes, nor did he engage in idle conversation. He was a one-way mirror — blunt, dependable, and heroic to himself. A woman had to take that reflection or leave it; it would not change. He dressed beautifully: stickpins beneath his starched collars, pleated and cuffed slacks that fell just so, cottony three-button roll suits. He could not stand unshined shoes. When the heels on his dress shoes began to show the slightest wear, they were replaced. Often he would size a man up by the kind of shoes he wore. Emily liked the fact he had a job in the Selma brickyards, never missed a day. "Anybody who had a job was somebody," says Aunt Bell, my grandmother's sister. Emily feared John Burke, and when she and Jimmy eloped to Anniston — a double ceremony with another couple — John Burke was livid.

Jimmy found work in Birmingham as a groundskeeper out at the Bob Riley Airport, pushing a broom, raking. Emily found work ironing and washing. She also sewed. Her Singer sewing machine had been a gift from her mother, Minnie, who had purchased it from a traveling salesman who traveled Alabama with the sewing machines swinging from the back of his mule. Emily had long black hair and high red cheekbones. She was part Cherokee. Her father, Thornton, had been an orphan during the Civil War. He roamed the woods, his pockets filled with red pepper. Cornered by strangers, he'd throw the pepper into their eyes and flee. I've seen pictures of Thornton Powell, my grandmother's father. He looks the way Booker T. Washington looks in all those schoolbooks: proud, severe, and unshakable.

In a span of two years Emily and Jimmy had three children

— the twins, Ira and my mother, Elvira, and their sister Creola — then abruptly stopped. My mother looked up one day into the sky and there was Jimmy, zooming over a field in an airplane. It was hard to believe. My mother and her brother and sister squealed. It had only been thirty-five years since the Wright brothers had first flown their wondrous contraption at Kitty Hawk. Now here was Jimmy Burke in an airplane. It was just a crop-duster, and he was just a passenger, but still, my mother talks about it to this day — the first black man she saw in an airplane, her daddy, floating, flying over segregated Birmingham.

Jimmy and Emily Burke wanted to leave Birmingham. There was always food on the table; no child under their roof ever felt hunger pangs. They just couldn't see opportunity in the South for their children. The children were always complaining about being out in the cotton fields; Jimmy's salary was paltry; Emily had to compete with all the other women who were ironing and washing clothes for pay. There was always news about big steel plants in the North, about jobs and better wages. The North was far enough away that sometimes it merely seemed like a dream. Then my great-great-uncle — Uncle Doc — hoboed his way up through the Carolinas, hopping trains, rumbling around the mountains of Kentucky: our Christopher Columbus. He landed in Columbus in 1939. That was a wicked year, and he was just happy to be out of Alabama.

Uncle Doc was a muscular man with a mouthful of pretty white teeth. He had a strong jawbone on his square face and bloodshot eyes. His voice was deep, musical. In Columbus he made his way over to Mt. Vernon Avenue. Already the avenue was in constant motion, all jumpy, some juke joints and all-night bars in action. Big bands were wailing over at the American Legion. Uncle Doc could feel the earth move a little on that avenue. He wished to stay put and found himself a room. Then he looked for work.

He found a job in construction, lifting cement in buckets to build the buildings downtown. He didn't bore ladies with his job description. He preferred chatting about the little quartet he had joined, singing up and down Mt. Vernon Avenue, grinning his milk-and-honey grin. Uncle Doc found time to write to Jimmy and Emily. They were flat, plain letters. Basically, they said this: Come north. Uncle Doc squeezed a little money into the envelopes — northern money.

It wasn't long before Uncle Doc walked into Vernon Tailors. Abraham Bonowitz, the proprietor, had a beautiful store, full of glass cases, shirts inside the glass cases. Bonowitz had fled persecution in Poland, hoarded his money when he got to Columbus, bought himself a tailor's shop. It wasn't long before Uncle Doc had a closetful of beautiful suits, hats perfectly blocked to match the suits, shoes perfectly shined. He lifted cement, but he dressed like a fancy-pants musician. Uncle Doc wore a diamond ring on his finger, told time by a gold-and-maroon watch. And he carried a walking stick. Uncle Doc was a long way from Alabama and knew it. When some of his relatives finally reached Columbus and saw him flashing money, raising that walking stick to point out directions, buying rounds of drinks inside bars on Mt. Vernon Avenue — the same Uncle Doc who had been living nickel to dime in Selma, who had been loading bales of cotton onto wagons — they were amused. "A so-called bigshot," sniffed Uncle Lacy when asked his first impressions upon seeing Uncle Doc in the North.

Uncle Doc's plain letters must have sounded like poetry to Jimmy and Emily. By the time Jimmy reached Columbus, Uncle Doc, who had now grown fastidious in his manners, was hosting guests where he lived, fussing with them to wipe their feet at the door to the single room he rented in a boarding house. He kept his walking stick in a corner of his room.

Jimmy Burke went to Columbus all alone in the summer of 1940. He was a cautious man and would not drag his wife and children up north without a job. Emily and the children waited in Birmingham. While they waited, they fretted, for Jimmy had never been so far away. Emily bent her back over her sewing machine. Her sewing kept food on the table. Jimmy quickly found work on the Pennsylvania Railroad, working at the Columbus roundhouse, fixing train parts, laying track. The roundhouse was set on a swath of land off Joyce Avenue on the city's north side. Uncle Doc showed Jimmy Columbus, showed him all of Mt. Vernon Avenue, and grinned in Jimmy's face, picking up the tab for drinks.

Jimmy saved his money and sent it south. Emily laid the money in her Bible. After six months of waiting, she packed her belongings, including her pretty Singer sewing machine, took her three children, and boarded a train north. "I remember the train ride was long and dusty," recalls my mother. She hunched up against the window; the land passed by like a series of postcards flapping just beyond the windows. When the train crossed the Ohio border, segregation fell away and they all went to roomier sections of the train.

The family moved into a small house on Nineteenth Avenue, within walking distance of the railroad yards where Jimmy worked. Sometimes in the mornings Jimmy saw men in his back yard, unfolding from sleep. They'd hopped off the trains during the night and taken to the ground. Jimmy didn't bother them and they didn't bother him. Emily quickly found work downtown at the Deschler Hotel, back in the kitchen, where she cooked.

In the next few years, five of my grandfather's brothers

came north. Every one brought his shotgun with him. Lacy, the mink hunter, was happy to get out of Alabama. With World War II, there was a shortage of metals, which meant there was a shortage of mink traps. Lacy was joined by Thomas, Joe Nathan, and David. Henry, the baby, remained in Alabama. When Joe Nathan took his wife, Suzy, back home to meet his father, it was Henry, dark and bony and quick to laugh, who met them at the train station. They bumped along the country roads in a horse and buggy, Henry full of questions about the North. It didn't take long before Henry joined his brothers in Columbus. He glided into World War II factory work. Just as Uncle Doc had showed Jimmy Mt. Vernon Avenue, now Jimmy showed the avenue to Henry. Henry wore baggy suits and had a country-boy whistle. He never missed a day of work, drank hard liquor, and bragged about the single-barrel shotgun he had brought north from Alabama.

The Burke brothers found jobs in the steel plants and at the post office. They spent time together, drinking, chasing women, letting Uncle Doc whisper them around town in his pink Cadillac. Jimmy, who drank homemade corn liquor in the South, drank barroom liquor up north. And he drank too much. He'd come home and lope off toward the kitchen, gulping icewater before he threw up, as if the ice and water would keep his insides from exploding. It rarely did. Thomas, the shyest Burke, the post office Burke, would look at Jimmy and shake his head. One night Jimmy keeled over, bleeding on the inside. The doctors told him if he kept drinking, he'd die. The brothers stepped into his hospital room in their soft-soled shoes. He lay there surrounded by them, the hard short Burke men, never very talkative, their language sometimes reduced to grunts, hard stares, the rubbing of the brim of a fedora. They told Jimmy what the doctors had told him.

*Twins run in the family: first my mother and her brother, Ira,
then my sister* WONDER *and me. Wonder beat me into the
world by a full minute.*

Jimmy lay there in his own silence. He was stubborn, and hardly a self-pitying man. No one could tell whether he wanted to live or die. Jimmy left the hospital and went home to Emily and his children. He never took another drink. He had resolve.

In his spare time, however, Jimmy took to gambling. He gambled on horses and dogs; he fancied greyhounds. Emily could not see how they could save money to buy a house. She had begun saving her money for a down payment on a house, which she wanted badly. She'd get what money she could from Jimmy before he hustled out to the racetrack. It was a slow way to save. It took years, but in 1955 they took a mortgage on a house at 1343 North Fifth Street, still on the north side. It was actually in that house that I first became aware of the colors of the world, that I first felt myself breathing outward.

There had already been a lot of dissatisfaction in my mother's life by 1954, the year I was born, along with my twin sister. Wilber and Wonder, twins, like Ira and Elvira. A year later Elvira Haygood, all of twenty-two years old with five children, had traveled the last mile of her brief marriage. She moved into the house her parents had just purchased.

Our neighborhood was working-class and integrated. It was surrounded by factories, by the Jeffrey Company and D. L. Auld. The house we lived in had four bedrooms, an attic, a basement, a small back porch, a large front porch lit by a single bulb at night, and, come springtime every year, a robin's nest on the underside of the gutter. The furniture, room to room, was solid and cared for; the carpet was thick, and it softened the walk of my grandmother, who stood on her feet nine hours a day, six days a week as a hotel cook.

My grandmother Emily was a gentle woman who rarely complained about anything. She had a fondness for roses, which she planted in the front yard. She also collected little metallic figurines, which she called woodknots, which sat on our mantel, atop TV sets, on bureaus, anyplace she could set them. The things were fragile and precious, and we were raised to honor their presence. When a woodknot was knocked to the floor and broke in hundreds of tiny pieces, we children scattered like baby seals, blaming each other, pointing, howling. We'd wait a few minutes, then drift back and circle around the shattered pieces, staring at them as if we could stare them back together, back to life.

I liked our banister, and when Jimmy and Emily and Elvira were not looking, I climbed onto it and slid down, banging head and body into the wall. Knots and bruises covered my head. Once, sliding down the banister, I lost my balance, lost the banister, and tumbled into the fish bowl. Not only fish and water scattered but so did some of my grandmother's woodknots. I lay crying and heaving; I had a broken leg, bruised arms. My grandmother's woodknots lay staring at me in tiny pieces. I groaned, crying with both pain and shame. When the leg cast was applied at the hospital, all gooey plaster at first, it felt as cool as cream. Emily and Elvira felt sorry for me. Jimmy was wordless. For years afterward, Emily would ask me whenever I returned home about my leg, remembering long after I had forgotten that it was the left leg I had broken.

I remember the smell of grass being cut in our neighborhood. It smelled like pine needles, fragrant. Summers, there were ladders everywhere, on the sides of houses, and open buckets of paint beside the ladders. You heard the click of lawnmowers, the kind you had to push. It sounded like the clicking of metal tongues. And I remember milk trucks rumbling down the alley through morning sunshine and men quietly setting bottles of milk at our back door. Sometimes I'd open the back door and there would sit our milk, in bottles, the bottles in a small cagelike case. It made me feel as if someone had left gifts in the noiseless morning for me and my sisters.

The Edgertons lived beside our house. They were from the Carolinas. Mrs. Edgerton always looked tired. She smiled quietly and mumbled her hellos. Mr. Edgerton, who was as wide as a bear, rarely spoke. He drove a construction truck. He would talk if you asked him a question, then turn his head away as he was uttering the last few words of his answer, as if he had used up enough air. I was always asking about Calvin, my friend, one of his sons. There were fourteen Edgerton children; eight still lived at home. And they lived in half of a double, unlike our house, which was a whole house. I wondered where they all slept. There was one sofa in the front room. I wondered where they all sat. When Mr. Edgerton wanted to be alone in the house with his wife, he told the kids to leave. When he was finished doing whatever it was he was doing with Mrs. Edgerton, he opened the door. The children paraded back into the house; once inside, they paraded right back outside, took their positions on their porch, and began fussing with each other.

Calvin and his brother Harry were two of the best football players in the neighborhood. They were as big as men, outran everyone. But Mr. Edgerton wouldn't let them play organized football. When they weren't in school, Harry and Calvin poured cement with their father. Sometimes they worked in the neighborhood. I'd come by and yell in their faces that it was time to go, to play, and they'd shake their heads, tell me they couldn't. They wore big workboots, and construction gloves covered their large hands. I sneaked sandwiches to give to Calvin and Harry sometimes. Calvin would raise a slice of bread, inspect the meat that lay underneath, then devour the sandwich. Spam, ham, bologna; I gave him all my Spam sandwiches. Standing on the Edgerton back porch, sometimes I'd peer into their kitchen. I always saw biscuits, pans of biscuits, stacked high. The Edgerton kids carried the biscuits — cold and hard — around almost playfully, like people carrying cookies.

Mrs. Dempsey lived on the other side of our house. She was a white lady. Her house was white. Her hair was white. She had a hunched back and a beaked nose. Sometimes the sight of her spooked me. The lights were rarely turned on inside her house, where she lived alone after her husband died. Sometimes at night you'd see her through curtains, sitting at a table alone, a candle burning. I do not remember her smiling, ever. Sunny days brought her outdoors. I'd notice her scouring the front yard, poking at the ground as if she'd lost something. The aprons Mrs. Dempsey wore were large and colorful. There was a grapevine in her back yard. Purple grapes hung from her vine. They tasted bitter, and when you chewed one and came across a touch of pure sweetness, you felt lucky. I'd sit on our back porch staring at her grapevine, remembering where certain bunches of grapes were hanging before going to bed, then checking the next morning to see if they were still there. She yelled at kids who climbed her fence and stole grapes. Jerry Lynn was always hopping her fence and making off with handfuls of the grapes. "I'll call the police," she'd yell, her body bent and stiff there beneath her grapevine, the grape thieves flying over the fence. Her eyes were flying all around the yard, like the eyes of a canine. She looked for stragglers, for cowards who might be squatting in the weeds, stilled there by her voice, unable to move.

My grandfather's word was the final word in our house, and as each child grew to understand the height of his words, so each child grew to understand to steer clear of Mrs. Dempsey's grapevine. At least once every summer Mrs. Dempsey would pick some grapes, put them in a bag, and reach over the hedges that separated our yards and hand the bag to me. She barely said a word. It seemed sometimes I had to wait until summer was nearly over for her to make her move. She'd hand me the bag of grapes and walk back into her house, as quiet as clouds, and close the door. I cannot recall a summer when she did not give me a bag of grapes. I'd sit there on the back porch with my bagful of grapes. I squinted when I swallowed them, and my fingertips turned purple.

Days warmly spun into each other, and my world seemed as soft as smoke. I wandered around our neighborhood. I wasn't allowed to go up to High Street or beyond Eleventh Avenue by myself. I'd get a whipping if I was spotted past those streets, where the cars seemed to move faster. I played and played. I threw rocks whenever I could. I leaned into gravel and searched for smooth round rocks, which zoomed straight through the air. You couldn't depend on flat rocks, because they'd arc outward, then back in, missing the target. Mostly I hurled rocks into abandoned buildings. Then I listened for glass to shatter. My body would twist in a kind of delighted agony when I heard glass shatter. I'd stand there, frozen, just for a moment. Then I'd bolt, scared and delighted that my rock had done what it was supposed to do.

A police officer strolled up the walkway in our back yard one morning. There were clothes billowing on my mother's clothesline. The officer was wearing a dark blue uniform, had pink skin, seemed taller than I'd ever grow to be. There had been some rock throwing; some windows had been broken; someone had spotted me; what did I have to say? I lied and lied, told the officer it wasn't me, told Elvira it wasn't me, turned back to face the officer, who turned to face Elvira, who looked down at me. The officer said he might have to take me to jail. I twitched; then I saw him wink at Elvira. He warned me: no more rock throwing. He smiled at my mother before leaving.

I loved movies, went to them every Sunday at the Garden Theatre, a fifteen-minute walk from our house. The Garden had seats with cushions, a mountain-wide screen, velvet curtains that parted slowly, and a balcony. Every Sunday there'd be a double bill, a large screenful of characters, most of the movies in black and white, some in Technicolor. Up in the darkened balcony a lot of boys put their hands up under girls' dresses. You'd hear moaning and squealing; you'd see cardigan sweaters lying on girls' laps, the boys' arms moving like snakes. My brother Harry took me to the Garden, but he'd disappear into the balcony, mostly with Rosanne, one of his steadier girlfriends. Elvira would give me fifty cents, two quarters. One quarter was the price of admission; the other quarter was for popcorn and a candy bar with vanilla insides called a bun. You had to go outside the theater to get your popcorn and candy, and it was a pain if it was cold, if there was a line.

I watched John Wayne punch Lee Marvin in *The Man Who Shot Liberty Valance*. I watched Dean Martin and Jerry Lewis movies, Elvis movies. On the large screen inside the Garden Theatre I saw, for the first time in my life, a woman's breasts. They were Elizabeth Taylor's breasts. She was sitting in a chair, having her portrait painted, nude. The artist was Charles Bronson. The movie was *The Sandpiper*. Even playing an artist, he looked hard. There were already a million lines in his face. I remember Elizabeth Taylor's breasts and I remember them exactly: they were full and lovely; the nipples were dark. I kept looking around for an usher to toss me from the theater. No one said a word, no one tapped me on the shoulder. I sat mesmerized, felt something rush through my body, as gentle as warm water. When I saw Bette Davis in *Hush Hush Sweet Charlotte*, I saw a woman drowning, and saw the drowning woman looking right at me, through the water and through the Garden Theatre screen. I couldn't shake her stare away. That night, at home, I cried out in my sleep, then rushed to Elvira's room, feeling my way down the darkened hallway toward her voice and bed.

On a sunny day on a playground I tripped and bit my tongue nearly in half. It had to be stitched back together. Chuckie Davis's German shepherd chased me down on my bicycle and bit me on my behind. Elvira had a fit, circling the hallway at the hospital with relatives, everyone wondering if the dog had rabies until Chuckie — a neighborhood bully — finally brought him to the hospital. It did not, and I was spared all those needle shots to my stomach. A skinny girl hit me in the back of the head with a brick after school one day. Doctors stitched me up. So I bled and I healed. I recently looked into a mirror to see if the scar on my chin left by that baseball bat Bobby Jordan was swinging when I ran up on him — it was an accident, we had just finished a softball game — was still there. I guess it always will be.

I sat on the wooden back porches of friends. The hours just floated by. The heat in summertime stayed up in our midwestern town. Adults mind heat, not children. I felt cool, like tall timber. I'd smell food through screen doors. Elvira always told me not to eat over at the houses of friends. Bad manners. Nonetheless, I ate over at the houses of friends. William Barnes's mother put slices of cheese on ham sandwiches, which I couldn't resist, and Skip White's mother made sloppy Joe sandwiches. I couldn't resist those either. After I had eaten I would wipe my hands and mouth well before walking home. Whenever I felt dusk coming on, I knew it was time to get home.

I loved our house, mostly, I think, because I found places to hide in there, places to vanish. The back rooms were like caves to me, doors flung open like giant bat wings. There were nooks and crannies in our basement, places to hide things, things I treasured. I hid my baseball glove beneath the basement steps, having lathered it with my sister's Royal Crown hair grease to soften it. I believed the basement's cool darkness, along with the grease, would turn the glove into something special. I hid my toys behind our furnace. Sometimes I left them for weeks. They'd get covered in spiderwebs. I would crush the spiders, blow the dust from my toys.

Emily and Jimmy slept in the front room of our basement on an old wooden bed that had a shiny headboard, all golden wood. There were few comforts in that basement. There was a radio on a nightstand, and two tall chifforobes, the kind you don't see anymore, in which my grandmother and grandfather hung their clothes. Atop the chifforobes were my grandmother's hatboxes. The hats were huge and full of feathers. I remember blue, pink, and white feathers. They looked mighty fussy. I always wondered how such big hats, once sprung from those boxes, could fit back inside. It seemed as difficult to imagine as a pigeon pulled from a magician's vest pocket, then returned to that very pocket. The radio stayed pitched low and played country music, and sometimes at night upstairs, in our living room, I'd put my ear to the floor heater, which had grates, and I'd hear twangy country singing rising up.

My grandfather didn't work on the railroad very long. It ruined his back. He found a job as head of the stockroom for a restaurant called Yolando's. Not once, however, did I see my grandfather go to work in overalls or khakis; Jimmy Burke wore suit pants to work, or one of dozens of pairs of dress slacks. He wore well-made leather shoes and kept them beautifully shined. There came a time when I wasn't allowed to leave that house unless my shoes were shined.

In 1962 I felt fear sweep our house for the first time. We were forced to stack food in the storage space of our basement. Actually, I stood in the kitchen as adults rushed by with cans of food in their arms, telling me to get out of the way. I just stood there sucking my thumb. Sometimes adults can tell you to get out of the way and not really mean it, because just as quickly they're on to another thought. But sometimes they can tell you to get out of the way and really mean it, the words flying out of their mouths flat and harsh and full of anger. This was one of those get-out-of-the-way orders that my mother didn't really mean. She said it sweetly; she was worried about a million other things. I guess she was worried about our safety. President Kennedy was challenging Khrushchev and the Russians. There was trouble in Cuba. Voices and stern faces crowded the black-and-white TV screen. There might be war. And we'd have to live in the basement, our makeshift bomb shelter. Elvira, my mother, fretted while lifting the cans in her arms.

Then one day the grownups brought the food back upstairs. There was laughter, deep throaty laughter, and hands placed on hips and adults leaning back on the kitchen counter and smiling. I smiled too and went on sucking my thumb. I sucked my thumb night and day. I was warned to stop and paid the warnings no mind. Uncle Ira, my mother's brother, sneaked into my room one night while I was asleep and put hot sauce on my thumb. When my thumb found its way back into my mouth, I cried out. But I kept sucking my thumb until it was raw. I'd raise it to Elvira's eyes and show her where the skin was starting to split and show her the pink insides from the cut, pink from my sucking it so much. I wanted sympathy. Elvira just pushed my thumb away.

We had a garage, as gray as a shack, that sat ten yards behind our house. Since no one in our family drove, or even owned a car, I used the dirt-floored garage as my play area, racing through it, kicking up dirt. It was cool and shadowy, and spiderwebs were everywhere. I held scout meetings in our garage and furnished it with scraps of furniture I found in the alley behind our house. I also hid treasures in our garage — comic books, cans filled with coins, jars with insects, my slingshot. I wasn't supposed to have a slingshot. I put rocks in my slingshot and fired at birds, the whirring hubcaps of passing cars, and people. I collected grasshoppers, punched holes in the jar lid so they wouldn't die. Sometimes they died anyway; I never thought to feed them. My friend Victor collected red ants, which he kept in a gigantic jar. Victor carried the jar everywhere he went, carried it under his arm like a football. Girls scattered when he came around. Victor liked his ants more than he liked girls.

I still remember the colors of this shirt: purple and yellow, one of my favorite combinations. I buttoned it to the neck, as if to ward off something. I was attending Weinland Park Elementary School. Mostly I wanted to stop stuttering; it embarrassed Elvira.

Many things came to me easily, kindly, but not words. I stuttered, and it was a mystery to my family why I stuttered. Single words caught me, and sometimes, in order to push a word past my lips — words that began with *p* or *t* were hellish — I'd raise one foot and then stamp it down, upon which the word would be released. Visitors to our house, forced to witness this, would become alarmed and stare at me, would stare at Elvira, Emily, Jimmy. I could tell that my stuttering embarrassed Elvira, because she'd look away, wouldn't even try to help me finish my sentences.

The stuttering began early in childhood. Jimmy said it was the result of tickling and sternly told my sisters not to tickle me in the stomach anymore. I got used to the laughter, the taunts, the mimicry. Then I was sent to a speech therapist at Weinland Park Elementary. I had a special pass just to walk out of class when it was time to go see the therapist. Machines were set up in her basement office; tape recorders and earphones sat on tables. The place looked like the controls of a space shuttle. I had to put earphones on and listen to my voice while looking into the big glass mirror in front of me. I hated it. It didn't help one bit. There were always other students in the sessions with me and the therapist. She'd sit with me ten minutes or so, then scoot her chair away to another student. I didn't mind stuttering at the world, if others didn't mind. Of course, Elvira was my mother. She'd have loved me if I were mute. But I could tell she minded my stuttering.

When I wasn't thinking of Mrs. Dempsey's grapes or staring for hours into Victor's ant glass or standing on the corner of Fourth Street at the stoplight along with my piano-playing friend Zachary, hoping we'd see a woman in a car with her skirt hiked up past her knees, I was playing marbles. Jerry Lynn was the best marble player around. He crisscrossed the neighborhood, alley to alley, trooping through neighbors' front yards with a pocketful of marbles. The neighbors would hiss at him, tell him to stop cutting across their yards, vow to tell his mother, to call the police, but Jerry didn't care. My friends and I knelt at the side of my house and played marbles, drawing circles in the dirt. There'd be a weird glint in Jerry's eyes; his tongue would be hanging from his mouth like a piece of uncooked meat. He would walk back home with his pants sagging because of all the marbles he had won, neighbors hissing at him once again. I traded marbles with Jerry sometimes, striped and paisley marbles for his solid-colored ones.

Then one day Jerry just stopped playing marbles. I guess he lost interest. I kept playing, my jeans showing holes at the knees from kneeling so much in the dirt. My mother just sewed patches where the holes were. There were even after-noons when I won a pocketful of marbles, afternoons when my own pants sagged. At night I'd put my marbles in a sack, close the top with a rubber band, and hide the sack in my bedroom closet. I was, however, afraid of the dark. I was afraid of seeing Bette Davis's chalky face from *Hush Hush Sweet Charlotte* in my dreams again. I was what I was: skinny, with a caved-in chest, and, because I sucked my thumb, buck-toothed. And I also believed in ghosts. But I was happy, rush-ing home from school with the fallen autumn leaves sticking to the soles of my shoes, the air cool and clear, Emily greeting me at the door, and there, Jimmy, chewing his tobacco, and somewhere in that house, Elvira, my mother.

My friend Zachary's mother — I called her Mrs. Ellis — worked downtown at the Union clothing store. She wore pretty clothes and smelled sweet, like a garden. When she was walking to her house from the bus stop, men would often slow their cars and whistle at her. Mrs. Ellis did not seem to like that too much. She made Zachary practice on the piano every day for two hours. Sometimes he went downtown to practice at a musical academy. And sometimes I went with him and sat downstairs while he was upstairs practicing. I had no interest in musical instruments: waiting for Zachary bored me till I was blue. But I waited; he was my friend, and Mrs. Ellis always gave him enough money to buy us both a milkshake.

Sports bored Zachary, so he didn't play. His new maroon loafers stayed new and maroon for a long time because he didn't run across the playground in them. Zachary wore thick glasses and was the first boy I knew who carried a briefcase. It seemed as large as a small suitcase to me. He had a key for the thing, and he was always locking and unlocking it. It was always bulging with papers and notebooks and music lessons. I think Zachary's mother thought I was ill-mannered, maybe because I didn't play any musical instruments, maybe because I liked eating over at her house. One summer Zachary's aunt from Georgia came to visit. She was pretty like Zachary's mother. Zachary told me his aunt slept without any clothes on. Totally naked. I made him swear. He did, but I still didn't believe it. I had never heard such a thing.

The grocery store at the end of our alley was called Mrs. Wilson's. It was a tiny brick store with two glass windows in the front. Mrs. Wilson was a plump lady with a pink face who wore a deep shade of red lipstick. My family had what was called a bill at Mrs. Wilson's. It was a line of credit, so every time my mother or grandmother would send me to the store, I'd get the items and say to Mrs. Wilson, "Put it on the bill." I believe I halfway sang those words out, they became so familiar. Mrs. Wilson would reach for a small notebook from behind the register and add up the items I'd bought. I'd add a banana or a plum or an apple for myself, then wolf the thing down before I got home.

"Are you sure your mother says it's okay for you to get this plum?" she'd ask.

"Yep," I'd say, grabbing the bag, bolting out the door.

During the Christmas holidays, Mrs. Wilson put toys in her windows. I'd stand looking at them, then beg my mother to tell Santa I wanted those very toys in Mrs. Wilson's windows. Many of them did end up under our tree for me on Christmas morning.

To keep me from mischief, my brother Harry — four years older — talked me into becoming a Cub Scout. I would learn things: rope-tying, commandments, honor. I hated scouting. I could never tie my knots properly, could never recite, cold, the scout pledges. Elvira ironed my blue scout uniform and I went to the meetings anyway. My scout tie looked silly and lazily tied; other boys' uniforms always seemed neater than mine, better ironed. Our scout meetings were held one street over, on Sixth Street, in the basement of a neighborhood family's house. I was nine when I went on my first camping trip. We left on a foggy morning. Elvira had a hangover and couldn't see me off. My friend Bubbles and I decided to share a tent. I told Bubbles that I had no idea how to tie the tent down, but he said he knew how. Bubbles was huge; he took up most of the space. Once the tent was tied down, we fell asleep, full of camp food and the extra food Bubbles had brought along. Then it started raining. Then the string holding the tent down snapped. Then the tent collapsed. I yelled at Bubbles. Neither of us was willing to go outside in the cold dark rain and retie the string. I shivered all night long, slept fitfully. The next morning I complained that I wanted to go home now, right away, please.

Bubbles lived right down the street from my house. We often went to get our hair cut together. Sometimes we went to Bax's Barber. Bax was a thin man. He yakked about everything under the sun. When he smiled, his jaws nearly disappeared into his mouth, as if he were sucking on something. Bax squeezed our heads too tight while he was cutting. He'd nick you with the clippers down around your neck. You'd jump, but Bax would just squeeze your head tighter. He wouldn't learn new hairstyles. He hated Afros — had taped, in fact, a sign in the window: NO AFROS. Every time a pretty woman walked by the window, Bax would stop cutting your hair and stare out at her.

But Bubbles and I stopped going to Bax's. We switched our allegiance to Fred Wallace. He was the neighborhood bootleg barber. He lived in a nice house and set up a barbershop in his basement. Really it was just a high-backed chair and a light bulb. He had a few pairs of clippers on a table. You had to watch your step down there; it was easy to trip over some old tools. Everyone in the neighborhood thought he could cut hair better than ole man Bax. He'd charge only fifty cents, and if you didn't have it, he'd let you pay on your next visit. Sometimes there'd be ten boys down in the basement waiting to get a haircut, and sometimes Mr. Wallace's wife would scream at him and he'd put down the clippers and vanish upstairs — for thirty whole minutes. We'd all stay put, cracking jokes at one another, admiring Mr. Wallace's son's motorcycle, hoping his pretty daughter would come down to the basement, maybe to grab some clothes from the washing machine. Heads barbered, we'd walk home through inky nights and await a new dawn.

3

I PLAYED BASKETBALL because my brother Harry played it, and in my neighborhood little brothers did mostly what their big brothers did. (There would come a time, soon enough, when I would play the game with a life-and-death fierceness.) Tutu and Bubbles and Dalton and I even played in cold weather, played until our noses ran with snot, until the tips of our fingers felt frozen. I'd just shove my hands inside my corduroy jacket, warm them, and play some more.

Winter turned to spring, which turned to summer. On a summer's day a bully by the name of Squirrel snatched my basketball from me. He tossed it across the pavement, told me to get off the court because he and his friends wanted to play. Just then my brother Harry was walking onto the court. He saw everything. Harry walked up to Squirrel and stood facing him like John Wayne. "Go get his ball," Harry said to him. A group of boys gathered, voices rising in their throats, expecting a fight. Squirrel went and got my ball, handed it to me delicately. My big brother was my big brother.

Mostly, though, I fished. When I didn't go fishing alone, I went with Tutu and Donnie Johns. Donnie's mother, Lily, was from Louisiana. She cursed a lot. Her voice was thick and hoarse. She slept all day because she worked at night as a waitress. She carried a knife in her pocketbook. About once a week in her back yard, in the clear light of day, with all the nosy neighbors staring, she'd threaten to cut someone's throat for messing with her children. "I'll cut your motherfucking throat," she'd say, wearing a pair of tight shorts. If you were a kid, you had to pretend you didn't hear the cursing part. Lily sometimes brought us pans of Cajun food, but we didn't like it. It would sit in the refrigerator until Lily called down to our house, asking for her pan back. Then I'd dump the stuff out and take her cleaned-up pan back to her.

Donnie could outfish anyone in the neighborhood, but I didn't like going fishing with him. He walked fast down High Street, half a block ahead of me, for no reason, as though the fish were planning to swim to another part of the state. Donnie would catch a lot of fish and then announce that he was ready to go try another fishing spot a mile away, and before I knew it he was already loping off, carrying his rods and reels, and because I hadn't caught any fish yet, I'd have to scoop my gear up and run after him, swearing at him. One of the good things about Donnie was that he could fight. A couple of times strange boys snarled at us. My chest would tighten. Donnie would drop his rod and reel, run after them, run them away.

After a while I stopped going fishing with Donnie. I started going fishing with Tutu. Tutu had a long neck, a head as big as my own, and large eyes. He dedicated himself with purpose to everything he did. He rode his bike down to Tuttle Park, taking the dangerous sloping hills so he could become the best bike rider. Emily and Jimmy would never allow me to take my bike down to Tuttle Park.

Sometimes I'd see Tutu walking fast behind our house, down the alley, carrying his fishing pole, all alone. I'd beg permission from Emily to go fishing, then hustle down the alley after him. We fished in the Olentangy River, which was a two-mile walk from my house. I enjoyed the walk down High Street, past the Garden Theatre, past stores, my fishing poles sticking out like lances. I carried two fishing poles, one a cane pole, one with a reel. When I got within twenty yards of the river, I could hear the water gushing from the dam. It sounded like a giant faucet. Every time I heard it, it sounded brand-new. I'd hustle down the hill leading to the dam, and there it was, gushing, silvery, and rolling: our dam.

We fished with red worms and cheap fishing lures. I kept my lures in a lime-green tackle box. Lures were expensive, and sometimes Tutu and I stole them from a hardware store near our house. We'd stroll along the aisles of the store and stand frozen in the tackle department and nod to each other when it looked okay to slip a lure into our pockets. Then we'd take a lure or two for purchase and walk up to the clerk. Little geniuses.

One day Tutu shoved several lures into his pockets. The lures were not in boxes; the hooks were exposed. I walked ahead of Tutu toward the checkout counter, wanting to get out of the store, to get fishing. The strolling yielded no lures for me. I needed the coast to be very, very clear before I would slide lures into my pockets. When I looked back down the aisle, I noticed Tutu limping, noticed a man following him. Tutu began to make faces, as if he were in pain. He said something, which I couldn't hear, a mutter. His jaw tightened. One of the hooks in his trousers had snagged his thigh, cutting into his flesh. I noticed a small circle of blood on his pants leg. We stopped at the counter to pay for the items we were buying. I walked briskly out of the store; Tutu hobbled briskly. Once outside, I pleaded with him to walk faster. He said he couldn't, said it angrily.

Before we reached the edge of the hardware store, a man reached us. I had seen the man inside the store, waltzing the aisle, and paid him no mind. He half circled both of us, looking us up and down with fast eyes.

"You two. Will you please follow me back inside the store?"

I froze. Tutu, in pain, admitted his thievery before we reached the manager's office. Then he begged help in removing the hook from his leg. I bent and looked at it. Then I yelled out my innocence. My mouth wouldn't stop; my granddaddy Jimmy would kill me anyway. I blurted out to Tutu that he was in trouble, big trouble. He shot me a cold look. The office we were taken to was small, with a single table. The store detective was quickly joined by another man. Both looked at us with that tough junior high school principal's look. I hadn't stolen anything. The manager said I could leave. He was still eyeballing me, as if a fishing lure might fall out of my ear. Tutu told me to go get his mother; hurry up, he said.

Tutu was put on punishment, and after his punishment we just went back to fishing. Calm rivers bored us. We liked action on a river's surface, dangerous rock crossings, believing that the harder the trek to the fish, the bigger the reward in the end. The Olentangy River dam gushed fiercely. Griggs dam was even fiercer. It was at Griggs dam that Tutu nearly died. The day had been raw and chilly, the wind high and hard. Tutu stood fishing at the edge of the water, ten feet above the dam on a concrete ledge. A gust of powerful wind came. He bent like taffy. Then he was gone, over the edge and into the water. He went under once, then popped up. I couldn't swim, not a lick. I yelled and yelled. Tutu popped up again, went under again. He looked terrified. A man, white — in those days everyone seemed identified by race: white man, colored man, white woman — appeared, jumped in, went under. When he came up he had Tutu with him. Tutu was coughing, arms flailing, eyes rolling like marbles, but saved. We shook on the riverbank, shook with fear, then shook ourselves free of fear. We thanked the white man, more than once, more than twice. Then he left.

My sister Diane — six years older than myself and the oldest of Jack and Elvira's brood — paid for me to take swimming lessons at the downtown YWCA. I didn't really want to take my swimming lessons at the girls' Y, but my sister got a discount because she worked there. The lessons were seven dollars a week. I hated the lessons, hated the cold water, the smell of chlorine and the sting of the water when it raced up into my nose. I failed lesson after lesson and was joyful when each class ended. But I did like going downtown alone. After my swimming lesson I'd go over to the Woolworth's and slide into a booth and order a banana split. In our town, at our Woolworth's, you got to pick a balloon off a string that stretched across the store right over the counter. In some of the balloons were little pieces of paper that said "1 cent," and if you chose one of those balloons, you'd get your banana split for a penny. It was like a game. There were many Saturday afternoons when I sat alone at the downtown Woolworth's spooning up a penny banana split. Sometimes the waitresses — all white — would smile as they pulled a pen from their pockets and punched the balloon. I'd catch the Indianola Avenue bus home from downtown, a rolled-up towel tucked beneath my arms, wet swimming trunks inside the towel.

There was a shotgun in our house. It stood upright beside my grandfather's bed in the basement. He had brought it north from Alabama. Jimmy said never touch it, and I certainly never did. I walked up on it a couple times, looked closely at the trigger. It was double-barreled and rusted, but I think I expected it to move. Jimmy kept some of the shells upstairs, inside a ceramic elephant beside the sofa he always sat on — the same ceramic elephant he kept his magnifying glasses in to read the racing forms and afternoon newspaper.

I saw my grandfather use that shotgun, but only verbally. Eddie, a tough neighborhood boy who drove a convertible and had an apple-shaped head, slapped my sister Diane. Eddie was Diane's boyfriend. Days later Eddie came over to the house to make up. He stood outside, at the bottom of the steps, demanding to see Diane. His apple head was jerking from side to side. Jimmy stood on the porch listening in silence. Alabama silence. Then he made up his mind: he had heard enough.

"Shit. Let me go get my shotgun."

Jimmy bounced inside, down to the basement. We followed him single file through the basement, from kitchen to dining room, from dining room to living room, from living room to screen door, where we stopped and peered. Jimmy walked out the door, told us to stay back. But we could see through the screen door. Eddie, tough Eddie, apple-head Eddie, was gone.

My grandfather did not drive a car. I never knew why. Everything important I saw my grandfather do, he did while standing on his two feet. Jimmy was a walker. He walked to the store, and he walked to the bakery. (You could smell the bread being baked inside the big red-brick building three blocks from our house.) Jimmy walked to the pharmacist, to his doctor's office, and he walked in his good leather shoes. When he let me, I walked with him. He had a nighttime job at a Greek restaurant on the corner of Eleventh and High, cleaning the place up after it had closed. He'd take me along. He wore dress slacks, as always, beautifully creased. And a fedora, gray, the brim bent just slightly at the front. I bounced from leatherette booth to booth inside the restaurant, mostly staying out of Jimmy's way and the swishing of the mop back and forth across the floor. I'd stare out the windows, eye pieces of candy, whistle to myself. When it was time to go, my grandfather would slide back one of the glass windows, take a couple of penny mints out, and hand them to me. I'd have preferred larger pieces of candy, but I dared not complain. We walked home in silence, the wind whipping, Jimmy's head down. I sucked my mint away.

Without a car in the family, we depended a lot on North-side Taxi. You'd call, and before you hung up you'd hear the man on the other end of the phone say, "Send a cab over to Jimmy's place." Then you'd stand with your nose pinched against the screen door looking for the white-and-orange taxi to turn the corner. Even now, in my hometown, in my grand-father's house, I can call Northside Taxi and someone will ask, "Ain't that Jimmy's place?" So without an automobile at our house, my sisters and I felt confined, locked in by our neigh-borhood. Uncle Ira rescued us.

Uncle Ira, my mother's brother, was a loping thick-shoul-dered man with a boy's young face. John Burke, my grand-father Jimmy's hardbitten father, doted on Ira, his firstborn grandson. He gave him nickels and dimes, took him into Selma when he ran errands in his Model T, surprised all those around him who thought he was a hateful and distant man. Uncle Ira loved his mother, Emily, deeply, sometimes phon-ing her several times a day as he grew older and left the house. But there was a distance between Uncle Ira and Jimmy, his father. It had to do with something that had happened during

Jimmy's drinking days: Jimmy, drunk, had raised a hand to Emily. He didn't strike her, but it was enough to raise Uncle Ira up from a chair. Uncle Ira was a Golden Gloves boxer. He balled a fist, a Golden Gloves fist, and told his father never to raise a hand to his mother again, ever. When a son climbs over that wall to get to his father, there's no going back in the other direction. The moment must have pained Jimmy — such a proud man, stared down like that, by his only son, in his own house.

A lot of people thought Uncle Ira actually looked like Joe Louis, the champ. They were both honey-brown in complexion. When Uncle Ira made it all the way to the Golden Gloves in Columbus, his bout was on TV. The family gathered at Emily's knee to watch. Uncle Ira took some punches, and it hurt my grandmother, who shook her head, clutched her hands, then stopped watching. Uncle Ira lost. Emily said little; she blinked away tears. When Uncle Ira went to work on the railroad, he gave up the boxing dream for good.

Uncle Ira moved his family around Columbus a lot, from Taylor Avenue on the east side into the house with us on North Fifth Street. Jimmy and Emily never complained when one of their three children had to come over and live for a while. I remember people sleeping on sofas downstairs, rumpled blankets, end chairs pulled together. I do not remember anyone's ever complaining. Then Uncle Ira moved his family into a big gray stone house on Jefferson Avenue. I liked that house. It seemed as huge as a castle. It had French doors, which opened wide. Jefferson Avenue had once been a well-heeled avenue for well-to-do Columbus families, but in the 1960s it was rundown. I romped and threw rocks at the empty house across the street when Uncle Ira wasn't looking. Years later I learned that James Thurber, the humorist and legendary *New Yorker* writer, had lived in that house with his parents. In 1962 I didn't know James Thurber from Howdy Doody, and when I aimed rocks at that house, which had been a boarding house by then, I aimed for the windows.

Uncle Ira knew how wild my sister Wonder and I were about going for rides in his car. He'd come by and pick us up, and it'd be a big surprise because he would just show up, like good weather, like sunshine. He'd double-park his car. "Y'all wanna go for a ride?" he'd ask, his arm hanging out the window. Words rolled from my Uncle Ira's mouth like words from a radio, even and soothing. My sister and I would beg our mother to let us go. Then we would run to the car. When we pulled away, we never knew where we were going. We might go anywhere, might go to the moon. The cars Uncle Ira drove were old cars. They smelled like old winter coats. They were the only cars I got to know as a child, and so they smelled divine to me. His cars never purred, either. They made noise — I mean noise. And Uncle Ira was always stopping to get gas, a dollar's worth, two dollars' worth, unfolding bills that had been crumpled up in his pockets like candy wrappers. A dollar's worth of gas seemed to be enough to get us going on our mystery rides.

I liked watching how Uncle Ira would steer with just one hand, whistling, telling us to settle down in the back seat but not really meaning it, because he'd say it in a soft voice, in between the whistling. We'd ride out into the country north of Columbus, where the air smelled flowery. We'd point to horses and cows, and we'd just wave at the land. Through Uncle Ira's car windows it all looked like a movie. Then we'd stop at the Dairy Queen, fill up on ice cream, let the ice cream drip on our shirts, get our hands sticky, and pile back into the car, sweetened and happy. We'd wipe our fingers on our shirts, on the car seat, tell on each other for wiping hands on the car seat, forget about telling on each other a second later. Then we'd pull off again, just riding, the wind blowing into the car. Then we'd see a fence and open sky and know our destination: a grassy area right next to the Columbus airport. We'd rush out of the car and slide our little rumps up onto the hood, and we'd settle down to watch airplanes land and take off. Our voices tingled; we'd finish each other's sentences; we'd crane our necks and watch the sky turn witchy and dark. Then the headlights of the planes coming in looked like white bowling balls hurtling our way. There were other families out there, watching, but they'd be far enough away so we never felt crowded. The sky felt like a big blue blanket being waved around. It was free entertainment, the magic of flight. Uncle Ira seemed happiest at such moments, sitting on the driver's side, the car door flung open, one leg inside the car, the other hanging out, the radio never on because it never worked. Maybe we kids were all the music he ever needed, sitting there in the dusky darkness, whistling, planes zooming overhead.

There were times when Uncle Ira would take us to drive-in movies. Our drive-in theater was off a bumpy road next to one of the big railroad yards in town. Monsters came down off the screen in the darkness. The speakers were on four-foot-high poles right next to the cars. Truth be told, the sound was often scratchy. Uncle Ira sometimes dozed off, tired. He worked at the ice house downtown, lifting and chipping big blocks of ice that came in on the Pennsylvania Railroad. We'd stand back and watch men in brown work clothes lift blocks of ice with huge hooks.

The men and women of my family, their whole lives, worked at low-paying jobs. Both my mother and her sister, my Aunt Creola, went into hotel kitchen work, just like their mother, Emily. They moved in and out of the big downtown Columbus hotels — the Deschler, the Christopher Inn, the Sheraton, the Chittenden — with relative ease, Emily recommended by former kitchen managers, the daughters recommended by their mother. My grandmother was never a head cook, but when cooks left one hotel and went to another, they had the ability — maybe it was just wisdom — to take some gifted members of their former cooking staff.

In our house there was always plenty of leftover hotel food, food wrapped in cellophane neatly stacked in the refrigerator, food in paper sacks, food stuffed into the freezer. There would be food left over from hotel banquets and food left over from holiday parties. I especially liked the Canadian bacon my mother would bring home. Also the dinner rolls my grandmother would bring home. She'd tear the roll-filled bag open and set it on the living room floor, where we'd be half circled around the TV set, watching the Bowery Boy serials on quiet Sunday afternoons. I grabbed the rolls with the tiny seeds on top. I got used to my mother and grandmother coming home and placing their huge black purses on the kitchen table and then reaching inside and pulling goodies out. My mother came home once and plopped something bright orange on the kitchen countertop. It had a hard shell and claws, and I couldn't imagine what it was, so I approached it slowly. Elvira cracked a part of it, and she became animated as she began pinching off pieces of its white meat to give us to sample. Her shoulders were wriggling. The taste was sweet and unforgettable; it would be years and years before I tasted another piece of lobster.

In our house no one ever died. The children were never rushed to the local hospital to sit in vigil for someone. Voices rose in anger, but only when a lie had been told. Sometimes we'd hear the doorbell ring and Jimmy would rise and open the door and it would be one of his children — Ira or Creola — clutching suitcases, back home. Aunt Creola came back in 1960. She had left home and married Joshua Talbert. Joshua came from a troubled family full of wild brothers. My mother read stories in the newspaper about their criminal exploits, making pitying noises in her throat while reading. Afterward, she'd fold up the newspaper with that particular story in it and place it beneath a mat on the dresser downstairs. She'd show it to other grownups, visiting. The grownups would read the story, shake their heads, start moaning. We kids knew not to touch that piece of newspaper under any circumstances.

Joshua was the one member of his family who had righted his life, clutched tight to a work ethic, meant to build a family life, found my Aunt Creola. He hauled cement between Ohio and Kentucky in a truck. On one of his runs his truck caught fire. It blew up, and Joshua died in the flames. No one ever knew what caused the explosion. Aunt Creola was a bride for less than a year. When she came back home, through Jimmy's front door, it was as if she left the pain of the outside world and what had happened behind. Life for her in that house just settled like a tossed blanket.

Aunt Creola brought her dog with her, a German shepherd. Geronimo was vicious, and I kept my distance as I stepped gingerly by him on the way to the garage to play. For some reason Aunt Creola doted on me. Every Easter she'd take me over to Mt. Vernon Avenue to buy my Easter suit. We'd walk into Lee's Style Shop. I'd pick out a sharkskin suit, matching handkerchief, and silk socks. The socks stretched up to my kneecaps. After church on Easter Sunday I'd hunt for Easter eggs in our back yard, still in my shiny suit.

The mention of Mt. Vernon Avenue carried a bit of mystery in our hometown. There were stores and nightclubs on Mt. Vernon Avenue, the likes of which were nowhere else in the city. My grandfather had long ago had his fun on the avenue. Now he wanted nothing to do with it and kept his distance. My grandmother went there to shop at Carl Brown's market.

Her doctor's office was also on the avenue. Sometimes she would take me on her doctor visits, both of us in the back seat of the taxi. (Jimmy never rode in the back seat of the taxi. Always the front seat. Sometimes, getting in the front, he seemed to startle the driver, who all of a sudden had to move newspapers, a clipboard, a hat, stuff, out of the way.) Dr. Percy Blount was my grandmother's doctor. I remember this about Dr. Blount's office: everything — the curtains, the carpet, the nurse, the doctor himself — seemed brown, sepia-toned. The doctor was a tall, severe-looking man. And everything in that office seemed quiet, nothing louder than the flapping of a magazine or maybe a grandmother telling a grandchild to be quiet, to hush, hush now. There was no candy for children in Dr. Blount's office, and there was no joy.

In our house there were lessons to be learned. A lot of them were taught by my grandfather. Jimmy always made us get a bag for anything we purchased at Mrs. Wilson's, or any other store, even if it was merely a single item. He figured it was easy for the police to accuse you of stealing if what you bought at the store wasn't in a bag. (To this day I will not walk out of a store without my purchased goods in a bag.) There was a lesson to be learned about money. My grandfather was scrupulous about the change due him when we returned from the store. He counted his change, every penny. He was an unlettered man, but full of wisdom. He knew the value of money, of honesty, and woe to the grandchild who tried to confuse him by losing the receipt. My grandfather would phone the store, have the goods itemized, count his change again. You sat frozen on the sofa. Then you'd suddenly find a dime, a quarter, in your back pocket, one you didn't know you had there — surprise, surprise — and you would start furiously patting the rest of yourself down, because Jimmy was loosening his belt now, the whipping was coming. Honesty was all. By evening you had forgotten you had been whipped. There might be scoops of homemade vanilla ice cream. A candy bar pulled by Jimmy from his ceramic elephant, a candy bar just for you. You felt comfortable in that house.

During rainstorms Emily let us sit on the porch, on a swing that had soft padding. Emily wanted us to feel close, to watch over one another. Raindrops would bounce off the railing and pop on us, tingling. We huddled close, but as soon as lightning came, we ran into the house like children in a fire drill.

When Selma and Birmingham became flashpoints during the civil rights movement, at different times during the early 1960s, Jimmy watched on one TV, Emily on another. They barely said a word. Sometimes long-distance phone calls were made down to Alabama. Long-distance phone calls were made in our house only in times of emergency. The calls never lasted more than ten minutes. They cost money, and as Elvira loved to holler, money don't grow on trees. When Emily would tell Jimmy someone was on the phone long distance, he'd jerk himself up from the sofa. Usually he rose from the sofa like a king, confident and unworried. Jimmy would get up in the middle of some of those civil rights broadcasts and go for walks. My grandmother would watch his backside until he disappeared from view, the gate creaking in the back yard and the sound of the creaking stretching back through the raised-up windows in summertime. My grandmother never returned to Alabama after she arrived in the north.

There was a lot of joy in our house when my grandfather's brothers came to visit, along with Uncle Doc. Big cars would pull up in front of our house, always on a Sunday, and children — my cousins — would rush from the cars. They always came after church, as if the Bible and the hymns and the gospel music had pushed them right to our doorstep. The brothers would emerge from their cars slowly, all hat-wearing men, then the wives, their smiles blossoming. The visits seemed marked by sunshine and clear air. There would be playing in the back yard, beneath our raspberry bush. (We were never allowed to eat the raspberries.) I'd shove cousins into our garage, and dust kicked up from the dirt floor would get on their shoes, on their Sunday clothes. I showed off the grasshoppers and praying mantises I kept in a jar.

The visits were glorious for my grandfather. He wanted his brothers, and his Uncle Doc, to know how happy he had made his household, how thoroughly his garden had been tilled. You could tell as he bounced through the house on those Sundays. He was short like Jimmy Cagney, and he moved the way short men sometimes move, quickly, without fuss, like a machine. He'd be in the living room, then the dining room, all in one motion, then standing there on the back porch churning vanilla ice cream in a rickety machine. It was a barrel, actually, with a metal contraption attached to it. It did not look like the kind of machine that could produce delicious ice cream. The vanilla ice cream had a yellow tint to it; I haven't tasted ice cream as good since. Then my grandfather would be running his hands through a bagful of roasted peanuts, peanuts that one of his brothers had just brought up from down south, from Alabama. You could see steam rising from the peanuts that Jimmy had just pulled from the oven. The peanuts smelled dry, smoky, and brown. My grandfather would stand over us children, shucking peanuts in his hands. The shucked shells floated to the ground as slowly as feathers. I'd grab a handful of peanuts to eat then and there, and another handful for later.

When it was time for the visitors to go — not really time to go, exactly, but time to unwind, to feign the act of leaving, to toss compliments, promise another visit soon — my grandmother would climb the stairs and come back down with clothes folded over her arms. Something someone had out-grown. Surely there was another cousin it would fit — Harry's suit, Diane's winter coat, my old jeans. Clothing was not tossed away in our house.

Age had climbed up on the backs of the Burke brothers gracefully, step by step. You could still believe that grouped together, they could rip a house apart, or infuse it with coun-try manners. As the brothers looked around at one another, preparing to leave, rubbing the brims of their hats, nodding to their wives, you could sense that they were happy to have tasted the comfort of another brother's home, back porch, back yard, cooked food. These were the same men who had rushed to one another's side in times of crisis, the same men who had pummeled men who had abused their daughters.

My grandfather and his brothers and Uncle Doc would loll for a while on the front porch. I remember playing in the yard, looking up at them, and seeing rows of baggy pants, men holding hats, holding cigars and tapping away the ash. Their Sunday shoes gleamed. I remember the smell on those Sun-day afternoons of the cigar smoke and my grandmother's red roses in the ground just in front of the porch and the men in the Stetson shoes. I remember a voice wafting over them, the voice of Joe Nuxhall, the Cincinnati Reds baseball announcer. Nuxhall's voice was like background music: it had just enough catch in it so that the men on the front porch could hear it clearly, could hear it just as clearly as they heard one another's voices. And when someone made a base hit or hit a home run, there would be a raised eyebrow, a curled lip, a handkerchief pulled without effort from the breast pocket to wipe the brow. There was never wild animation among Burke men, probably not forty years earlier, not now. They'd stand there together, brothers standing their ground. They had been raised on the old Negro Baseball League teams of the Deep South, the Birmingham Giants and Selma Cloverleafs. Even if the old

Negro League was gone, my uncles still loved the game, the integrated game now, loved it in repose, the gift of thinking backward, the radio voice following them from the living room out onto the front porch.

They seemed to tell each other in their own way, in silence, when it was time really to start leaving, to lift their feet from the porch and down onto the steps. Their cars, always tended to like good clothing, eased off, just a whir above silence. There would be waving, and I would be waving, and Jimmy, after they pulled off, would scan the sky as if looking for rain. He'd tell us children to stay out of my grandmother's roses, then he'd walk back into the house and the sound of Joe Nuxhall's voice on the radio. The screen door closed slowly: that was Jimmy's doing, tinkering with hinges and screws until he got it to close softly, uneventfully, exactly the way he wanted it to close.

My grandfather's uncle, Uncle Doc, remained childless and a bachelor his entire life. After he arrived in Columbus from Alabama, he never lived anyplace other than that room in that rooming house on Mt. Vernon Avenue. He worked odd jobs and spent his money as freely on strangers as on relatives. He was, like my grandfather Jimmy, a fastidious dresser. He also believed strongly in family. A man hit my mother once. Jimmy and two of his brothers left the house in search of the man. When Uncle Doc drove up and asked where they were going, they told him they were going to whip the man who had struck Elvira. "Now wait a minute," Uncle Doc said. Everyone knew Uncle Doc was crazy about my mother. He scanned the faces of his nephews and a thought came to him: "Y'all got kids. I ain't got no kids. I can afford to go to the penitentiary. So let me go kill the son of a bitch." They never found the man.

There had been a lady in Uncle Doc's life in Columbus. She lived in a big fine home on the city's south side. Sometimes Uncle Doc took my mother and her brother over there for Sunday dinners. They were children then. My mother remembers those dinners as southern in style: heaps of food, Uncle Doc's lady friend showing off her beautiful manners, slices of cake brought to them around the table and eaten. Then Uncle Doc would escort them out to his car, the pink Cadillac. But Uncle Doc refused to move in with the lady, or marry her.

Uncle Doc died in 1970. Months before his death, he lay in a hospital bed, quite sick. His nephews didn't make it to the hospital to see him because no one had told them he was there. By the time they got there, Uncle Doc had already left. As soon as he was released from the hospital, he went to Schoedinger's Funeral Home — a white funeral home in downtown Columbus — and paid for his funeral in advance. "Damn niggers wouldn't come see me in the hospital, how in the hell they going to take care of my funeral?" Uncle Doc told my Aunt Suzie. The nephews tried explaining, but each one would go only so far with words, then he'd stop. That was the kind of men they were — the kind of men who felt they owed the world, and anyone, one explanation for any given matter, and only one. As they tried to explain to Uncle Doc that they hadn't even known he was in the hospital, the air filled with angry silence, theirs and Uncle Doc's.

When he died, the nephews and their wives gathered in a room at the funeral home. They felt a little funny in that white funeral home, at a service without music or hymns, the air conditioner chilling them too much. Uncle Doc had left instructions that he was to be cremated. His ashes were spread over downtown Columbus. He did not owe a soul in the world a penny when he died. He left his lovely suits and jewelry — among the jewelry a gold-and-maroon watch — to my grandfather Jimmy.

4

My GRANDMOTHER worked at several downtown Columbus hotels before finally settling, in 1962, on the one she
would work at the longest, the Christopher Inn. It wasn't
really an inn at all but a quite fancy hotel, twenty stories high
and circular. Emily rose in darkness, at 4:30 every morning. She never set an alarm clock, just used her own body's
clock. (I picked up the habit and to this day do not need an
alarm clock to wake me at eerie morning hours.) She would
walk to the bus stop on Summit Street, wearing soft-soled
white shoes, the kind of shoes nurses wear in hospitals. Twelve
hours later she'd catch the 4:10 Indianola Avenue bus home
from downtown. The ride took about twenty minutes. The
bus rolled past the huge Smith Brothers warehouse, past
the Wonder Bread bakery, past the D. L. Auld factory (they
made car parts), and on across the Fifth Avenue intersec-
tion. Sometimes I'd rush out into the alley to wait for my
grandmother, and when I'd see her turn the corner into the

alley, I'd dash to her. She'd smile and hand me the bags in her arms.

My grandmother was always tired coming home, but you'd never know it. There'd be a few minutes sitting in a chair before she rose again, off to the kitchen to prepare food for us, the grandchildren who crowded that house. There was something gentle and orderly and even masterful about my grandmother in a kitchen. Even tired, she was in command. She'd tie on yet another apron. She'd turn on the oven. She'd slice potatoes, slide them into boiling water. She'd season meat, spanking it until it was tender, pinching herbs between her fingers, then sprinkling them over it. She'd reach for another pot, another pan; she'd check the oven. And she'd talk to us — the grandbabies, as she called us — and to Elvira, my mother, and the conversations would flow into one another and her concentration would never waver. My mother helped my grandmother in her kitchen, but there was never any doubt it was my grandmother's kitchen. So Emily would pull something from the oven and she'd lay a kitchen towel on top of it to cool it off. No written recipes in that kitchen, just stored knowledge.

Of course my grandmother did the same thing at work. But downtown at the Christopher Inn she cooked for hundreds of faceless people she never saw from the cave of the kitchen, mere strangers. I like to think now that she saved the lovely things about kitchen work for us, the delicate movements, the reverence for food, for brown sugar, for honey, for basil. My grandmother's gravy wasn't just gravy; it was something delicious and spicy, doctored up to a point where I was able to eat white rice, which I hated, when she lathered it with her brown gravy. Before you knew it an aroma would be all over the house. There would be steam rising from okra, from beneath the towels laid on top of cornbread; steam from chicken and macaroni and mashed potatoes. There would be piping steam from brown gravy. Chairs would be pulled out from the dining room table, a huge pitcher of Kool-Aid would be centered on the table (you could see sugar piled a quarter-inch high at the bottom of the pitcher: I put it there), and a blessing to Jesus Christ would be uttered: God is great, God is good, let us thank him for this food. That's mostly what I said. Then we ate.

Elvira, my mother, was there in that house, behind the kitchen steam. But it was sometimes hard to see her, hard to hear her words. I latched on to my grandmother, fastened myself tight. My grandmother always had a special plate of food for my grandfather because he had a sensitive stomach. After I finished my meal — I chewed with my mouth open and I never ate enough, was always skinny — I'd take my grandfather's plate to the kitchen, because Jimmy ate from a small table in front of the sofa where he sat. He ate hunched over, like a man at a face bowl, and he ate in stone silence. Finished, he would pull a hankie from his pocket, wipe his mouth, and reach for his pouch of chewing tobacco. "Time to get your lessons," Emily would say to us after dinner. She was talking about schoolwork.

It was impossible when I was a young boy eight years old, ten even, to think of my grandmother and grandfather as a romantic couple. Physically, an outsider might not have matched them. Emily was tall, taller than Jimmy, and she was big-boned. Her cheeks glowed red from her Cherokee Indian blood, and her hair was long and black, plain beautiful. Jimmy was short, as dark as a shadow, and blunt in both words and movement. He walked down the street fast, no-nonsense-like, just a blur.

Jimmy had a hard face and flat eyes. He was quick to frown. Emily was quick to smile. Emily's voice was soothing. Jimmy's

EMILY, *my grandmother, in the 1940s.*
She swam in kindness, and saved us all.

voice was gruff, and you wanted to understand what he said when he said it, because you didn't want to ask a second time. You could sweet-talk Emily out of a spanking, but not Jimmy, because he had your number, once and always. When you misbehaved — heisted someone else's cupcake from the refrigerator — Jimmy would look at you with those flat unblinking eyes. "Get upstairs," he'd say. You'd look back over your shoulder as you were climbing the stairs and you'd get a peek at him taking off his belt. You had the option, once at the top of the stairs, to choose any room, and usually you'd

JIMMY BURKE, *my grandfather, who taught me important things. A bricklayer, he dressed like a dandy. This photo was taken in 1941 in Selma. Already, though, he was looking north, toward Columbus.*

choose your own room because you knew it so well, knew which corner to run to and crouch in, knew which dresser you could stand beside so the dresser would absorb the swings of the belt. Jimmy climbed the stairs slowly: the drama leading up to the whipping was the most unmerciful part. It ended quickly, and there you were, seated on the edge of the bed, crying like some great child actor, like Spanky on *Our Gang*. Then you'd come downstairs and find out you missed dessert, but you didn't really miss it because someone — Emily? Elvira? Jimmy? — had left you a big piece of lemon cake on the kitchen counter.

Emily liked gospel music, listened to it on the radio every Sunday morning, listened to Eddie Saunders, who hosted *Sermons and Songs* on WVKO. The voices of Mahalia Jackson and the Mighty Clouds of Joy filled our house on Sunday mornings. Emily hummed to herself. Lying in bed on Sunday mornings, we children could hear the music as it floated up the stairs and into our bedrooms through the radiators. That music stayed right on the edge of your sleep, and it was soothing, you felt dreamy. It floated right by Jimmy; I don't think he was moved. Emily said "Amen" for reasons you didn't know, prayed softly, belonged to the Order of the Eastern Star, a Masonic group.

We were raised as Baptists. Mostly we attended storefront churches in our neighborhood. Wonder and I dressed on Sunday mornings and set out on neighborhood journeys, climbing the steps of churches that were there one month, gone the next. Our family souls were fastened, however, to a church on the east side called Trinity Baptist. The Reverend E. A. Parham preached from the pulpit on the rare Sundays we went together as a family to Trinity. There was never a car, but sometimes relatives came by to pick us up. I'd suck on candy in church, stick chewing gum beneath pews, fall asleep. Even when my grandmother couldn't make it to church, she pressed dollar bills into our hands — they were always folded tightly — and told us to drop them in the offering for her.

Trinity sat one block from Mt. Vernon Avenue. The grandest Baptist church in Columbus was Shiloh Baptist. It was right down the street from Trinity, and it was upper-crust, several cuts above the common Burkes, the holding-on Haygoods. A lot of the folks who went to Shiloh had college degrees.

Jimmy didn't attend church. He hated nothing more than relatives who showed up announcing themselves preachers. Several of my cousins at different times arrived at our front door, Bible in hand, inviting the entire family to church to see them preach. Jimmy badgered them about their training, which they didn't have. Asked where the church was located, how many members it had, asked what had happened to the previous minister. Jimmy could put the words "fool" and "preacher" in the same sentence while reaching for tobacco from his pouch, his eyes still glancing at the black-and-white TV. Wasn't it enough simply to reach down, deep down, and find religion, find it like a gift hidden behind a tree, savor it and want to share it with the outside world, hold it up higher than the sky itself? Maybe to Emily; not to Jimmy. Jimmy didn't like shortcutters, fakers, counterfeiters. "Jackleg preacher," he'd say as soon as our relative left the house, full of Emily's sweet blessings.

Jimmy was a lone wolf, had no male friends who came by to visit from the neighborhood, didn't yak on the phone for pleasure. He didn't care for jewelry and wore only a gold ring, which he never took off — a signature of the secret society to which he belonged. Emily was sociable, loved the ladies of her Masonic order. Emily welcomed traveling salesmen into our house. Jimmy let traveling salesmen get five, maybe ten words out of their mouths, then he was closing the door, bidding them goodbye. I saw him more than once raise a hand, palm out, as if to say *enough*.

Jimmy liked country music, the shriek of banjos on the TV. We'd sit at his knee and watch *Hee Haw*, ladies in plaid on bales of hay singing their hearts out. Jimmy watched in silence, his jaw puffy with chewing tobacco. He also watched Lawrence Welk, who held a baton and directed ballroom musicians. I wouldn't watch Lawrence Welk with my grandfather; I'd bolt for the front door and outside. I'd rather snatch lightning bugs from the darkness around Emily's rosebushes and put them quickly in my jar than watch Lawrence Welk.

The money Emily wasn't spending on her grandchildren, her home, food, she tried to save. Jimmy spent his money on the horses and fleet greyhounds out at Scioto Downs and at Beulah Park, racetracks on the outskirts of town.

Jimmy believed in paying cash for everything, carried his money in a silver money clip. He thought interest paid on credit accounts was what was keeping the world blind, poor folk poor. Emily had credit accounts at several downtown shopping stores. She kept them a secret from Jimmy.

Emily walked through our house softly, undisturbingly. When you were sick, there she'd be in your bedroom, just home from work, ghost quiet. Jimmy stomped, banged doors wide open, flicked on lights hard. "Get up," he'd say if you had chores to do, and he'd wait outside the bedroom door until you got up, standing out there like a man, ready to kick the door in. You got up.

Jimmy gave people who worked on the house — carpenters, welders, plumbers, neighborhood Mr. Fix-Its — one chance to prove themselves. White or black, they had one chance. He'd stand over them while they worked, hands in his pockets, a dead cigar in his mouth. My grandfather seemed hardest on blacks. Emily gave everyone the benefit of the doubt. She gave fifty dollars to two men who showed up at the house raising money for missionary work. She wasn't the only one in our neighborhood who fell for the con. Jimmy was livid, went silent. He searched for the men, on foot, and it was a difficult chore.

I never saw them touch. I certainly never saw them kiss. Maybe their devotion was filed away in some kind of vault, and they drew on it like people drawing on a bank account, when they needed it. Love's a mystery.

They watched each other climbing up and down the steep steps in our house, listening for signs of ailing, for odd throat noises, as if ready to issue a medical alert. Jimmy would walk to Mrs. Wilson's store to get whatever Emily wanted. He would often bring back other things, things she didn't know she needed but she needed. Like Epsom salts. Or baking powder. Or Doan's kidney pills. Or rubbing alcohol. My grandmother was crazy about rubbing alcohol. She soaked her feet in a bucket of alcohol and warm water. She must have ached like a hospital patient. Jimmy must have known that.

She did not like his going to the racetrack, wanted him to put his money to better use. But she kept silent and he kept going. My grandfather used a magnifying glass to read the fine print of the racing forms. The instrument had a black stem; the thing looked elegant. I was glad he went to the racetrack. Often I'd go along. The taxi — Jimmy must have spent a fortune on taxis, because the track was far away, out in the country, through miles and miles of trees, of daylight — would swoop through farmland, heading to Scioto Downs, the meter clicking and making a sound like someone sucking food from a cavity. I'd roll from one side of the taxi to the other in the back seat, scanning hillsides for deer. Never saw a one. I can't help but think my grandfather lost more than he won over the years at the track. But he had not only Burke stubbornness but a gambler's stubbornness: he'd even the odds, he'd win his lost money back, he was smarter than the oddsmakers. (Jimmy always kept our taxi fare to get back home in a separate pocket in his dress slacks.)

When I didn't go to the racetrack with my grandfather, I'd run to the living room window at the sound of a car door closing — Jimmy's taxi. I'd see a hat, the tip of a cigar, baggy pants. When he came into the house, you never knew if he'd won or lost, because he'd always have the same expression on his face, flat, no trace of emotion. Jimmy gave away nothing, the true gambler's best expression. He'd take off his coat and hat, ask about phone calls, sit down, grab his tobacco pouch, take off his shoes. If he'd won at the track, he'd walk into the dining room after a few minutes and stand over the table where Emily always sat. He'd stand there, his feet as wide

apart as his shoulders. Then he'd lift his wallet slowly —
maroon leather, soft and well worn, the only wallet I ever
knew him to carry — from his trousers, all the while working
the wad of tobacco from one side of his jaw to the other. He'd
start pulling money from the wallet and laying it out neatly on
the table, ten-dollar bills, twenty-dollar bills. More than once
I saw a hundred-dollar bill. Sometimes my mother rushed
from the dining room at the sight of so much. Maybe it
frightened her, all that money; maybe this ritual was mostly
between Jimmy and Emily. First Jimmy would give money to
Emily. Then he'd call out to Elvira, my mother, and give her
money. She folded it and stuffed it inside her bra. We kids
would get a few dollars. We'd run to hide our money. I'd put
mine in my jar. Emily would take care of her bills. She always
worried about her medical bills from Dr. Blount's office out
on Mt. Vernon Avenue.

So sometimes Jimmy beat the odds. But mostly he didn't.
A lot of times he'd have to come back to Emily a week later
and borrow some of the money back. I guess all the love in
Jimmy for Emily was in the original giving, in the joy that
swept our house when he won, in that act of sharing, no
strings attached, just two people from the woods of Alabama
now in the North. Two souls seesawing through life. The love
in Emily for Jimmy was shrewd and smart. As much as my
grandmother loved the clothing at Madison's, a classy downtown department store, not many items actually left the store
and made their way into her closet in the basement. She did
more window shopping than actual buying. Emily believed in
turning a nickel into a dime, a dime into a quarter, bad luck on
its head. And she believed in rainy days. My grandmother
hoarded her money. When Jimmy came back to her, asking —
in a low voice, which we could barely hear; quite uncharacter-
istic for him, mind you — for the money he had won at the

racetrack, the money he had told her to go shopping with, she retrieved that money. And she passed it back to him without words.

With the exception of my grandfather's jackpot nights at the racetrack, which were quite rare, the passing around of money in my family was done slyly, conspiratorially, in tiny whispers. It was done almost with a touch of artistry. My sister Diane worked a part-time job when she was young. She washed diapers; hated the job. She'd motion to me and Wonder with her eyes. We were to follow her into the kitchen. Once in the kitchen, she passed the money into our palms, as quiet as a spy — a dollar apiece, sometimes a little more. Money was passed from palm to palm on our front porch, in the hallway upstairs, on the stairs leading to the basement — my father to my mother, Jimmy to one of his brothers, Emily to Jimmy, Creola to Emily. Even now, with years gone by, I pass my money along to family members quietly, wanting no bells to ring, nothing to go off, just *Take this.*

5

Eʟᴠɪʀᴀ ᴄᴏᴜʟᴅ ʜᴀʀᴅʟʏ compete against Emily in our household, so she remained on the edges. There was something ghostly about her. On some weekends she disappeared. Elvira went out to meet men, to be met by men, on Mt. Vernon Avenue. My mother loved getting dressed up to go out. It was a ritual for her. I'd sit on the rim of our bathtub watching her apply makeup to her face. She'd stretch her eyelids, applying mascara. She'd powder her face, and wisps of the nut-brown face powder would float through the air like dust. It smelled perfumy. There was a little mole on my mother's face, like a dot. She even dressed up the mole by putting a touch of mascara on it.

I believe my mother was the only person in our whole neighborhood who ordered her dress clothes from Frederick's of Hollywood. She scanned for their ads in *True Confessions* magazine, her broad shoulders collapsed into the sofa, the magazine posed upright on her tummy. Of course, Frederick's

I like this picture of my mother enjoying herself on Mt. Vernon Avenue. Of all her hairstyles/wigs, this was my favorite. Her eyes seem as happy as her smile. The man behind her has keeled over, poor soul.

also had its own magazine. It came to my mother in the mail. If she laid it on the coffee table and went to the store, we were not allowed to touch it. The mailman would come to the door weeks after she had ordered her clothing, carrying a package wrapped in brown. Sometimes the neighbors would be peeking over onto our porch. I'd rush to find Elvira's purse so she could dig for her money to pay the mailman. The things she ordered were always frilly, and they glittered, and they had straps over the shoulder, straps as thin as spaghetti. My mother wore a lot of black clothing. The outfits were imitations of what Hollywood actresses were wearing at the time. I'm talking Dorothy Dandridge, Eartha Kitt, Diana

Sands — black actresses. My mother sometimes mentioned their names, so casually you'd have thought she knew them personally.

After my mother had dressed she'd start tearing through her jewelry box, lifting out bracelets, necklaces, fake pearls (as if I could tell), earrings with loops. Some of the earrings were as big as my school eraser. Then she'd start scavenging for matching high heels. While her head was rolling around like a coconut, I'd beg for pizza money. "Look in my purse." She'd say it as if she were out of breath. There was always makeup powder at the bottom of my mother's purse; it got all over my hands. But I didn't mind.

Then there'd be a car horn blowing outside, and my mother would walk down the steps of our house, slowly, one hand on the banister, dressed up and smelling like the cosmetics counter at the Lazarus department store downtown. Neighbors whistled at her from behind darkness; then she was gone, sometimes in a taxi, sometimes with her wild friend Lily, who had a car. Lily would be blowing her horn out front for my mother as if a dam had broken, as if the flood were coming. Even before my mother got out of sight, I'd miss her.

It wasn't always at night that my mother went over to Mt. Vernon Avenue. She went sometimes to sit beneath tents and listen to evangelists who were crisscrossing the country, spreading their brands of gospel. Elvira didn't trust streetcorner preachers, men who carried Bibles and screamed to the heavens, then asked for money in the same breath. So why'd she go and sit there and listen? On a lazy afternoon in 1963 in Columbus, Ohio, it was something to do. Listen to the screaming preachers; have a soda at Tyler's on the avenue; glide home in the soft Sunday darkness.

In temperament my mother was like Jimmy, my grandfather. She was blunt, given to bouts of silence, not quick to touch. My mother had perfected the art of rolling her eyes. She rolled them hard at people who bothered her, at her own children, at me. You'd feel a little dark ocean wave come over you when she rolled her eyes. You'd reach out and try to find the source of that wave and sometimes you just couldn't; it just came, without warning, whooshing. But my mother was popular. Relatives liked being around her; Uncle Doc called her his favorite niece. Relatives now confide to me that this was because of a kind of flinty frailty that she possessed. My mother's laughter — loud, bent-over laughter, teary laughter — circled a room. She seemed to laugh for people who had lost reason to laugh. Her laughter untamed tamed rooms.

For a woman, my mother had good height. She stood five feet eight inches. That didn't satisfy her, however, and she wore spiked high heels. She towered over her girlfriends. She stood tall enough to look men in the eye. My mother was never short of dates. Men wanted to do things for her. She let them. Some of the men lasted a mere week; a couple visits and they were gone. Elvira's inner timer had run out on them. Jerry lasted the longest. I was crazy about Jerry. Jerry was a magician.

My mother met Jerry in 1952. At the time she was married to my father. When she and my father were divorced and she moved back home with Jimmy and Emily, Jerry began paying visits. He did odd jobs around town. He got up early in the mornings, climbed into his pickup truck, and rolled off into the world of Columbus, going wherever a body and a truck were needed. He hauled junk, scrap metal, iron. I never heard him complain about his work. I never knew where Jerry lived, not even which side of town he lived on, but he seemed to me a happy man. He had his truck, and he had Elvira in her Hollywood dresses. Jerry thought my mother was a tall, skinny gift, something he'd be able to treasure

forever. Most of the time when he came to our back door —
you were special if you had the okay to come to Jimmy's back
door — he came with hands full: pots of homemade stew,
beans, cabbage; sacks of fruit; dead squirrels and dead rabbits,
because my mother was wild about rabbit. And there was
always a jack-in-the-box grin on Jerry's face. He'd pile the
goods onto the kitchen cabinet. Then he'd turn to my mother.
"Give me some sugar," he'd say, meaning a kiss. She'd roll her
eyes, but she'd smile too. That wasn't the hard ocean-wave
roll of the eyes. That was an affectionate and girlish roll of the
eyes. My mother liked it when Jerry weighed our refrigerator
down with things to eat.

He did more than just haul junk. He also fixed things. I
thought he could fix anything. I think much of the world
seemed broken to Jerry, seemed unhinged, and he wanted
to put the world back together, steady it, tighten it. As he
searched for tools in his toolbox, he'd start whistling. Spotting
the tool, he'd snatch it up, as if it were trying to run.

Many men who knew my mother lied right to my face on
our back porch. A man promised to buy me a kite. A man
promised to buy me inner tubes for my bicycle. A man promised to buy me a new glove. I guess they simply said things to
make a child go away. To inch closer to a child's mother. Jerry
made promises and kept every one. He never lied. One evening my red bicycle broke, which broke me up. I called Jerry.
He told me to set my bicycle on our front porch — no one
would steal your bike in our neighborhood — and he'd come
by and fix it. The next morning I rushed out to the front
porch and there on its kickstand was my bicycle, fixed. Jerry
fixed things in the night, while I was dreaming. And when my
sisters and I were sick, down with colds — Jimmy had held
our heads back, his hands pressed to our foreheads, hard, and
poured castor oil down our throats — Jerry would come visit.

He'd kneel beside my bed, smiling. He'd pull quarters from behind my ear. He'd pull a handkerchief from his pocket, tuck it into a balled fist, puff out the handkerchief, and make figures appear on the wall from the handkerchief's shadows: lions, horses, giraffes. I laughed and I felt better. Elvira, however, held to her two fixed reactions to Jerry. Either she'd smile, or — and this could come as quick as a pulled knife — she'd roll her eyes. Jerry didn't mind. Either reaction, he'd grin. In a cold world, my mother was all the fire Jerry needed.

On holidays Jerry's pickup rumbled down our alley. We couldn't wait to hear the noise: we'd run circles around the raspberry bush in the back yard waiting for him. All of the junk would be gone from the back of his truck and it would be filled with hay. We were going to the river. Every summer holiday Jerry took us to the river. We had our own special family spot on the banks of the Scioto. It was first come, first served, but we always got there real early and always went to the same spot. As soon as Jerry arrived to pick us up from our house, he would hop down from the pickup and we'd run to him, then we'd hop up into the back of the truck, into the hay. Elvira took her time coming out of the house and getting into the truck, the front passenger seat, cleaned up just for her, all hers. The truck rumbled toward the river, I and my sisters and cousins piled high in the back, our laughter rising. The hay smelled faintly of cows and horses, like the insides of a barn. And the more you smelled that smell, the more you liked it. We never knew where Jerry got the hay from: magic. In the back of that truck, caught between hay and blue sky, we felt light, airy. It seemed as though we drove for hours. Years later I took that same ride, driving myself; the trip took all of twenty minutes. The world slows for children.

As soon as we reached our spot on the river, we children scattered into the shade and sun and across the grass. The adults spread blankets. Grills were set up, bags of charcoal upended, meat laid on top of the grills. I strolled along the riverbank, poked sticks at dead fish lying there, walked through the woods, got hungry. While the food was cooking, the grownups sat on blankets, sipping liquor, pouring delicately from the bottle of Seagram's into one another's paper cups. They became woozy from the drinks, the sunshine, the green grass. I rarely saw Aunt Alice, Aunt Louise, Uncle Henry, Uncle Ira, Jerry, Elvira herself, any happier than on that grass beside that river, their children safe and within shout's reach. You'd hear laughter rising from grownups' bellies, and the sound sounded good. We played games through shiny afternoons. By dusk the Seagram's had put Elvira right to sleep. She slept like a mummy.

At night I'd climb into the back of the pickup, tired. I'd lie on my back and stare up at the sky, the stars, the blue-blackness up there. But in that truck, lying on my back, hay poking my skin, I felt safe, even if I did hear things: trees, wind, crickets, a wheezing river. Jerry set lanterns around our campsite. They glowed yellow. Soon enough I would hear the morning, see the fog, smell bacon mixed with morning, see Jerry at the grill, smiling, talking in a low voice to Elvira, Elvira suffering from a hangover, begging Jerry to get her some Anacin.

There were times when my aunts and uncles brought friends along to the river. Raymond, a friend of the family's — a friend of my mother's, specifically — came once. Raymond had a smooth face, dark, memorable eyes, a handsome smile. He didn't look as though he did a lot of hard work. Even out at the river Raymond wore dress-up clothes, alligator shoes, swinging jewelry. There was drinking, and angry words were exchanged between Jerry and Raymond with the slicked-back hair. Something to do with Elvira. Jerry inched close to Raymond and demanded an apology. Raymond stepped back. He put his hand in his pocket, as if he were going for something. A lot of fancy-dressing men like Raymond carried switchblades. But Jerry let loose with a roundhouse right. It came so quick, and so viciously, you had to blink to comprehend what you had just seen. "Don't put your hand in your pocket again," Jerry said to Raymond. Raymond did, and again Jerry's fist flew through the air, and again Raymond dropped onto the grass, falling as though he had had a heart attack. There was blood; Raymond turned puffy. It was over just like that. There was a lot we didn't know about Jerry. He looked at us, embarrassed, ashamed that he had done what he had done. I didn't like him any less. I guess all my sisters and I needed to know about him was that he was the second finest man walking the earth. (The first was our grandfather.)

One summer day in 1962, when the weather was clear and gentle, Jerry the magician disappeared. My sister Wonder and I saw him before the disappearance. Elvira had vanished one weekend, out with another man. Jerry went looking for her, like a detective, getting up close to people, whispering in their ears, knocking on doors. He thought people were lying to him. But he found out what he didn't want to find out. That summer day in 1962, Jerry came over to our house to see me and my sister. He must have known Elvira wasn't going to be there. The three of us sat on the ground on a little slope behind our garage, backs to the garage wall, huddled like soldiers. "I'm going to go away," he said to us. Jerry never lied, so he really was going to go away. His voice was hollow. His shoulders drooped. My sister began to cry, which made me cry. I remember Jerry looking up and down the alley, looking to see if Elvira might turn the corner down by Mrs. Wilson's grocery store. She didn't. Then he walked away. His legs were bowed, like the legs of a cowboy. He hopped up into his pickup, drove off, didn't even look back. Maybe he caught sight of us in his rearview mirror. Even after all these years, I want to believe he did. My sister and I ran into our house, the one house where we had always been safe, kept from darkness and terrible hurt. Not this time. Elvira had come into the house through the front door. We ran up to her, told her Jerry was gone, told her he said he wasn't coming back, pleaded with her to find him. Elvira put her hands on her hips, rolled her eyes.

Who knows if the dots can be connected: two months later — during which time we hadn't seen him — Jerry was arrested for stealing a load of baling wire off a railroad car over at the railyard. Just picked the stuff up and loaded it onto his truck and hauled butt. He was convicted and sent to the Ohio State Penitentiary. Things are kept from children, as they should be. This wasn't the first time Jerry had been sent away to the penitentiary. He was a smallish man, but coiled, well built. He had been the Ohio State Penitentiary lightweight boxing champion. That was no small feat: the place was a maximum security prison, a gray-walled building in downtown Columbus with the hardest cons. To climb the ladder of fighters inside a place like that, a small man would have to be tough, and brutal with his fists. Out by the river, our family friend Raymond never stood a chance against Jerry. I recently asked my mother if she ever went to visit Jerry while he was in prison. She didn't. "They used to have so many riots in there," she said.

It wasn't until four years later, in 1966, that I heard Jerry's knock at the back door again. We had been sitting around the dining room table. An autumn day had flowed into darkness. We had no idea Jerry had been released from the penitentiary until my mother pulled back the curtains on the back door, saw his face, and hollered his name. They hugged for what seemed like an hour. I rushed up to Jerry, along with Wonder.

He hugged us, rubbed our shoulders as if we were wearing silk, stared at everyone. He looked thin and weak, and older. His voice had dropped a little; his words trickled out. Something seemed to have happened to him, and we didn't know how to put it into words, even silent words, at that moment. My mother, who by now had moved on to other men — Elvira didn't wait for men — fixed Jerry a huge welcome-home meal. He gripped his fork tight and ate his food quickly, quietly, and completely. Just like James Cagney in those old prison movies. I loved the sight of him sitting there, but wasn't sure if I still knew him the way I had known him. Jerry was older; I was older; my red bicycle was gone. Jimmy sat in the living room, mostly silent. Jobless men were the second most annoying thing to my grandfather, the first being jackleg preachers. Jobless men just released from the penitentiary must have really annoyed him.

After dinner Jerry reached into his back pocket and pulled out a brown wallet. It was leather and, for a man's wallet, beautiful. There was black stitching on the edge of it. Jerry passed it around, showing it off.

"Where'd you get that?" my grandfather asked.

"Made it behind the wall," Jerry said, referring to the penitentiary.

And my grandfather was through talking for the night.

After that, Jerry stopped coming around, drifted from our lives. I last saw him sitting on the front lawn of the state capitol in downtown Columbus. It was 1976; I was fresh from college. He was waiting for the bus. He looked to be shriveling up; his clothes were too big. There was a pornographic book — I saw a picture of a naked woman on the cover — poking from the pocket of the tweed coat he was wearing. I felt bad about losing touch, and even now, writing these words, I feel ashamed that I couldn't have been braver, couldn't have gone looking for him around Columbus.

"How are your sisters?" he asked. "And Harry. How's Harry?" His bus came and he shuffled across the pavement. He looked back, but not with his eyes — with his ears, as if he imagined I had called something out, which I had not.

I was in another city when news of Jerry's death came. He was, among other things, a good man who made me and my sisters very happy. Sometimes he even made Elvira happy.

There was nothing like news of the beginning of the Ohio State Fair every summer in our hometown. I'd save up my allowance and count the money in my jars. Sometimes I'd sell some of my marbles, but never the solid-colored ones, because they were too precious. The fair, which had been taking place since 1849, was a kind of extravaganza of Middle America. That meant corn on the cob, rides on the carousel with music humming in the background, cowboys dressed in bright colors and clicking their spurs at the rodeo. And of course the freak shows, with men and women with large heads — but never as large as on the poster outside the tent — looking you right between the eyes and scaring the daylights out of you. Every year, on the first day, Wonder and I walked to the fair from our house. We knew how lucky we were to live mere blocks from the fairgrounds, to be able to walk up on it like that. At night we'd run up to Elvira's room before she went to bed and look through the window in the direction of the fair, across all the rooftops and treetops. The sky would be lit up in all different colors from the reflection of the rides at the fairgrounds.

On the morning the fair opened, I woke up early. I did my chores. I retrieved my money and put it in my front pocket, then patted myself down to make sure it was secure. My sister and I walked to the fair: then, when we couldn't stop our feet, there we were, running, brushing past startled folk until the fair itself rose over us like something magical and gothic —

our Oz. A lot of my friends sneaked into the fair. You could sneak in by following a crowd at the front gate, then, as soon as you got up to the ticket window, take off running, running for your life, with the ticket-takers screaming at you and for the police. Or you could climb the fence at the north end of the fairgrounds — right in front of the catfish pond — and take off running once over it. (A lot of my friends snagged their legs on the fence; they'd howl with pain.) I wasn't brave enough to do either, so I just paid at the front gate. Once inside, my sister and I roamed like lost children in and out of barns, where we'd stare at roosters, pigs, cows, sheep, exotic birds, shiny horses. We'd go to the freak shows beneath billowing dusty tents. We'd see someone with a glass eye, or maybe a missing arm, or maybe a terrible skin rash: the crocodile man. Someone would give a talk about how the crocodile man was captured "in the wilds of Florida." There'd always be someone standing there with a microphone, giving us the life story of each freak. The so-called freaks sat there on stools, a few cheery but most sad-eyed. Many looked just like everybody else. Sometimes they'd be finishing off their lunch, right in front of us. We'd shake our heads and gawk.

But the part I enjoyed most, even more than getting on the rides, was the rodeo: the cowboys and the angry bulls breaking free, the invisible announcer with the twang in his voice, which came from someplace up in the shadowy rafters, the smell of manure, and the jingly clicking of those spurs on those cowboy boots. I'd sit and watch the rodeo for hours, and while I was doing it, I'd pray for a cowboy hat for Christmas. After the rodeo I'd go out in back of the open-air stadium and get up real close to the cowboys and their horses. I'd watch them unsaddle the horses. Sometimes the cowboys just squinted; sometimes they said hi. I wanted to watch them ride off into the sunset, but the cowboys just led their horses back over to another barn for the night. Sometimes, hanging out back there with the cowboys, I'd get manure on the bottom of my sneakers. I'd walk home kicking the manure off at curbsides.

In the winter, my brother Harry would take me to the fairgrounds to watch big-time wrestling. The wrestlers were huge, like animals. I watched them from the stands with my mouth wide open. Bo Bo Brazil and Sweet Daddy Seekee were about the two most favorite wrestlers in our neighborhood. They were the only two black wrestlers on the circuit. Days before the event would begin, someone would tape flyers to the telephone poles all around the neighborhood: "Bo Bo Brazil. Sweet Daddy Seekee. See Big-time Wrestling. Ohio State Fairgrounds. $1.50 admission." I'd stare at Bo Bo Brazil's picture on the flyer as if I expected him to come flying down off the telephone pole. Jimmy would give me money to go to the wrestling event. He'd lay it on the dining room table, just lay it there, and it was my grandmother who actually told me it was my money, to go see wrestling. I'd scamper by Jimmy and thank him and run upstairs to count it.

There were times when I had to go to the fairgrounds and I hated it, times when I had to go to the fairgrounds for food. When my mother wasn't working we'd go back on welfare. The sight of her monthly check — it came in a colorless envelope — thrilled us for some reason. When my mother could get work, she worked. She got jobs at hotels, and mostly it was seasonal work. Once she even got a job out at the Scioto Country Club, in the clubhouse attached to the racetrack. She'd catch a city bus to the end of the line and then stand where she stepped off the bus and wait for someone from the country club to come out and pick her up. She must have gotten quite cold in the wintertime. But eventually she got laid off from that job as well. And as soon as my mother was laid off, we'd go back on welfare and I'd grab my little red wagon for the walk to the fairgrounds, where we'd get our commodities, in a great big warehouse.

It'd be just me and Elvira. I begged my mother to take shortcuts so friends in the neighborhood wouldn't see me. I was embarrassed. She did sometimes, scooting up back alleys with me, my wagon rolling over gravel. Sometimes I heard screen doors creak open, heard friends howling my name; I didn't dare look back. Elvira walked quickly, with long strides. But then there were times when she was not in the mood to take shortcuts, when she walked right up Fifth Street, right in front of all my friends, who knew where we were going because I had my empty red wagon. When I walked through the fairgrounds when there were no rides up, no rodeo announcer's twang from the stadium, no sightings of candy apples, no Ohio State Fair, the place seemed spooky and quiet. We'd go into the warehouse, where people were lined up waiting for their food, and once we reached the front of the line we'd start loading up my red wagon with cans of peanut butter and Spam, boxes of margarine, sacks of flour, powdered milk. The stuff felt as heavy as cement. Then we'd walk back home, Elvira holding one of my hands, my other hand clutching the handle of the red wagon, the wagon bumping along. I'd keep looking back over my shoulder to make sure nothing fell out.

We stored the commodities down in the basement, like Pilgrims burying their goods. The peanut butter was oily, the milk, when watered, still had lumps in it, and the Spam was horrible. I'd throw my Spam sandwiches in a garbage can on the way to school and beg William Barnes to let me eat lunch over at his house, because his mother always fixed those ham sandwiches with slices of cheese on them. She also had about ten different kinds of cookies. And she'd let me drink as much Kool-Aid as I wanted.

The one journey my sister and I feared most was to the dentist. Because my mother was on welfare more often than not, we had dental care provided by welfare. The dentist was a mean black man with a moon face and eyes like dots. His office was downtown, across from the public library. You'd never see him until the last moment. Then he'd step from behind a curtain, pick up some tools, push back your head, and yank out a tooth. Then he'd vanish again, like some strange Oz-like figure, and a nurse would come in and wipe away the blood. There were good teeth he took out, I believe, teeth I want back, badly. I'd cry, my sister would cry. We'd bleed all over the place. We'd hold hands on the way home. At home Emily and Jimmy would give us sweets as soon as we healed.

Jimmy was my grandfather — and my father. It was sometimes confusing to friends. I called him Daddy. I barely knew my real father, Jack Haygood. By the time I was eight he had remarried, though he still lived in Columbus, over on the east side of town. But he'd visit us often enough, mostly on weekends, and the sight of him excited me. He drove a Hudson automobile, purple with a soft beige cloth interior, and some mornings I'd wake up and hear his voice downstairs in our Fifth Street home, coming at me from the dining room or from the front porch, floating upstairs to me through screen windows. My father's voice was deep and smooth and it carried like echoes. I'd pull back the curtains and see his car parked in front of our house, spotless, with whitewalled tires, there like a trophy. I'd rush downstairs, and for some reason I'd feel jumpy, as if it were a holiday or something. Jack and Elvira would talk in the house, then they'd go out to the car and talk some more. I'd be up on the porch, playing, and I could almost make out what they were saying, but not quite; what I heard just sounded like two people whispering to each other. Jack's hat would be on the dashboard. You could see

JACK, *my daddy, as a navy cook.*
I felt tingly when he showed up.

Elvira behind the windshield rolling her eyes, being silent, smoking a cigarette. Before he drove off, my sisters and I would run out to the car and badger the man for money. He'd raise coins from his pockets, sometimes a dollar bill or two, and he'd drive off in that beautiful car. We might not see him again for two weeks. We never complained.

My sisters and I were lucky that we got to know our father's family, his sisters and brothers, who lived in Cincinnati. Jack's brothers were tall light-skinned men, handsome. Uncle Falvin was a preacher with a church across the border in Kentucky. Another, Uncle Duke, was funny, loud, and charming; he died in a car accident on a dark Georgia road. One sister, Aunt Gussie, left Ohio to live in Los Angeles. She did maid work and dated a man who dressed beautifully and worked in Hollywood: janitor, back lot, Paramount Studios — the mov-

My father's sister, AUNT BERTHA,
took a shine to me. I'm grateful.

ies. Another sister, Aunt Bertha, doted on me. I'd cry for two
weeks about wanting to go see Aunt Bertha, until finally
Elvira would put me on the bus to Cincinnati to go visit her.
I'd ride with my face pressed against the window, flat farmland
rolling by.

My Aunt Bertha and her husband, Uncle Willie Grover,
weren't rich. They just seemed rich to me. There was all kinds
of food in their refrigerator, none of it commodities. Aunt
Bertha told me I could have anything I wanted from the
refrigerator, at any time. I ate like a wolf. They had a car; had
two cars, in fact. I played and fought in the big yard with
my cousins. We loved kickball. One sunny afternoon the ball
bounded up into an old dilapidated truck in the adjacent yard.

I scampered after it, up into the truck, and a swarm of bum-blebees buzzed right into my face. I screamed for my Aunt Bertha, my Uncle Willie Grover, my cousins. They rushed me to the hospital. My face swelled, but I was fine.

Except through school maps, deep-hearted wishing, imagina-tion, I never traveled. More than anything in the world I wanted to travel, to visit any place beyond Ohio. There were times when I felt the rest of the world was calling my name. It was like a great pulling. I satisfied some of the desire by sending away for fishing magazines, for art supplies, and star-ing for hours at the faraway post office box numbers, the different states my packages arrived from: Illinois, Missouri, New York. I wondered who in Missouri had wrapped my package, had typed my name on the label; I wondered if they thought of me, all the way in Ohio, if they wondered how tall I was, what color I was; I wondered if they thought we'd ever meet. When friends returned from vacation, I pum-meled them with questions about the out-of-state locale, the weather, the hills, the people, the food — especially the food. I wanted to know how long it took to get there in a car. I wanted to know if there was anything like our Ohio State Fair. I talked until they got tired of my questions.

In the summer of 1964 I packed excitedly to take my first journey out of the state of Ohio. I was going south, to Geor-gia, with Aunt Bertha and her family. It would be the first time I had laid eyes on my father's mother, my grandmother Frances. It was hard to imagine that there was another entire family of Haygoods off in the distance, waiting to meet me, Jack's boy — pulling at me from the outside world.

We left Cincinnati in the middle of the night, and the hours blurred by. It wasn't long before the sun came up. Uncle Willie Grover did all of the driving. There were six of us in the car: Uncle Willie Grover and Aunt Bertha up front, me and my cousins — Alberta, Joyce, and Willie Junior — in the back. I was ten that summer, Alberta nine. The two of us fussed the whole trip. Somewhere between Kentucky and Tennessee, Alberta told me she hated me. Uncle Willie Grover drove with a pistol under his seat, the driver's seat. I had no idea why. Of course the grownups knew why: the South, the sixties.

Uncle Willie Grover was a big man, dark-skinned. He had a country voice; that is to say, his words sometimes seemed to pause in his throat, in his eyes, rolling around, joyfully so. Everything he said seemed to surprise even himself. "Godawmighty" was one of his favorite words. Uncle Willie Grover made words sound elegant. His upper lip had spots of pink on it. When he had been a kid in Georgia, an aunt had been making some peanut brittle in a frying pan. Uncle Willie Grover tried to slurp some of it up — he was just a boy — and it stuck and singed his lip. His full name was Willie Grover Browning. No one called him Willie, always Willie Grover. I've come to love the double stitching of southern names: always as if the middle name were pulling the first name along.

Aunt Bertha was a kind, tall, butter-colored woman, generous in her affections. She fascinated me. She could do many things at once: watch the road signs, fix Uncle Willie Grover a sandwich, settle me down in the back seat, pour my cousins lemonade to drink — all with the voice of an angel. Aunt Bertha had taken the best of the Deep South — family love, love of food, faithfulness, and common sense — and raised her family with those ingredients.

We arrived in Statham, Georgia, on a crisp morning. Fog hugged the roadsides. Crops were everywhere in fields. The corn, I distinctly remember, was up high from the ground. An

Ohio boy can recognize a cornfield a mile away. The Georgia morning smelled wet, grassy. And you could smell pine trees in the air too. I rubbed sleep from my eyes. When the farmhouse came into view through the mist, my grandmother Frances, whom I had never before seen in my life, though I knew she was my grandmother as soon as I did see her, was on the porch, her hands resting on her apron. She was dressed all in black and wore tiny eyeglasses, the frames perfectly round. I was the only stranger to her eyes who stepped out of that car that morning. She pulled me up close to her bosom. An old lady, a soft lady. "This here's Jack's boy, all right," she said, seeing my father in me, the Haygood in me. I had to pee; I wanted to eat; I wanted to run and play; I wanted to go fishing; I wanted to see where I'd sleep; I wanted to find the candy store. I could smell fresh-baked biscuits from the porch.

I ran around that first day, looking out over vast stretches of land, watching cars rumble up and down the dusty roads, sizing up my grandmother's mule, wondering if I'd ever ride the thing. Then I was told what chores I'd be responsible for every morning: fetching water from the well, collecting eggs from the chicken coop. I'd climb up on the well and lean over it, staring down at the darkness down there. Sometimes, if the sun was high, I'd be able to catch the sheen on the surface of the water down below. The well water had a metallic, sweet taste to it, quite unlike our water up north. It was also as cold as ice, and I soon began looking forward to gulping a mouthful. The chickens in the coop ran around like crazy, pecking my hand when I reached for eggs. I dropped some eggs and didn't care. The ones I successfully scooped up I bragged about.

An uncle told me never to walk up behind a mule, so I didn't. I found my grandmother's mule out in the middle of a

FRANCES HAYGOOD, *my paternal grandmother.*
It broke her heart when she came to Columbus
looking for Macaroni and couldn't find him.
We decided not to tell her he was in a
place called San Quentin.

field, the sun beating down on its back and my head. Its eyes were like giant black olives. My cousin Willie Grover Junior lifted me up on the mule. The longer I rode, the more I felt the bone sticking up from the mule's backside. It made the ride grueling. I smacked the mule with the back of my hand. I yelled at the thing, *getty-up*, ten times, forty times, but it just walked up and down and across my grandmother's fields. It was as if someone had already whispered in the mule's ear where to take me, how far to go before turning around.

The land stretched for miles, all Haygood land. My grandmother's father, the Reverend Harrison Vincent, had been a big shot with the National Baptist Association: old men meeting in meeting halls, talking about the crops and Jesus Christ as though Jesus Christ lived down the road. My great-grandfather had been a respected landowner who had left each of his children land in Statham. His sons — my grandmother's brothers — were the men I'd see on porches. They looked ancient to me. I'd walk the roads near our farm and stumble upon them, silent men in straw hats, rocking, enough room in their baggy pants for another human being.

"You Jack's boy, ain't you?"

They knew the answer before I answered.

"Yes sir," I'd say.

They'd look me up and down from beneath the straw hats, smiling brightly. They'd raise an arm to their wives, pointing at me, looking at the wife. "This Jack's boy." It hardly mattered to them that I barely knew Jack.

A long road ran beside my grandmother's cabin. At the end of that road, going south, sat two cabins a few yards apart from each other. Children were all over the place. They were my cousins, Uncle R.D.'s children. It was hard to tell whether they lived inside or outside. The front yard was full of things — chairs, buckets, tables, something that looked like a cross between a washing machine and a robot. Uncle R.D. sat on the porch of one of the cabins all day long, his red eyes looking off into the distance. He never said a word to me during my entire visit. A few times I thought he was on the verge of saying something, because I saw his Adam's apple move. It moved like a ventriloquist's. But nothing came out. I squinted when I looked at him.

The Georgia nights were as dark as sleep, unlike any dark I had ever known. At night I'd stand in the front yard, a lantern hanging from my hand, and look out into the surrounding forest. Everything was scary black. And the forest was no longer visible, just thick darkness, the kind of darkness that would just swallow your imagination up whole. Soon as I heard something move, or even imagined I heard something move, I'd take my lantern and hurry back inside.

The inside of my grandmother's house was all wood. The floor was wood and the furniture was wood and the doors leading from room to room were wood. In one room there were cans of food — farm food — stored for the winter. Green beans and yams. Pickles in green pickle juice; beets in red beet juice. The house smelled like food, and all day every day there was someone in the kitchen cooking — breakfast, lunch, dinner. The smell kept me hungry.

I slept in a room with my grandmother, in a bed next to hers. Thick colorful quilts lay on top of the beds. I told my grandmother I couldn't go to the outhouse at night, told her I was afraid of tripping, of falling over something. She knew what I was afraid of: out there, the dark. So she set a bucket beside my bed and told me to pee in it. "Drop water in this," she said. The nights were coolish, and I slept balled up beneath my quilt. I ran so much during the day that at night I collapsed and fell asleep, free of dreams. Mornings I bathed in a wide tin tub, the kind you sometimes see in cowboy movies. I shivered sitting in that bucket, causing water to splash on the wood floor. My teeth chattered. My knees knocked.

After I did my morning chores, most days I'd walk into town with Willie Junior. One day I walked alongside him with a ten-dollar bill in my pocket. My sister Diane had sent it to me by mail, and when it came I danced around my grandmother's front yard. At the country store I bought myself a soda pop and candy and bought Willie Junior a soda pop and candy too. The clerk behind the counter smiled widely at me. I think he could tell by my accent that I was a stranger. The town was tiny — a couple of feed stores, a country store, little stores that sold plaid shirts and coveralls. Dust was always blowing in my face. Willie and I just roamed.

Willie Junior was a far better country boy than I'd ever be. He knew the woods, knew where to fish, knew secret hiding places. When we were walking through the woods, he'd walk ahead of me, whacking his way through thick weeds. He carried a long knife, twirling it when he wasn't whacking away at something. Weeds hit my bare legs and I shrieked. Willie Junior never shrieked, just kept telling me to keep up.

One afternoon at a creek, tired of sitting, of not catching any fish, I told Willie Junior I was leaving, going back to the farm. I was also hungry. Willie told me not to walk away, to stay put and wait for him. But I was already walking. I told him I'd find my way home: over there, then up that road, then a ways down that way, through those woods, which I was already pointing to. Away from Jimmy and Emily and Elvira back in Columbus, I could be — to use one of Elvira's favorite words — hardheaded.

Before I realized it, however, I was deep in the woods. Stretches of land looked just like other stretches of land. I wanted to see my grandmother's farm, her mule in the fields, but I didn't see those things. There was not a rooftop in sight. I looked over my shoulder and yelled Willie Junior's name; he didn't answer. I walked onward, onward until the moment when I realized I was lost. I began walking faster, hopping over logs and huge rocks. Then I came upon a clearing. Tall white marble stones, evenly spaced apart, stones as tall as me. All the stones said "Haygood." I had stumbled across the Haygood cemetery, the final resting place for aunts and uncles

My knee is bent, my face is scowling: I'm in my father's Georgia with WILLIE GROVER JUNIOR, *who whacked his way through the woods as if he owned them.*

I had never known, for my great-grandfather, the man who had purchased the land I was lost on. I saw tiny photographs of Haygoods on some of the stones. It was a common practice in the thirties, forties, and fifties to put a little picture of the dead person on his or her stone. The pictures had small rounded glass coverings on them. But I had no time to appreciate the artistry. The stones were blocking my path, and it was getting dark, and I didn't like being there in the cemetery. I started to bolt; then some voices reached me. It was my Aunt Frances (named after my grandmother) and her husband. They were among those sent looking for me, and they had noticed me through the trees. "I got lost," I cried out to them.

Back at the farm, my grandmother spanked me good. She also lit into Willie Junior for letting me out of his sight. Willie didn't say a word to me the whole night, half of the next day. After my spanking, though, my grandmother fed me. She cooked the food I had helped pick off the land — okra, tomatoes, green beans, lima beans, corn. My grandmother fried our corn and it was wonderful, buttery and sweet. She fixed homemade biscuits and let me spoon grape jelly from a canning jar onto them. There were open jars of relishes and peppers and beets on the dinner table. You didn't have to ask for anything, you could get as much as you wanted. My grandmother kept telling me to eat. When I was finished, she would tell me to eat some more, look over at my Aunt Bertha, and pronounce that I was too skinny.

Some conversations between Aunt Bertha and my grandmother came out muddled, as if they were standing behind a curtain, but they weren't. They just lowered their voices. I heard talk now and then about Gary, my other brother, my father Jack's bastard son, who had been raised right here on this farm. I couldn't say anything, because I had never laid eyes on Gary. (Once, in our home in Columbus, I had been handed the telephone. I listened to someone on the other end — his voice was strong and chipper — tell me he was my brother. It was Gary, calling from the penitentiary. I handed the phone back to my sister, went to play.)

I went to visit all of my aunts and uncles the day before I left. I found Uncle R.D. on his porch at the end of the road. His children scampered around him as if he were invisible. His Adam's apple was jumpy. He didn't move an inch, said not one word to me. I even wondered if he remembered I was Jack's boy.

Home pulled at me; I was not unhappy to leave. On the day I left, my grandmother and my cousins stood in her front yard and waved us away. There were so many cousins that I could hardly remember all of their names. I waved goodbye with purpose, as they did.

I looked forward to my return to Ohio. I missed Jimmy and Emily — and Elvira too. I wondered if they missed me as much as I missed them.

Alberta and I resumed our bickering in the back seat before we had left the tall trees of Georgia. Aunt Bertha said we were fighting so much because we secretly liked each other. Uncle Willie Grover let out a long squealing chuckle. Alberta shook her head — no no no, she did not secretly like me. Not at all.

Just before I was about to enter eighth grade, on the cusp of turning thirteen, I fell deeply in love — with basketball. Before this, I could take the game or leave it, just as I could take or leave baseball, football, kite flying. But now the game of basketball had drifted inside me, and I knew it was there to stay, like shadows in a wide forest. It was a pretty game: a player taking a jump shot from the top of the key and floating back downcourt, or pausing for a split second, then bolting like a fired bullet toward the rim and a layup; or you yourself doing something you had never done before on a basketball court and listening to the music from the mouths of others who knew you had never done it before — and you might not ever do it again. You couldn't play baseball or football by yourself. Basketball called out to the lonely: I'd shoot baskets for hours, just me and the sky and the gentle wind. I'd rise from bed at the sound of someone bouncing a basketball down the alley. I'd walk to empty playgrounds and just stare at the rim, at the net. I'd borrow basketballs that belonged to grown men, sweet-talking their wives at the screen door, then thanking them for trusting me to bring their husband's ball back before dark. I'd return the ball, then rush back to the playground, playing some more with whoever remained on the court. I didn't mind the dark. It was as if my eyes reversed the dark, the dark turned to daylight; I saw clearly, learned the sound of my friends' voices in the dark. I wasn't playing with or against daylight, with or against darkness; I was just play-ing. I liked the game, the quickness of it, the simplicity. All you were asked to do was fill up the air around you with bodily movements.

It helped to be born with the grace the game required. You could spend a lifetime looking for such grace. Basketball seemed the perfect game for a skinny boy with a caved-in chest who believed he had a little grace. When my cousin Talbert got a job at the mental hospital in Columbus, when he told me there was a gymnasium, when he told me he had the keys to the gymnasium, I begged him to let me go to work with him on Saturday mornings. Talbert was a big brute, moody. He wore sunglasses at night, listened to Miles Davis all the time. I played while patients peered at me, their faces pressed to the window of the bolted door. And when Talbert was fired — for nearly choking a patient to death — I was sad.

I entered Indianola Junior High School in 1966. It was an old gothic brick school set beside railroad tracks. Trees surrounded the school grounds. We were a bunch of black and white kids, children of factory workers, auto mechanics, waitresses — all neighborhood kids. It was a mile-and-a-half walk from my house through alleys with my friends, Bubbles and Tutu and Dalton. I ran and looked at the gym on the first day. By the second day I was shooting baskets on my lunch break. It felt nearly romantic to be inside that small boxlike gymnasium. A lot of times, on the way home from school we'd stop at Lawson's grocery store. We'd crowd around each other, shielding whoever was brave enough on any given afternoon to pick up cupcakes and drop them into our duffel bags. Bubbles was especially good at shielding us because he was so big. Back out in the alley, we'd walk fast and look over our shoulders.

I didn't make the basketball team in the seventh grade. The coach said something about my being "weak." I lacked muscle; other boys were bullying me during tryouts. I sulked, cried even. I did strengthening exercises; I shot baskets on my own outside in the cold. In class I flicked through basketball magazines and daydreamed.

We were always being called out of class to attend an assembly. A scratchy voice would come over the school audio system and we'd be marched off to the auditorium. We seemed to have the same speaker every time: Mayor M. E. Sensenbrenner. Did he do all of his speaking to schoolkids? He was a tall, bony man with skin as white as chalk. His eyes were dark and his hair shone like the tips of my grandfather's shined shoes. After his speeches he always stood at the back of the auditorium handing out these itty-bitty American flags. We'd take them and fling them at each other during detention hour, which was held every day after school in the cafeteria.

The next year rolled around. I aimed to make the basketball team. I flexed my muscles in mirrors. The night before try-outs, however, I fretted: I still didn't have my physical examination form filled out. I didn't want to make a fuss to Elvira about taking me to the clinic for a physical. She might have said it cost too much; she might have just told me to forget about playing basketball. My brother Harry always forged his physical exams. He'd just fill out the form and scribble an un-recognizable name at the bottom. The night before my try-outs, Harry closed the door to our bedroom and forged my physical for me. He signed a phantom doctor's signature with a wild flourish of the hand. No one could make out the name of that doctor. Harry pronounced me in excellent physical condition, and the next morning at school I handed the form to the coach. He just filed it away with the rest of the examination forms.

The light in the gymnasium at Indianola Junior High al-ways seemed gauzy to me. It was an old gym with brick walls and wood floors. The floors still gleamed, but the place smelled musty. Yet every time I stepped onto that gym floor, I felt lifted up. I felt nervous too. I'd shiver and sweat at the same time. My arms and legs were always ashen, as though I had been rubbed down in chalk. Mornings before taking off for school I'd rub myself, arms and legs, with my sister's Royal Crown hair grease, which gave my skin a sheen. I shone like a new dime. After practice my friends and I would walk home from school beside the railroad tracks, throwing rocks at trains, betting who would make the team, who'd not make it. We'd say funny things about Coach Magoo — that was really his name.

Coach Magoo cut me again.

Only this time was worse. I felt painfully and forever cut loose from my friends, from shooting baskets and sweating and dribbling, from walking home from school together after practice in the twilight beside the railroad tracks, swinging our duffel bags, stealing cupcakes. I lost sleep at home that night, said nothing about being cut.

The next day after school I floated into the dressing room. I do not believe I could have stopped myself. I got dressed in silence. My friends knew I had been cut and they were surprised to see me in the locker room. Skip White looked at me as if I had just murdered someone. He shook his head coldly. But not my friend Tutu. Tutu looked at me as cleanly and kindly as a friend might. There was nothing in his eyes to condemn me. I hustled out onto the gym floor, startled Coach Magoo, and begged him for another chance. I stood there in front of everyone, begging through dry lips. The coach looked at me, then away from me, then turned to me again. He sent me into the warm-up drills. For three straight days I practiced. I played hard, hearty, reckless. Coach Magoo put me on the team. Skip White resented my being on the team. He whispered unkind things behind my back. I didn't care.

Harry bought me my first pair of Converse All-Star sneakers, white hightops. I'd sit on the end of our wooden bench during games, looking at the blurring play in front of me, scanning the students in the seats. I rarely got into games. I'd sit on the bench, shivering and sweating as always. I was happy to have a uniform, even if it was too big for me. I was happy to walk home with my friends after practice and games — the darkness draping us, the old Pennsylvania railcars rumbling by — swinging our duffel bags, drawing our shoulders in from the cold, a team.

Harry was a star athlete at North High School by his eleventh-grade year. He ran track and won trophies. He started center for the basketball team. My friend Bubbles and I caught the city bus to North High's games. Dwight Lamar, also a star for North High School, showed up at one game in a lime-green suit and sunglasses, with a walking stick. He stood in the doorway of the gym before disappearing to the varsity locker room. The crowd went crazy. But toward the end of Harry's basketball season in the eleventh grade, my brother got in an argument with the coach about which position it was best for him to play. Harry wanted to play forward, not center. The coach said he was the coach, he made the decisions. Harry threatened to quit the team; then he actually quit, shocking both school and coach. My brother was called a quitter; he joined with the school rebels. I went to North High's tournament game at the fairgrounds, taking my shortcut, the one I took to get our commodities. Harry showed up in street clothes with some of his friends. He was wearing a black leather coat. He looked cool, and lost, staring out at the court, watching his teammates. North High fans were yelling at him, asking him why he wasn't out on the court. He laughed, shook hands, and walked out of the coliseum, his unbuttoned leather coat flapping.

Harry stayed out late at night. Elvira peered out the windows. He didn't have basketball practice to hold him down; she wondered where he went after school. Harry suddenly announced he was going to quit school altogether. Our grandfather was passionate about education. We were not late for school; the thought of playing hooky never crossed our minds. My grandfather told Harry that if he quit school, he'd have to leave the house, find another roof to cover his head. And he said this with that Ten Commandments look on his face, that Burke look. There was no retreat from that look. Emily and Elvira just sat and listened. Jimmy had closed the door on the matter.

The standoff was awkward. My brother quit school and joined the navy. He wanted to be a man before he was a man. Nervousness swept our house: Vietnam, the war. Emily and Elvira fretted. Jimmy was as quiet as stone. My brother went off to a naval base in Florida, then sailed on the USS *Saratoga*. He sent a framed photograph of himself to Emily. It was his graduation photo from naval school. My grandmother set the photograph atop her TV set, at eye level. She watched newsreel footage of the Vietnam war on TV some evenings, rubbed herself with her rubbing alcohol, soaked her feet, and thought of Harry. In that photo atop my grandmother's TV set, Harry was dressed in his navy blues. He had a thin mustache, and he also wore a silky white ascot. Years later I came across another picture of Harry in navy uniform, only as I looked closer, I realized it wasn't Harry. It was Jack, our father: the same smooth skin, the same thin mustache. The same eyes.

I missed my brother and prayed he'd write letters.

I still put baby powder on the outside of the sneakers Harry had bought for me. The powder kept them milky white. I did not score a single point on the basketball team the entire season. When I got into a game, I shook with fear. The lights seemed too brittle. The students in the stands seemed too noisy, even if there were a mere dozen or so for our JV games.

I raced home after school to look for letters from my brother, which never came.

When Diane began talking to our mother in a low voice behind closed doors, I knew something was wrong. Diane, all of seventeen years old, was pregnant. Little skinny Eddie, apple-head Eddie, the tough guy, had gotten her pregnant. She'd sit on the back porch looking out over the yard, wondering what she'd do, where she'd go. She was afraid of how angry Jimmy would surely be. She decided she'd go away to Detroit or Cincinnati, live with relatives and finish her schooling in one of those cities. Our cousin Lois, fanciful and carefree, invited Diane to come live with her. Lois had come to visit us on several occasions. She lived in Cincinnati, took long drags on her cigarettes, talked loudly, laughed loudly, and wore hippie clothes.

When Jimmy came home from work one day, my mother told him that Diane was pregnant, said she'd be leaving soon. Jimmy stood facing Emily and Elvira and said that Diane wasn't going anywhere, said that he never wanted to hear such talk again, said that Diane was already at home and she and the baby would stay right there, upstairs. Emily nodded, didn't say a word.

Diane's baby came, a boy. She named him Tony. He looked just like Eddie. But by that time my mother was already announcing plans to move. Move? The idea sounded ridiculous to my sisters and me. This was the only house we knew. But there was a relatively new housing project on the east side called Bolivar Arms, and my mother had applied and been accepted. She hadn't been out in the world since 1951, when she and my father married. The end of that relationship stung my mother. She found a cocoon with her parents. But in 1968 my mother was only thirty-six years old. She wanted to leave the cocoon. There was still time for her to set her compass.

On the last day of school at Indianola — it was a bright day — I stood on the edge of the baseball diamond in back of the school. I huddled with my friends, saying goodbye. I knew next to nothing about the east side of Columbus, about the new school I would be attending. But I knew the east side had a reputation: it was tough, rowdy. It could be dangerous. And the basketball players were better, quicker, bigger.

We packed our clothes in old worn suitcases, in large bags, in pillowcases.

Uncle Ira came to get me and my sisters and baby Tony on the day we moved. My brother was a million miles away, and I wished he were not. Elvira was already in our new apartment, having slept there the previous two nights on blankets. Our new furniture had not yet arrived. Jimmy had told her not to sleep in the apartment by herself, with no bed, but my mother was both anxious and eager; she believed someone else might be given her promised apartment.

The day Uncle Ira came for us was sunny and clear. His car lumbered down Fifth Avenue and made a right onto St. Clair Avenue, heading for the St. Clair Avenue bridge. This bridge was popular in our town. It was the bridge that carried you straight to Mt. Vernon Avenue. There was a hump in the middle of it. My sisters and I always liked riding over that hump in a fast car, because it felt for a moment like a carnival ride, bouncing up and down in the back seat. But this time, approaching the bridge in Uncle Ira's car, I didn't feel any excitement. I was leaving my friends behind, and Jimmy and Emily. Something was about to snap, and suddenly I realized it.

When we reached the hump in the bridge, I saw the rooftops of the cement structures where we'd be living. I saw open sky. Then Uncle Ira's car went over the hump and I felt as if I were being swallowed down into something. We rolled down a road adjacent to the railroad tracks, and just shy of a smelly stockyard turned right and rolled into Bolivar Arms. The eyes of kids I had never seen in my life landed on me like hungry insects. Every apartment looked like every other apartment. Every small tree planted in front of every apartment looked like every other tree. Elvira walked out to the car and toward us like someone coming down off a movie screen. Her head was held high. Her shoulders were squared. She glowed like that colored actress Miss Dorothy Dandridge. My mother looked proud. We dragged our belongings into the new apartment. People watched from the sidewalk, stared down from windows, started mumbling.

I had no idea what it would be like to live with my mother alone. My mother was going solo. For some reason that frightened me.

6

Bolivar arms, a three-acre public housing complex, consisted of five units, each a cul-de-sac, each a dream come true for the families that occupied the apartments. It had been built in 1964. It replaced shacks, lean-tos with outdoor plumbing, muddy fields. The area had been a huge eyesore; it made the city fathers grimace. So they were delighted to see the complex rise. Its style was military barracks, with each unit looking exactly the same — the same beige brick, the same little tree planted in front of each apartment. Mayor Sensenbrenner strolled around the site at the opening, tall and chalky, as happy as someone at a revival, handing out his miniature American flags, smiling.

There was something different I noticed about Bolivar Arms right away: it was all black. We had moved from our integrated neighborhood to a segregated neighborhood. I guess my mother had to take what she could get.

I had, for the first time in my life, a room all my own. It was small, but it was mine. I papered the walls with pictures of sports figures. Campy Campeneris of the Oakland A's: he wore white cleats. Oscar Robertson of the Cincinnati Royals: he wore number 14; he never smiled on the court, all business. I hung my clothes neatly in my closet. I shut the door when I felt like it. I pulled back my curtains and peered out over my new surroundings, spied people sitting on cars, stared at strangers coming and going, listened for the bounce of basketballs. At night I bent down on my knees, leaned on my bed, and said my prayers, as Emily, my grandmother, would expect me to do.

The first grown man I met in our new apartment was Bo. Diane came home with him one evening. Bo wore brown lizard shoes. He told me they cost ninety dollars. I gaped, stared at them during the whole evening, prayed I'd own a pair of shoes like that someday. Bo asked me questions about school, books, my hobbies. He concentrated on me as if he wanted to study me. "You're smart," he told me, elevating me to a position I doubted I deserved.

Bo had kind but sleepy eyes and talked out of the side of his mouth in a raspy voice. It sounded always on the verge of a cough. His mustache looked like a caterpillar on his lip. He was too old for Diane, but she liked him. He never hit her, as crazy Eddie had done. He took her to the nightclubs up on Mt. Vernon Avenue. Bo was a hustler and a heroin addict. (He was honest about the hustling; I didn't learn about the heroin till years later.) Sometimes I'd still be up when they returned, Bo coming through the door jauntily in his lizard shoes. He may have hustled, may have shot heroin, but he was also a gentleman, had fine manners, graceful movements, respected my mother. One night Bo told me that hustling scared him, scared him because he made so much money and he didn't know what to do with all of it. I thought he might then and there give me a handful of money, but he didn't. Bo could talk for hours, and I could listen for hours. He'd talk about politics, the streets, self-confidence, faraway places. Sometimes I'd see him walking along Bolivar Avenue in a long tan trenchcoat, hands stuffed in the pockets of the trenchcoat, lizard shoes moving like live lizards, and wonder how come he didn't have a car if he really did make so much money.

It did not take long for a voice to begin to surface in our new apartment. It was my mother's voice, racing up the stairs, bouncing off the walls. My mother's voice charged ahead, took on a new texture. It was the final commandment given in our new home. There was no more Jimmy and no more Emily, no more buffering, no more higher authority, nothing to shave the anger from her voice — just Elvira. My mother's voice carried. My mother screamed. If she was drinking, her voice cracked walls.

For years my mother had been as dim to me as faraway candlelight. I could not distinguish her strengths from her weaknesses. I thought of her as fragile, and told myself that Jimmy and Emily, my grandparents, would defend me from the monsters of the world. But now, in 1968 — America's apocalyptic year, Elvira's apocalyptic year too — my mother began to emerge with the force of a just-turned-on blast furnace. I tilted various ways from the heat. Loose in the world, as I was about to see for the first time, my mother stood on her bony legs, laughed, cried, and made mistakes. That year was the first time I had ever seen my mother cry. One night not long after we moved into Bolivar Arms, there she was, downstairs, lying on the sofa, balled up. I think I knew why she lay there crying: there wasn't enough money in the house; bills were piling up already; long hot nights had already begun to suck in my sisters; the world was darker than she had imagined. I stood at the bottom of the stair railing, staring at her, mumbling; then I bolted back up the stairs, full of fear and incomprehension. But the next morning she rose, flinty and fierce, and went about the job of standing her ground, protecting her children.

My mother prayed standing on her feet, standing over the kitchen stove. "Sweet Jesus," she'd say. When we heard that utterance, we knew what had happened: she had lost another kitchen job; the rent was behind. Her strength was not always noticeable, but it was there and it helped me become the man I am today. My mother clutched my hand crossing streets, tight. She slapped me when I deserved to be slapped, which was when I laughed cruelly, when I mocked an older brother for going scoreless in a basketball game.

Who knows what would have become of my mother if she had stayed in the South, in Selma? Maybe a lifetime of working in a chicken factory; maybe a farmer's wife and ten children. As it was, when she moved to the east side of Columbus in 1968, Alabama was pretty much on fire with civil rights demonstrations. While the South was struggling to keep from falling apart, Elvira Haygood was trying to put her life back together. If you wanted to connect to the American South in Columbus, Ohio, in 1968, all you had to do was go to the east side. So many of the people who lived there were from the South, from Mississippi and Alabama and Georgia, from teeny-tiny towns whose names we didn't even know how to pronounce in geography class. The east side of Columbus may have been strange and even exotic to my sisters and me, but not to Elvira. She knew Mt. Vernon Avenue: she knew the Macon Club and she knew the Idle-a-While and she knew Tyler's Drugstore. She knew Carl Brown's grocery store and she knew the Pythian Theatre and she knew the Flamingo Club. In 1968 my mother knew where we were going, even if we didn't.

Not long after we had moved into our new apartment, my mother started working again, back at Yolando's restaurant, where my grandfather worked, where, off and on, she worked over the years. She put on her waitress uniform again, which she had gone rifling through the closets to find. She'd arrive home late, tired. I'd pull back the curtains, look outside, see her, the moon, the darkness. And I'd soon hear the clink of glasses.

My mother drank. She couldn't hold it at all, but she preferred bourbon. "That was my drink — a shot of bourbon," she remembers. When she drank, she wanted to dance. She also wanted to philosophize. She'd return home from Mt. Vernon Avenue, where she sometimes stopped after work for a drink, which always turned into several drinks, which led her to the dance floor. Sometimes she'd call from the bar to check on me and my sisters; I'd hear music in the background, and loud people, their voices scattering. When she arrived home, after she had finished opening and shutting cabinets downstairs, after she had fried herself something to eat, she'd climb the stairs, talking to herself, with grease from the fried food still on her lips, still on her cheeks. She'd come into my bedroom, sit on the edge of the bed, lean against the moonlight coming through the curtains. She'd talk about life, about relatives, about slights done to her. She'd talk about men, about my sisters, about my brother away in the navy. "Are you listening to me?" she'd ask, her head rolling like a whole pineapple. I lay as limp as someone on ether. I wanted sleep and wished her to go away. But she talked on, filling my lightless room with slurring words, with her hurt. After a while she'd stand, and before leaving the room, she'd tiptoe in the darkness over to my dresser, unball her fist, and lay quarters — sometimes dimes — on my dresser. Her waitress tips; my school lunch money.

Elvira Burke had a difficult time adapting to school when she arrived in Columbus. She was from Alabama. The northern kids would make fun of new arrivals from the Deep South, make fun of their accents, their clothes. Thirty years later, in our neighborhood on the north side of Columbus, I'd do the same thing, mocking southern kids, pointing at their ragged clothing. I couldn't do it within earshot of Elvira; I'd surely have been slapped.

By the time Elvira entered Everett Junior High in 1946, she had a wide chip on her shoulder. Protection against other kids, against teachers, especially against kids with easy lives. She wouldn't back down from any fight or any challenge. And there *were* fights, my mother swinging her long skinny arms and her sharp elbows, then being marched off to the principal's office. She was so fragile she was almost weightless. Her sister, Creola, would rush to her side when she was losing or outnumbered. Elvira would be sent home from school.

Actually, the school wished to be rid of Elvira Burke, the tall, skinny girl from the Alabama woods. Soon enough the authorities suggested in no uncertain terms that she'd be better off at trade school. Elvira's final year in junior high was the eighth grade. Jimmy, pained, said little, leaving the raising of the girls to Emily, their mother.

My mother caught a bus to the outskirts of the city to attend trade school. She sat in sewing and cooking classes, bored, rolling her eyes. Like her fellow students, she was branded a troublemaker, someone the public schools had tired of, a castaway. Elvira didn't like the school, didn't like the teachers, didn't like the discipline. The bus ride to get there took too long; she thought she knew enough about cooking. Sometimes she missed the bus — on purpose. She lasted a year and didn't graduate.

Elvira began hanging out on Mt. Vernon Avenue, twirling on a stool inside Skurdy's Bar. Skurdy's sold wonderful crab-cakes, had a killer jukebox — Nat King Cole, Arthur Prysock, Jackie Wilson, all humming in your ear. My mother knew all

*The inside of Skurdy's Bar, on Mt. Vernon Avenue. It was one of my
mother's favorites: the jukebox, the crabcakes. That's* SKURDY *himself
behind the bar, holding aloft a bottle of beer.*

the Jackie Wilson songs by heart. One day, dreaming fancy
dreams about being a fashion model, she walked into George
Pierce's photography studio. Pierce would take a slew of photographs of strollers on the avenue; those he really liked he'd
put in his window, hoping they would attract other strollers.

Elvira Burke got her photograph put in George Pierce's window. "He kept it there for a whole month," she remembers. The whole world saw her. My mother was nineteen years old. Anything could happen. The world might flower. Her sister chaperoned her on the avenue on weekend nights. Elvira had no idea what she'd do with her life. Uncle Doc flashed a diamond ring at her and told her it was hers — if she went to nursing school. But her dreams of modeling and nursing just started dreamily slipping away.

She met Jack Haygood at a carnival on the avenue. They'd have carnivals in the summertime, right there on a spit of land beside the Pythian Theatre — rickety rides set up on the playground of the all-black Garfield Elementary School, people selling cotton candy, candy apples, bags of popcorn. Jack's attraction was immediate. He was a war vet with a thin mustache. In those days, thin mustaches were in. Elvira lay in bed at night thinking about him. Then she'd convince Creola to ask their parents if they could go out. Creola would promise to keep an eye on Elvira. They just wanted to go for ice cream, to a movie on the big screen at the Pythian — Elvira liked melodramas; Jack wasn't picky. They'd be back by ten. But they'd always end up on Mt. Vernon Avenue, beneath the glittering neon lights. Soon as they got there, Jack would be waiting, the evening deepening toward darkness. "And soon as I saw him, we'd go off together and Creola would go her own way," says my mother. Jack and Elvira would go into the nightclubs that lined that street — Skurdy's, the Manhattan Club, the Trocaveria. (The Troc, as it was called, was renowned for the Pearl Box Revue, a group of men dressed like women who shimmied across the stage. Tom Page, the owner, made a mint off his transvestite revue.) "Your mother could dance real good," my father recalls. "She'd dance with other men. Of course, I didn't much like that."

Elvira found a going-nowhere job in a greasy spoon of a restaurant on St. Clair Avenue. It was jewelry and makeup and clothes money, a little money for Jimmy and Emily to help pay the bills. Then she became pregnant by Jack. They started having children. In a four-year period came Diane, then Harry, then Geraldine. All born to my mother — and I didn't realize this fact until I went noseying around, looking at records — out of wedlock. All Jack's children, and he proudly claimed every one. Jack was working at the Packard auto company over on Long Street, fixing engines, reupholstering interiors. Jack Haygood fell in love with cars. Elvira was raising the kids, listening to her blues on the phonograph.

They married in the summer of 1952, on the front porch of Jimmy and Emily's house on Nineteenth Street. The little affair started at six in the evening. My mother's bridesmaid was Barbara Jean Sims, one of her best friends. (Barbara Jean's father was Jerry, later to become my mother's boyfriend and my giant on this earth. As I said, Elvira liked melodrama.) Jimmy stood down off the porch, in the yard, quiet. Elvira clutched a little white Bible in her hand as the ceremony took place. That Bible, tattered, now sits atop my bedroom dresser. That evening — the weather was beautiful, my parents remember — Jack took his new bride out to Gahanna, a small town northeast of Columbus. You had to take a winding two-lane road to get there, past farmland and strangers and thick trees. There was a little place in Gahanna for blacks called the Big Walnut Country Club. "They had a place out there where you could sit under trees and they'd serve you," recalls my father.

Jack and Elvira moved into a large rooming house on Gibbard Avenue. A man named Bill Taylor owned the house. Elvira insisted on kitchen privileges; she had three children. I remember nothing at all about the two years my mother lived on Gibbard Avenue before moving back home with her parents. My twin sister remembers the howling of a dog, then her memory draws to a close. Diane remembers a little more: "There were always loud arguments and loud music. The place was terrible. It was dirty. There were rats, and one night a rat bit Geraldine." The mattresses lay spread out on the floor. The rat would only have had to hop up on the mattress to get to Geraldine. Jack and Elvira were as poor as pennies.

By the time my mother moved to the east side of Columbus, she hadn't been out flying on her own wings since 1953. Fifteen years, some of them hard, had rolled by. Now time and fate had pushed her to a new part of town. There was something else that attracted her to the east side. Now she was within walking distance of Mt. Vernon Avenue. At night, from our apartment windows, you could see the flickering neon lights of that mysterious avenue.

My mother bought three whole rooms of furniture from Spicer's furniture store for our new apartment. The floors were tile, the walls cement. The windows in the living and dining rooms, facing the back of our apartment, slid open sideways. There was nothing out there except a road, and across the road, railroad tracks and rusting train cars. It took me a month to get used to the train whistle and the trains humming by. Down the roadway, less than a quarter of a mile, lay a stockyard. On real warm days you could smell the manure rising. But we got used to that.

It was easy to tell that Elvira was proud of our apartment. Even as our days and weeks started to add up, we wanted to keep it brand-new. Weekends my sisters and I cleaned, mopping and scrubbing, up early just like Elvira. On those early mornings my mother moved through our house quickly, a piece of cloth tied around her head to keep her hair in place. She'd hum to herself and she'd sing along to the tunes coming from the radio, which we kept tuned to WVKO, rhythm and blues. Sometimes I'd hear her talking to people through the screen door, their voices low like people in a theater balcony. Salesmen were always coming by in cars — insurance salesmen, carpet salesmen, men in short-sleeved shirts and skinny ties. The carpet salesmen came in vans and lugged in pieces of carpet for my mother to look at. We couldn't afford carpet.

My mother didn't rise early every weekend morning, especially when she had been out on Mt. Vernon Avenue on Friday nights. Those mornings after, she'd rise late, around noontime. She'd descend the stairs, and just before stepping off the last step she'd pause, as motionless as a nervous robber, as if she were trying to steady herself. Then there she'd be, complaining of a headache, walking woozily, grabbing something to eat, then back upstairs to bed.

I did all of my cleaning chores, but not always up to my mother's standards. She would stand with her back to me, looking inside the pantry at the floor and cupboards that I had just cleaned. "You ain't done nothing but given this place a lick and a promise," she'd say, hands on hips. Once a month we had inspections: the military touch. On the days before inspection, we'd clean like beavers. Then the dreaded day would come: someone from management would come around, clipboard in hand, and check the apartment, scribble words in the notebook. Sometimes it would be Harold Sawyer. Mr. Sawyer had flown in World War II with the famous, black Tuskegee airmen. After the war many of those airmen were restationed at Rickenbacker Air Base, on the flat, wide-open fields just outside of Columbus. Mr. Sawyer looked like a black Clark Gable. My mother feared inspections, feared losing her apartment. She'd stand around while the place was being inspected, running her fingers through her hair, shifting on her feet. I felt worried for her. But we always passed.

My mother's mail-order deliveries from Frederick's of Hollywood continued to catch up to her in Bolivar Arms. Men and women knocked on our door bearing C.O.D. slips, sending my mother searching for her cash. She never kept her money in banks. She did not believe in banks. She shoved her money beneath her mattress, hid it in shoeboxes. Elvira needed to be able to see her money when she wanted to see it. Sometimes she forgot where she had put it. We'd set about tearing the apartment apart.

There was actually one white family in Bolivar Arms, just one. The Robinson family had come from West Virginia. Four teenage girls and their mother, poor whites. They lived in our circle. The girls stood out. They were loud, wore red lipstick, and talked with the sassiness of black people. They listened to black music, walked cool like black people. You could tell they wanted to be black. It was kind of funny. Over time I also came to see how kind they were. "You new, ain't you?" Florence, one of the daughters asked me that first week. She was sitting on her stoop in a pair of hot pants. I looked at her legs. They were big and fleshy. The Robinson family was taunted sometimes by outsiders, black visitors to Bolivar Arms. Then the blacks in the circle would rally around them. "I'd tell my kids we had just as much of a right as everyone else to live in Bolivar Arms," Mrs. Catherine Robinson told me not long ago.

The kids in Bolivar Arms were not like the kids on the north side. They seemed quicker on their feet, stayed out later at night. They dressed differently, in loud clothes purchased from stores on Mt. Vernon Avenue. I wanted to fit in. I aimed to fit in. I wore sandals, wore beads around my neck as well, persuaded Elvira to let me buy a couple of shirts with Nehru collars. I dressed like a hippie one day, a revolutionary the next. I didn't know any revolutionaries. I had personally never met a hippie, but on the north side of town, near our old house, which was near Ohio State University, I had seen plenty of them. The hippies smelled fragrant, from the incense they burned. For some reason they talked softly. On the north side, my friend Dennis became a hippie, started wearing vests and beads and knee-high boots, smelling like incense; started waving the peace sign, even at strangers. Dennis was a great basketball player, tall and fluid. When he became a hippie he didn't stop playing basketball; he'd show up on the playground, though, with a shoulder bag on his shoulder, wearing a shirt that looked as if it had been splashed with paint.

During those first weeks in Bolivar Arms, people were always coming up to me and introducing themselves. I'd sit beneath a canopy on the Felton Street playground wearing beads and sunglasses and sandals and polyester Nehru shirts in the hot sun. A boy named Chin was among the first to introduce himself. Everyone called him Chin because he had a long chin. We became friends because of basketball. A pipe stretched across the outside of every apartment, and there was a space of about twelve inches between the pipe and the cement it hung from, enough room to shoot a basketball through. Chin and I would shoot baskets through the pipe for hours. We banged into the cement, scraped our elbows, ignored our bleeding, and played until it got dark. Chin had eight brothers and sisters. Everyone in Bolivar Arms, it seemed, had large families.

I liked going into friends' apartments for the first time. You never knew what you'd see. You'd be able right off to tell who was living pretty well and who was not, who had furniture and who didn't. I had never been inside an apartment like Chin's. When you walked in, you had to take your shoes off. You'd have thought they were a Japanese family. The floors gleamed and the place was spotless. This was hardly my mother's lick and a promise; here everything had been gorgeously licked; a million promises had been kept. The place was beautiful. The drapes on the windows matched the furniture, and furniture was everywhere. Oddly, the furniture was set at angles, like furniture is sometimes set inside a furniture store. A red chair might be placed, just so, next to a pink chair, which might be placed, just so, in front of a gray divan. If Chin moved a sofa eight inches to the left while we were sliding around the house — only when his mother was away, of course — he'd know exactly which position to move it back to. I thought such a talent amazing. (Elvira thought Chin's mother had bad nerves, which accounted for her fastidiousness.) When his mother, who worked at the local laundromat, returned home, she'd look around the apartment at each piece of furniture as if something were unfolding in her mind: that something was a picture of how everything had looked when she left. Chin and I stood nearby, braced for anything that might set her off.

Chin's mother liked me. She didn't mind when I came to visit, so long as I took my shoes off when entering the apartment. Some boys would come to visit Chin, boys his mother had determined were ruffians, and she would meet them at the screen door. "I don't want you near my apartment," she'd say, her eyes wide and wild. Only once do I remember her flying into a rage about furniture that had been moved around in the apartment. I grabbed my shoes and flew from the house, stayed away for several days, phoned Chin when I thought the coast might be clear.

Featherstone's was at the end of the apartment complex, a tiny store like Mrs. Wilson's on the north side. Only no one had a bill at this store; nothing was purchased on credit. Cash or scram. Mr. Featherstone wore glasses and never smiled. His shoulders were thick and heavy. He watched every move you made, followed you with his long neck, his eyes. There would be no stealing of cupcakes in Featherstone's, and no smiles would be offered by old man Featherstone. Sometimes his wife would be in the store with him. They barely said a word to each other.

Girls were everywhere in Bolivar Arms. They sat on their stoops, sat on the big ugly green generators in the middle of the apartment circles playing pattycake, skipped rope in sneakers. I was thirteen and shy; Chin was thirteen and shy. We didn't know what to do about girls, how to make friends with them. We circled the ugly generators and sneaked looks up under their dresses.

Lona Cobb lived around the bend from Chin. Her eyes were huge and happy. I thought she was pretty, and I thought she had been giving me the eye ever since I had moved into the apartment complex. She'd walk by me, twisting herself, and she'd smile. Halfway through the summer one day she told me to meet her at the side of her apartment. I did, eagerly, a pair of hippie beads swinging from my neck. There she leaned into me, hard, then kissed me, hard. I had never been kissed like that. In fact, I had never been kissed by a girl. When she pulled back from her kiss, there was a strange smile on her face. I had an erection. Then she slapped me.

"What did you do that for?" I yelled, stunned.

"Let's kiss some more," she said, the strange smile still on her face.

The slap had been so hard that tears began to well up. To her it looked as if I were crying. I turned and walked away; she yelled at me to come back; I kept walking, double-stepping away from her and that strange smile. I walked straight home and dabbed my eyes with toilet paper. Chin later told me that he had thought all along that Lona Cobb was crazy.

Then I met Toni. She lived just down the walkway from

Chin. Chin liked Toni, but he knew she didn't like him, so I was free to let her not like me too. For weeks I watched her skipping rope with friends, playing on her porch. Her clothes were always ironed, full of ironed-in creases. Her hair was always combed, pretty, always shiny. If you got real close to her, you could see a little hair grease on her forehead. When Chin and I would spot her sitting on the big ugly green generator, we'd circle the thing and try to sneak peeks up under her dress. Her hands would start moving like baby snakes, pulling her skirt down past her knees, fingering its edges, ladying herself up. And even that little bit of motion was pretty to look at, and I was grateful for it.

One morning, walking to Chin's past her apartment, I saw Toni in hair rollers and a houserobe out on her porch. It was early in the morning, and the world seemed empty, just me and her. She had always looked so neat, as neat as a school-teacher. But not this morning. She squealed and rushed back inside her apartment when she saw me looking in her direction. Just before closing the door, she looked at me through the screen. That was all I needed. That was the moment that convinced me that she liked me. If not, why feel so ashamed at my seeing her? I had embarrassed her; I had caught her off-guard; she wanted to look good for me.

I thought of her through the warm days and warm nights. Chin told me her bedroom was on the left, facing out, and I stared up into it when the sun went down, seeing only shadows and silhouettes. I wondered if she was lying across her bed thinking of me. And I wondered if she had asked any of my sisters for my phone number. She had not. So I looked her number up in the phone book. I called. Her three brothers — always getting into fights in Bolivar Arms — were tough and hung together like the Jesse James gang. They laughed when I stuttered on the playground. I could hear one of them laughing as he went to tell her I was on the phone, stuttering. Even invisible, even through telephone wires, there was something powerful and sweet about Toni. Her voice was so sure and confident; it touched me like a switched-on ceiling light. But she tried to rush me off the phone. How bizarre, I thought. She was busy, she said; could I call another time, she asked; someone had to use the phone, she repeated; bye. Weird.

7

My sisters gloried in our new home. With my mother working at night and spending more and more time up on Mt. Vernon Avenue, they were freer than they'd ever been. There were no Emily and no Jimmy around. Wonder played with her girlfriends, walked around, couldn't wait to grow up, to be older. Geraldine — at sixteen, three years older than me and my twin sister — pronounced herself older than she was by hopping into the passenger seats of cars driven by men, by returning home late, by arguing with Elvira, by walking from unit to unit in the noonday sun in hot pants. Then her stomach started to swell: she was pregnant, by a boy named Tommy. I couldn't imagine what she saw in him. He was nearly as short as one of those midgets at the Ohio State Fair. He had been coming over in the evenings, dangling his car keys, crossing his little legs, talking down to me, even though he didn't know a thing about basketball.

Diane, my oldest sister — all of nineteen — took night

courses at Central High School so she could get her high school diploma. She had married Eddie, the tough guy, but the marriage didn't last. He kept begging her to come back. He'd call me, ask me to deliver messages to her; standing nearby, Diane would tell me to hang up the phone, and I'd hang it up. She figured that Eddie — who was still shooting basketball for money on the Weinland Park Elementary School playground in the afternoons, who was still swinging at her when he felt like it, who was still two-timing her — was crazy. Some nights I rocked Diane's baby, Tony, to sleep and pulled the curtains back and looked out onto our new world from the bedroom window. A lot of nights Elvira would be out there somewhere — where, I didn't know — and I'd wonder if she was safe.

There was a family living on each side of us in our new apartment. I didn't know the family who lived in apartment 29, because they rarely came out. When they did, they scurried by wordlessly. Mrs. Erma and her son, Martin, lived in apartment 31, on the left side of us. Mrs. Erma was thin and yellow-skinned; her son was also thin and yellow-skinned. They looked more like brother and sister than mother and son. Both of them, when they weren't standing stock still, moved about in a jittery fashion, as if something were about to pop out of their bodies at any moment.

I'd sometimes see Mrs. Erma from my bedroom window, standing in her front yard, the yard just a little spit of grass, standing as still as a pole. Standing there on the grass, she'd have one arm crossed at her chest, the other arm crooked up to her mouth, a cigarette at her lips. The hour would be past midnight. She'd be staring up at the sky. Mrs. Erma believed in Martians. She'd tell me and Wonder about life in outer space. Sometimes she'd stop in mid-sentence, just as her voice was starting to go flat, and her eyes would get wide, and she'd turn and bolt into the house and not come back. Confused, I'd stand there like someone stranded at earth's edge.

A lot of grownups steered clear of Mrs. Erma, but not Elvira. My mother sailed toward outsiders, strangers, the slightly off-center. She and Mrs. Erma shared beers, cigarettes, exchanged pots of food, got loud together. When we didn't see Mrs. Erma for days, my mother would get worried. She'd send me next door to knock on Mrs. Erma's door. I'd pound, and when I didn't get an answer, I'd pound some more. She'd finally come to the door, open it with the chain still attached, and peer out at me through those two inches between chain and door.

"What do you want?" she'd scream.

I'd tell her my mother was worried about her and ask if everything was all right.

"Tell Mrs. Elvira I'm fine." Then she'd abruptly slam the door in my face.

Martin, her son, never wanted to go to the playground with me and play basketball. He sat in a lawn chair and smoked dope, often right in front of his mother. He smiled easily and smelled like marijuana. Martin would sometimes leave the apartment early in the morning. He said he was off to summer school. Maybe he was, but he never carried any books. Once, with the afternoon fading, he walked up on me and some of my friends playing basketball. He took off his jacket and demanded the basketball and ran around the court with a cigarette in his mouth. He had a kind of zany Jerry Lewis body. He ran around as if someone had wound him up like a toy. We just shook our heads. "Later," he said, after he was finished disrupting our game. Then he walked on home with his jacket flung across his shoulder and beads of sweat on his forehead.

Every circled unit of apartments had one triple-decker, set aside for extremely large families. Mostly these were southern

Me and UNCLE ED, *just finishing a day's worth of fishing at Paradise Valley Fishing Lake, outside Columbus. You had to pay to fish the lake. When we didn't catch fish, Uncle Ed yelled conspiracy; when we did catch fish, he boasted of his skill. (I notice Uncle Ed has on a pair of waders, as if he's Hemingway. I never saw him set foot in the water.)*

families. The Wests lived in the triple-decker in our unit. There were fifteen West children. You could never sort out their names. All the boys were tough, especially Tom, who was short, well built, and short-tempered. When he talked, his lips hardly moved; he was scary, and I avoided him. Ricky West had a gap in his front teeth and could get any girl he wanted. I hated to play basketball with Ricky, because he would dispute every foul called; he'd walk around the court with the ball tucked under his arm, smoking a cigarette and yelling. Ronald West, whom everyone called Fatman, kept to himself, studied hard, and liked Wonder, who paid no attention to him. The West girls were as quiet as nuns. Boys said little to them for fear of Tom swinging his hard fists at them.

I spent time reading *Field & Stream* magazine, leafing through pages, gathering information about faraway bass tournaments I'd never get to go to. There was no place around Bolivar Arms to fish. So I was thrilled on those Saturday mornings that Uncle Henry, my grandfather Jimmy's brother — the last brother to leave the Alabama woods — would come pick me up and take me fishing with him. I'd rise with the dawn, wash the dishes Elvira had used during the night after work, then pack up my lime-green tackle box. First we'd stop at the stockyard, directly across from the railroad, just yards from our apartment. The soft black dirt in the stockyard, which felt cushiony, was ideal for red worms, and we'd crawl under the white fence and start digging with our hands. The reddish pink worms were everywhere in the soil. Every few minutes or so, Uncle Henry would raise his back up and look over his shoulder for police. But we never had any problems and dug for the worms in peace, scooping them up by the handfuls and tossing them in our buckets. When we had enough worms, we tossed the buckets in the trunk of the car. Uncle Henry was a miser; he'd drive several miles out of the way to get the cheapest fishing tackle. He had half a dozen poles in his car trunk, some tangled up with the others, but once we reached the riverbank he would untangle them right away, with ease.

Uncle Henry worked at Buckeye Steel, the huge steel plant on the city's south side. He was the tallest of the Burke brothers, at times the most talkative. He had six daughters and a son. When a pimp came sniffing around one of his daughters, Uncle Henry beat him up with his bare hands. He was charged with assault. In court, Uncle Henry explained to the judge why he had beaten the man: his daughter, a pimp, the breaking of his heart. "You ought to be commended for what you did," the judge said. The case was dropped.

Ed was Uncle Henry's best friend, and we'd always have to go pick Ed up. I started calling Ed Uncle Ed; he didn't seem to mind. He was a heavy drinker. Once we went to pick him up and were startled by the sight of him running out his girlfriend's back door: bleeding, with a knife poking from his side. His girlfriend, Louise, who had stabbed him, ran behind him with a large bucket. She motioned for him to take it, told him to let the blood drip in the bucket, not on her grass. She stood looking at Ed as if he had just dropped from the sky onto her lawn. Ed moaned, reached for the bucket, blinked his alcoholic eyes, cursed all the way to the hospital. That day we had to cancel our fishing trip. When Ed got back home, Louise fixed him something to eat.

On the riverbank, Uncle Henry and I would sit on logs for hours. He whistled, scanned the river's surface with his bloodshot eyes, and caught fish after fish after fish. Uncle Henry kept even the little fish. "Good eatin'," he'd say. I'd sometimes sit for hours and not get a bite. Ed, however, could fish no better than I. He'd tell me stories about fishing in rivers all over Ohio. When the game wardens came by to check fishing licenses, Ed would snarl, show them his license, then curse them as soon as they disappeared. He moved as if he had been put together by a machine and all the parts didn't connect. He moved stiffly; it was the alcohol sliding through him. Sometimes we went to Paradise Valley, a lake where you had to pay to fish. Uncle Henry always paid my way in. The lake was moon-shaped and tall weeds circled it. Ed would sit, not catching any fish, drinking from a bottle wrapped in a brown paper bag. He'd curse the owners, who were sitting in a lodge on a nearby hill; he'd call them con men, he'd say there were no fish in the lake, he'd demand that Uncle Henry take him home. Uncle Henry reeled in fish after fish, paid Ed no mind.

Uncle Henry always gave me some of his fish to give to Elvira. She'd freeze them, then thaw them out later for a dinner. My mother lathered our fish in cornmeal and dropped them in a skillet of hissing grease. She'd fry a panful of green tomatoes to go with them. Our freezer, in fact, stayed full of frozen bluegill fish. I half expected their tiny eyes to move when I opened the door. Dead fish stare.

I knew nothing about politics in the South, or in Columbus, for that matter. I knew nothing about student revolution and protest. I knew what I was supposed to know: fishing, basketball, my Uncle Ira's phone number by heart, Jimmy and Emily's phone number by heart, all the hiding places my mother had in our apartment for her bottles of bourbon. So when the tanks arrived on a quiet summer's day in the summer of 1968, I was shocked. They were National Guard tanks and they rolled right into Bolivar Arms, having been called out by the governor because of rioting up on Mt. Vernon Avenue and across the east side. The tanks surrounded Bolivar Arms; through bullhorns, the soldiers barked orders to get off the streets. All you could do was run, stop, turn around and look at them, then take off running again. "I had never seen anything like that," my mother now says. "Tanks coming up on the sidewalks." We watched through the screen door. I bounced from window to window. The soldiers wore helmets and didn't crack any smiles. There were news bulletins. Our phone started ringing: Jimmy and Emily. A curfew was put into effect. Any kids going to the store had to have a note from their parents. Elvira wrote out my permission notes on lined paper. I'd fold the note up and put it in my back pocket. Then I'd walk to the store, looking at the soldiers looking at me. I'd walk all the way to Featherstone's, buy what I was supposed to buy, watch mean Mr. Featherstone not even say thank you as he bagged my groceries. Then I'd walk back home. Elvira would stand inside the screen door until I returned. A few days after they arrived, the soldiers disappeared. Everyone could go out and play again.

I raced off to play basketball every day after doing my cleaning. I'd stop by Chin's, and if he had finished with his chores, he'd come along, smelling as if he had been freshly scrubbed, wearing starched white sneakers, wearing blue jeans that had been pressed, wearing shirts that had been unfolded and still had crease lines in them. We played on the basketball courts behind Monroe Junior High School. There were no nets on the rim, so we didn't hear the swishing sound when the basketball went cleanly through the hoop. We heard banging, the ball banging against the rim, rattling before it rolled in, if it went in. Sometimes we heard nothing, just saw the ball arc into the air and down through the rim, cleanly.

Friends on the north side had warned me that I'd have to fight in Bolivar Arms. It didn't take long before I got into my first scuffle. I accidentally tripped Chandler on the playground while playing basketball. He picked up the basketball and threw it at me hard, striking my chest. I caught my breath, picked up the ball, and threw it back at him hard. He ducked. "Motherfucker," he said. Then he ran across the court toward me. For some reason I lit out across the field of overgrown grass that lay between my apartment and the playground. He caught up to me and began pummeling me with his fists. I swung at him; he swung back, harder. Chin was coming up on us, circling. I broke loose and ran home. Chandler stopped just yards from my screen door and lolled there like a hunter stalking big game, shaking his fists. I was terrified.

A day later Chin told me Bobby Chandler sniffed glue; he

was nutty, Chin testified. I didn't need proof. Then Chin warned me that I would be seeing a lot of Chandler when basketball practice started, because he had played varsity the year before. Days later, back on the playground, I ran into him again. I started calling him Gluesniffer, though never to his face. He acted as if the scuffle had never happened. And I did too.

We played basketball almost every day — me, Prune, Gluesniffer, Chin, Fatman, Jazzy Joe Wade, Worm, all apartment kids — and we played right through the heat, through the sunset, as our bodies and souls began leaning into autumn. I think I liked nothing better than making new friends with a basketball rolling off my fingertips. Prune was as dark as a prune, never passed the ball, always gunned it, shot it every time he touched it. He lied with a straight, calm face: his father was a big shot in the military; the family would be moving out of the projects any day to join him; the family actually had quite a bit of money; the good family furniture was in storage, to guard against theft. When he talked to you, Prune held his head up high, and his chin would poke out like a snobbish Englishman's. We laughed at him, felt sorry for him because he often wore the same clothes several days in a row.

Sometimes Jimmy, my grandfather, came out to visit, the cigar in his mouth. His taxi would pull up in front of our apartment. He didn't stay long — had given the taxi driver specific instructions, in fact, on when to return. He looked around the complex, shook his head — so many hellion children — slyly slipped my mother some cash, and waited for his taxi to come take him home.

Returning to our apartment one day that first summer, I saw a taxi parked in front of the apartment. Maybe my grandfather. When I reached it, I looked inside, but it wasn't my grandfather. There were two women in the back seat. I had never seen them before. I opened our screen door and there, sitting in a chair in an orange two-piece suit, silk, was my brother — my half-brother — Macaroni. I had never seen him before. I had talked to him once on the telephone, when he was in prison. I had heard whispers about him down in Georgia. Sometimes I had even thought about him, mostly about how he might look.

"Hey boy, how you doing?" he asked.

When he smiled, his teeth were so bright it was as if he were throwing them at you. Words jumped from his mouth like sounds from a jukebox. He talked in a rush of words. He had just been released from prison over in Mansfield. "I just got home," he said, not mentioning the prison part. He said we had to get together, to get to know each other, said he played a lot of basketball, swore he was better than me. But he had to go right now, he had just wanted to wait around to meet me. He stood up and walked outside to the waiting taxi, to the girls inside that taxi, because they were his girls.

His name was Gary, but everyone called him Macaroni. He walked with a kind of jump, as if he had just won something. My sisters had always whispered it out, as if it were a secret, the secret that everyone knew: Macaroni was a pimp. He came by his money dishonestly. He was the kind of man my Uncle Henry would have killed with his bare hands, the kind of man my sisters were curious to know more about.

And there I was a short time later, standing with Diane downtown, at the Franklin County Jail. Months after his release, Macaroni was arrested again, on a forgery charge. The Franklin County Jail was a big white stucco building just a stone's throw from the old brick-walled Ohio State Penitentiary. Macaroni stood talking to us behind Plexiglas, telling us not to worry, it was nothing, he'd be out any day. He didn't look worried at all. He had talked back to a guard. It was my first visit inside a jail; I was scared. I wondered why Diane had dragged me there. But it was just like Diane. Diane threw lifesavers to family members in distress. She hated it that Macaroni had been lost to us — out there, far away, as lost to us as one of Mrs. Erma's Martians. Diane decided that we'd never lose sight of Macaroni again.

Every day around noontime a strange-looking truck appeared in the middle of our circle of apartments. It was big and boxy, just like an old ice cream truck. It had a bell on its side, and the bell rang like crazy. The truck was multicolored — red, blue, green, and pink — and "The Goody Wagon" was stenciled on its side. It looked as if it had escaped from a circus. But it was a grocery store on wheels. I had never seen anything like it. A man parked the truck, pulled the keys from the ignition, pulled up a little window from inside, and pronounced himself open for business. If you didn't hurry outside when you first heard the noisy engine and the bells, there'd be a line by the time you reached the truck. Then you'd have to stand there and worry about whether the man behind the window would run out of what you wanted. I'd stand on tiptoes, peering into the truck, scanning the shelves. The insides were shadowy even in daylight, but you could spot bread, milk, cookies, sodas, boxes of grits, oatmeal, sometimes boxes of pancake mix, on its shelves. I'd buy milk, boxes of grits, popsicles for myself and my sister. Everyone liked the fat dill pickles, which would be soaking in juice in a jar on a shelf. Almost always I had to buy a box of Anacin for Elvira's hangovers. My mother slept past noon a lot of days, because she didn't go to work until late in the evening. I'd wake her up when the truck came, shaking her bony shoulder, asking her if she wanted anything. After I bought our goods, I'd go back in the house and fix my mother some grits. (Often I'd keep her change from the Goody Wagon. My mother wasn't like Jimmy. She hardly ever counted her coins.)

Grits were always a challenge to cook. You had to stir them quickly or else lumps would appear in them. I'd spoon the grits for her onto a dish; steam puffed over the plate like tiny white clouds. Sometimes I fried her up a couple of sausages, even if she didn't ask for them. Then I'd climb the stairs with the plate and her two Anacins in the palm of my hand, along with her glass of water. I learned how to balance everything while walking up the steps, the grits in one hand, the glass of water in the other, with the Anacins tucked into the hand with which I carried the plate of grits. It got to be easy. Palming so much, I was as mindful of my steps as a butler. I liked knowing, for some reason, that my mother was eating a hearty breakfast. About ten minutes later I'd hear her screaming from behind her bedroom door; I'd hustle upstairs to get her empty plate. When she was fed and content, I'd amble back downstairs, light on my feet, content as well.

The Goody Wagon certainly didn't have everything Elvira needed, so she'd send me up to Mt. Vernon Avenue. A lot of times I went to get her a pork chop sandwich at the Chesapeake Bar & Grill. "Have them put some hot sauce on it," she'd say, her voice cracking walls. "And come straight back!" It didn't matter to my mother that the Chesapeake was a hole in the wall. My mother liked hole-in-the-wall places, preferred them to fancy places. Just like she preferred loud, predictable friends to quiet and deceitful people. "Seddity" was one of my mother's favorite words for her enemies. Once she had marked someone as seddity, that was pretty much it; it was their scarlet letter as far as she was concerned. A couple of men in suits and ties came around wooing my mother, one in alligator shoes and swinging a briefcase. In the beginning, she

*My mother's dates always seemed to
be as tall as trees. I remember this one,
Bob: a baritone voice but too quiet.
I didn't like him.*

liked their money and their bourbon. She liked it a lot when
they hustled up to Carl Brown's store and returned with bags
of groceries for her children. My mother laid her cards on the
table: she had kids, she was alone, life was hard. Then, after a
while, it started — words my mother couldn't understand flying from the mouths of the seddity men; the same men bragging about who they knew, places they had been. She deci-
phered it all pretty quickly: just another example of someone
turning seddity. First she'd start rolling her eyes. Then she'd

start putting her skinny hands on her hips, standing with her lip slightly curled, her silence crackling like glass breaking. Then she'd just ask the man to leave, not to come around anymore. And then there went the *click click click* of the alligator shoes right out the front door.

My route up to Mt. Vernon Avenue was simple. I'd dash out the apartment door and up a stretch of pavement that led out of the circle of apartments. Then I'd angle off to the left into a field of weeds and old houses, and once through a pathway that had been footmarked in the weeds, I'd come to an opening, which would be Twentieth Street. I'd pass the Refuge Baptist Church and then the Macon Bar. Then there I was, on Mt. Vernon Avenue. It was as busy as fire. People would be everywhere. The stores had big glass windows. Cars were parked everywhere. Car horns were honking in the distance. I'd look inside the store windows, look at the clothes on the mannequins, at the shoes on the feet of the mannequins. I'd read fishing magazines at Tyler's Drugstore. I'd wolf down a couple of doughnuts at Brassfield's bakery. If Elvira had known I was spending her money before I'd even bought her pork chop sandwich, she'd have killed me.

I lingered one afternoon, bouncing from brick storefront to brick storefront, letting my mother's sandwich get cold. I'd get lost on the avenue, lost in thought, my mind churning like an engine. Walking home from Mt. Vernon Avenue that day, suddenly in a rush, I hustled past the Macon Bar and galloped into the field of weeds that hugged the rows of abandoned houses. The weeds were child-high. I never saw the man following me. I think I felt him, though, like breath. He walked right by me. It was a heavy and purposeful walk. Then I looked up and he was standing in the doorway of one of the abandoned houses. It was green. He had come into focus, and he seemed as large as a doorway itself.

"Come in here," he said. "I want to get between your legs." His eyes fixed on my legs. The words had just floated away from his mouth, but evilly. I froze. The air had turned gluey, sticky. The man reached out to me; his arm looked as thick as a log. I inched backward. Then I bolted into the weeds and the sun. I ran fast, then faster, my throat burning. I never looked back. I wanted to talk and I wanted to yell, but I couldn't, because to keep going I had to breathe, and I couldn't breathe and talk and yell at the same time. At least I didn't think I could. Then I was home.

I collapsed onto our new sofa. Elvira came downstairs. She was in her waitress uniform, getting ready for work, smelling like nutmeg-brown face powder. She asked me why I was out of breath. Nothing seemed to make my mother more nervous than my running into our apartment at breakneck speed. That first summer in Bolivar Arms I did a lot of running into our apartment. I told her what had happened, some strange man, his words. Elvira's neck yanked like a chicken's, and she ran to the screen door and looked into the distance. Then she ran to the telephone and snatched the receiver up into her hands. I did not know about such dark things.

The policeman was friendly and spoke in a tone to comfort. He told me I could sit in the front of the car. It was the first time I had ever been inside a police car. We rode over near the abandoned houses, along Twentieth Street, then up and down Mt. Vernon Avenue, looking for the man. I told the policeman he was dressed in a brown corduroy jacket and that he had on a beret. Then, there, in front of the Idle-a-While, I saw him. He was walking, very slowly, all alone. The officer arrested him on the spot. Another police car arrived and the man was put into the back seat. I looked at him through the glass window of the car I was still in. The arrested man in the beret, big and powerfully built, looked frightened, like an animal caught in a trap. And I felt a tiny bit of sorrow for him. A crowd had gathered. I wanted to go home.

Back in Bolivar Arms, word about what had happened spread from circle to circle. My friend Chin asked me if the man had done anything to me. Then he told me that word had spread that the man had done something to me.

"No. Hell no," I said.

Toni, the girl I liked, was in fact in love with, the girl who still seemed as impossible for me to touch as a diamond, asked me if the man had done anything to me. She was sitting on her stoop with a small knot of other girls. I said no. Her girl-friends giggled like Munchkins.

The summer wasn't over yet, and already I had been punched by a glue-sniffing basketball player, seen soldiers in tanks with rifles drawn riding past our front yard, met my half-brother the pimp, and escaped from a would-be child molester.

There were times when I missed Jimmy and Emily and the north side.

There were times when I wondered what my mother had gotten me and my sisters into.

The notice to appear in court found its way into our mail-box one day. I enjoyed journeys, anywhere. Elvira and I caught a city bus downtown, to the courthouse, so I could testify against the man. I sat in a high-backed chair on the witness stand. I felt swallowed up in the chair. The air in the courtroom seemed tight and uncomfortable. After the judge instructed me, I explained what had happened and pointed to the man, who never raised his head to look at me. There was talking between the judge and the lawyers; their words floated by me like bubbles. The man was led away in handcuffs, later sentenced to prison.

Leaving the courtroom that day, I felt happy for some reason. I laughed because the man had been handcuffed, led away. When I laughed, right there at the corner of Town and High streets, in the cold daylight, with people nearby, Elvira slapped me across my face. I do not know why. Slapped me and yanked on my shirt collar. Maybe it was the pain of seeing another black man going off to prison. I do know my eyes welled. We waited at the bus stop for our bus.

Elvira and I.

My mother and I.

I was crazy about my mother.

That September I prepared to enroll at my new junior high school. The night before the first day of classes, I laid my new clothes out on the bed, admiring their newness, swiping at imaginary lint. Elvira had given me money to buy a new pair of shoes. It wasn't enough money to buy a pair of lizard shoes, the kind my sister's boyfriend Bo wore, so I bought a pair of white straw shoes, low-heeled slip-ons, and I thought they were beautiful. They were not sensible shoes; winter would be rushing into view soon. But I didn't care; style interested me as much as common sense.

Monroe Junior High was the first all-black school I had ever attended. Sometimes there'd be picketers outside the school, holding up signs about integration. I had classes to get to, and I walked right by them. I knew that as soon as school started I had to find Bob Marsh, the basketball coach. He was muscular and wore a crew cut. He had been a Marine. I told him I desperately wanted to make the basketball team. He was walking away already, across the gym floor, which was so shiny the wood looked yellow. A million keys jangled on his belt loop. "Good luck," he said. And that's all he said. He always walked like that — as if he were on his way to stamp something out.

Chin warned me that I'd be tested during the first days of school; he said someone would try to pick a fight with me and I must not back down. If I did, I'd be labeled a sissy forever. So when Bobby Montgomery shoved me on the playground during a recess, I wheeled and sucker-punched him. I had never sucker-punched anyone before. Montgomery was dazed, and I was dazed — and suddenly sorry I had hit him. He made a lazy lunge at me; someone separated us; he never shoved me again.

Chin worked after school, had himself a job right inside the school, as a janitor. He'd run a dust mop up and down the hallways and inside the auditorium. He walked down each row in the auditorium, lifting up every single seat and dusting. It took forever. I often helped him, and when I'd miss a row, he'd get upset. Chin was a good janitor. On the evenings I couldn't hang around with him, he'd get a real attitude, question my friendship, so I tried to stay with him after school as often as I could. I'd sit in a chair in the back of the auditorium and watch him when I didn't feel like helping him sweep and clean. I'd make up lists of who I thought would make the basketball team and who I thought would get cut, trying to manipulate my imagination so my own name would never fall from the right list. Glenn would make the team, Harvey would not; Bobby would make the team, no way Ricky would make it. I'd holler my analysis out to Chin to get his reaction. Glenn would not make the team, he said: bad grades. Harvey would not make the team because he preferred playing on the renegade after-school basketball team for truants and boys with bad grades. Ricky would not make the team either, because he had a loony jumpshot. Chin said all these things with authority. I was impressed and eager as the list of casualties rolled off his tongue and he pushed the dust mop along. There were another half-dozen players Chin told me not to worry about: wild boys whom Coach Marsh wouldn't fool with, didn't like.

I was a long shot to make the team. I was an outsider, I had only one year remaining as a junior high student, I did not bring any sterling credentials to Monroe from my old junior high. I would have to hustle. And I would have to pray. Chin could not tell me whether I would make the team or not.

Our tryouts began.

Our practices were happy and sweaty affairs, long lanky boys racing up and down the court. Coach Marsh strolled along the sidelines, back and forth, a clipboard in his hands. He scowled a lot, blew his whistle a lot; I couldn't tell if he realized I was on earth. He paid a lot of attention to his returning lettermen. There were Tiny and Eli Barrett and Aaron James Summerall and Gluesniffer. They were good. I had played with them during the summer. Sometimes when I had shown up on the playground, Eli — whom everyone called Worm — would be there by himself in the hot sun, racing up and down the court, a white towel around his neck, a jug of water nearby. Worm was already playing with grown men, and beating them.

After practice, after we showered, Chin and I would go get his dust mops and sweep up. I'd sit there in the yellow-lighted auditorium, my voice growing desperate as the days dwindled to when we'd know the final roster. I began to doubt my mathematical calculations about who would and would not make the team. I began to question Chin's analysis. I also realized that Chin and I would be competing for the same position — guard — and that Chin had not played varsity the year before. He had never played on the basketball team at Monroe. We were both on the slippery side of the ship and we knew it.

Yet during practices I could tell that Tiny wanted me to

make the team. I didn't know why. He was always calling my name out so the coach could hear. "Nice shot, Haygood," he'd say. I'd catch the coach glancing my way.

Tiny was one of the best-dressed boys in the school. Darrell Williams, who lived in my circle, was the absolute best-dressed. Darrell worked a construction job after school. He was only fourteen, but he had sideburns and looked much older. I think he spent all of his money on clothes. He brought them home in huge shopping bags — silk shirts, silk pants, long flowing coats that hung as loose as capes. You'd see him up on Mt. Vernon Avenue, swinging bags, shopping bags full of fine clothes, in a carefree motion.

Darrell may have been the best-dressed, but Tiny had the best style. Tiny was partial to wearing scarves around his neck, the kind Mexican bandits wear in the movies. Some days he'd show up not with a scarf but an ascot, the kind the English wear in the movies. He looked cool in an ascot. He had a whole line of silk shirts. We suspected that some of them were Caveman's shirts; Caveman was Tiny's older brother, and they were both the same size. But we never said anything to Tiny about it. And Tiny wore two-piece suits to school, not even for any special occasion. He'd wear a suit and sit in study hall brushing it with his hands, tugging at the lapels. He'd grin when any of us reached out to feel the material.

Some evenings after practice, Tiny would come over to my apartment. Elvira would be at work. Often before she left she would fix my dinner. I'd come home and it would be on the stove, something in a pot with a lid on top of it. But I also cooked a lot for myself. I liked pork and beans and wieners. I'd open a can of pork and beans, then I'd chop up three wieners and drop them in. I'd pour sugar into the pot and stir. It's still one of my favorite meals. I'd offer Tiny food, but he'd always say no. He was shy. Or maybe someone had once told him not to eat over at the houses of his friends — bad manners. But one night as Tiny was leaving through the kitchen, I saw him reach down and scoop some of my leftover pork and beans and wieners up into his mouth with his bare hands. He sucked the bean juice off his fingertips and walked on out the door.

Tiny had spent part of the previous year in reform school for stealing cars. He was short. Everyone joked that he had to have a pillow to sit on in the driver's seat as he was zooming around town with the police hot on his tail. He lived over on Starr Avenue, which was across the St. Clair Avenue bridge. I walked over to visit him one Saturday. His place was a wood frame house, brown. It was also huge, and it looked quite old. There was broken-down furniture on the front porch. The door was closed, and the curtains were so dark and uninviting that you wondered if anyone lived there. The door creaked open: Tiny was grinning. Day and night, Tiny grinned, a big wide toothy grin. He never discussed his mother and father; we didn't even know if they lived in Columbus. Tiny lived with a guardian, and I looked forward to meeting her. I think I believed a guardian might somehow look different from someone's real mother. She was a big lady with thick arms. Her hair was as wild as a witch's. When Tiny introduced me to her, she nodded and said something as she walked by, but it came from her throat, a husky mumble, and I couldn't make it out. It turned out that Tiny lived in a rooming house, which I didn't know until I started walking around, bumping into strange men. Tiny told me not to say anything to them, so I didn't. He led me to his bedroom, pulled a key from his pocket, looked to the right, then the left, then put the key in and opened the lock. I had never known anyone who had a bedroom with a lock on the door. Tiny explained that it was on account of the boarders. He closed and locked the door behind us after we entered.

The bedroom was as neat as a hospital room. And it was a shrine to Tiny himself. Basketball trophies were all over the place, set beautifully in a diagonal display. There were framed pictures of Tiny in his basketball uniform, in street clothes, grinning as he always grinned, as if he were the luckiest kid on earth, just happy to be alive. I didn't have a bedroom like Tiny's, and I suddenly wished I did. A large window threw daylight onto everything. Tiny pulled his scrapbook down from a shelf. He walked it over to me very importantly, like a butler bringing a tray of tea. He opened it for me to look at and gently scolded me about lifting any picture or newspaper clipping from beneath the cellophane. Then he took a seat on the edge of the bed and watched as I sat in the chair and turned page after page, allowing his life to unfold. He looked delighted, and sometimes he'd hop up real fast when he saw a picture that he thought needed additional commentary or adjustment beneath the cellophane. Outside the door I heard footsteps coming and going, conversations that trailed off.

When I had finished looking at the scrapbook, Tiny stood and motioned that it was time to go. Standing out in the hallway, he pulled the key from his pocket and locked the door. As we were angling toward the steps, a couple of boarders were coming up the stairs. When they reached us and slowed, Tiny stared them down with a scowl on his face. "Move out the way now," he said to them. His voice was gruff, no-nonsense. I was pretty amazed. The men seemed afraid of him. It was as if Tiny himself ran the boarding house.

I asked Tiny often if he thought I would make the basketball team. He always said yes. "You should make it" is how he actually put it. I didn't want to have to beg myself onto the team as I had done at Indianola Junior High.

My palms were sweaty on the morning the final roster was to be announced. I hustled down the hallway to scan the list attached to the coach's office door. When I saw my name on it, I howled, I was so happy. I think I was as happy as I'd ever been about anything. I couldn't wait to tell Elvira. Chin made the team too. I'd need new sneakers. I'd need new wristbands. I'd have to ask Elvira to let me go up on Mt. Vernon Avenue and buy some new ties to wear to the games. I couldn't wait to tell Jimmy and Emily. My sister's boyfriend Bo told me he knew all along I'd make the team. Sometimes Bo could sound like a genie. Elvira would roll her eyes at Bo when he started sounding like that.

Practices grew more intense. Coach Marsh barked more often; his voice grew heavier. The old Marine resurfaced. Sometimes a few of the school rebels — Harvey, Glenn, Ezel — would stand at the doorway of the gym and watch us practice. Marsh could turn on them, however, in a fury, and scream them away. After practice I would follow Chin to the auditorium, help him sweep up.

I could soon tell, however, that I wouldn't play much in games. Tiny and Hook — he had a long nose — were the starting guards. Gluesniffer and Mel Stanley were second-string guards. I would only play, it seemed, after they had played. But I didn't care — at least, not in the beginning. Being part of the team, I was wanted, and I wanted to be wanted.

Worm and Aaron James were our starting forwards. There was probably no other forward in America like Aaron James. The kneepad he wore mostly covered up his wooden leg, but you could sometimes hear the clickety-clack of the leg as he ran up and down the court in practice. It must have been quite a struggle for him to run with a leg made of solid oak, like dragging a piece of log. After our first three games, Aaron James was leading our team in rebounds. A TV station came out to do a story on him during one of our practices. Then a reporter for the *Call & Post*, the local weekly newspaper, wrote up a piece. Of course, the major reason for the interest was the wooden leg.

It had happened when Aaron James was eight years old. He had been out playing along the railroad tracks. When he crossed the tracks, his leg got snared. Lying there, lying back with the train's wind on his chest, keeping him down, the roar of the engine in his ears, he was forced to witness the whole episode, to pray the engineer would spot him, would stop the train. Then his leg was gone, just like that. Paul, his brother, reached him first, picked him up like a sack of potatoes and lit out running. Aaron James would have to face the world on a leg and a half. There were a dozen children in the Summerall family, too many for the parents to baby Aaron James. So from then on he hobbled along, tough and hard, reaching out with everything he had for the basketball being thrown in his direction.

Every day in practice Aaron James had to face Coach Marsh, who never let him slack off, who pushed him as hard as he pushed everyone else. There was a kind of Tin Man stiffness to Aaron James's style of play. He knew exactly what he could do, how far he could and couldn't depend on the wooden leg. He was an old-fashioned player, never doing anything fancy, no behind-the-back dribbles. Watching him, you noticed extreme efficiency, a beautiful economy of motion, nothing at all wasted. The leg made him play almost as if the game were a new invention to him and the world. Sometimes, dribbling, slipping between two defenders, going up, bouncing the ball off the backboard and watching it go in, then stopping — as if he quickly had to insert a part of his basketball-playing brain into the wooden leg before taking off again — he looked as fluid as a snake.

Nights before our basketball games, I'd wash my game socks on my mother's washboard. She brought the thing with her to Bolivar Arms from the north side. It was a square wooden board with metallic ridges. You set the washboard in the bathtub, ran some water, then scrubbed your piece of clothing up and down the ridges. It was scrubbing and it was hard work. But it got your clothing clean. I'd also polish my black dress shoes with liquid shoe polish. On game days we had to dress up. I'd crack the bedroom window so my polished shoes would dry from the fresh air. Then I'd turn on my transistor radio and lean back on the bed, listening to professional basketball games from Indianapolis and Cincinnati. Oscar Robertson played for the Cincinnati Royals, and he was about my favorite player. I even saw him once at an exhibition game at the Ohio State Fairgrounds. I watched the way he walked out onto the court, the way he sat down, the way he chatted with the referee. Robertson never smiled, treated the game like a science, was as methodical as a mathematician, but I smiled plenty watching him. Sometimes — though I'd have to hold the radio up to my ear — I could even get the Virginia Squires from way over in Virginia. There'd be static, but I could still hear. I could imagine the size of the gymnasiums out there in the distance, the size of the crowds. Nights and faraway basketball games vanished into me. Most nights I slept peacefully.

I loved game days. Loved how the janitors had closed the gym doors and how the bleachers had been pulled out and the gym floor swept clean and pretty. All for us, the Monroe Mustangs. There was a hum inside our gymnasium on game days. I think we had the prettiest uniforms in Columbus; at least, that's what Tiny said. They were gold and green, pure silk, and they made a swishing noise. We had long silvery zippers on the sides of our warmup slacks. We wore green kneepads and cottony white wristbands. Tiny, being the captain, led us out of the gym onto the floor. I rarely played. I sat and rooted. I sat and badly wanted to be in the game. During timeouts I scanned the crowds to see who was there. I saw my friend Harvey Frazier at every game, wearing his three-quarters-length leather coat. Harvey, as dark as a raisin, strutted across the gym floor during timeouts, scuffing it, daring any teacher to say anything to him. Mr. Wood, the truant officer, would yell something at him, but Harvey would just keep walking, paid him no mind. Sometimes he even showed up at away games, especially if he thought kids from the host school were planning to jump us after the game: Harvey was there to protect. "Haygooooood!" he'd yell whenever he saw me, sounding like a crazed boxing announcer. I liked Harvey's sister, Karen, but she liked Fatman — and she was nearly a foot taller than Fatman. I stopped liking her.

After our practices, after Chin had finished sweeping up the auditorium and some of the hallways, he and I would walk with a fast step — it had turned nippy during basketball season — up to Mt. Vernon Avenue. We'd go right to Sandy's, a neon-bathed hamburger joint that sat across from the old Pythian Theatre. The Pythian, where my mother had gone to see movies and live stage shows, wasn't showing movies or stage shows any longer. Now it was mostly offices inside. We were lucky, because Drac, our friend, worked behind the counter of Sandy's. Though his real name was Ronald, we called him Drac because he had deep-set eyes that looked like two bullet holes in a piece of brown wood. He would be wearing a white apron and a silly hat that looked like a sailor's cap. I'd order a burger and french fries. When I got outside I'd look in the bag and there'd always be a couple extra hamburgers, sometimes even a fried apple pie. I'd look back over my shoulder through the glass, and Drac would just smile, and I'd thank him with a smile of my own. There was no place to eat inside Sandy's. Chin and I would stand outside beneath the light and wolf down the burgers as if we'd never eaten decently before.

Jazzy Joe Wade also always hung out at Sandy's. He too was in the ninth grade. He used big words, seemed wise beyond his years, wore silk shirts and patent leather shoes without socks. He had false teeth, and I liked him. If we'd had a class poet, it would have been Jazzy Joe. He got straight A's in algebra and English. But ours was just a gritty inner-city junior high on the east side of Columbus, Ohio. Jazzy Joe, like most of us, would have to find his own poetry. Sometimes you'd see huge football players who played for Woody Hayes at Ohio State eating their hamburgers in the parking lot of Sandy's. They'd be in their scarlet-and-gray letter jackets and they'd be friendly. Their windows would be rolled down; sweet soul music blared from their car radios.

I prayed to get into our basketball games, but I didn't get into them. I sat far down the bench, dressed in my green-and-gold silk uniform, my white wristbands, my green kneepads; dressed to kill, dressed to play, flat-out dressed. But I didn't play. Worm and Tiny and Aaron James played beautifully, manhandling teams we played against. When Gluesniffer got into the game, he'd gun it up, shoot nearly every time he touched the ball. His eyes were bloodshot, and he'd be wheezing out there on the court. But his shots went in, *swish, swish,* right through the net, so Coach Marsh had to play him. During timeouts Gluesniffer would wheeze, trying to catch his breath. Chin and I would snicker. I'd sit on the bench and watch the game and I'd also watch Toni, who was a cheerleader. She'd do cartwheels. For some reason it was exciting to watch her wipe sweat from her brow. Her sneakers were as white as salt. But by the time basketball season came around she was going with Rodney Smith. Rodney had green eyes and wore his leather coat unbuttoned. All the girls liked him. I'd see him and Toni walking home from school together sometimes, laughing off in the distance, as happy as clowns. I wondered all the time if they had kissed. I wondered if Rodney had touched her in any secret places. Chin said he was pretty sure Rodney had touched her.

Elvira was happy when my brother Harry came home on leave from the navy. I was also happy. It was basketball season and it was cold. My brother was wrapped in wool. He strolled through Bolivar Arms in his navy blues, all cocky and head held high as if he were anxious to get back to "the war," as he called it. Actually my brother spent most of his time during "the war" at sea, along the coast of Spain. He sent us pictures of Barcelona, pictures of him surrounded by Spanish girls. In one photo he held a bottle of beer in his hand, had his arm wrapped around a girl's shoulder; the girl was holding a cigarette between her fingers, and everyone was laughing. My brother never fired a shot in the war, nor did the ship he sailed on.

It was a wonderful moment for me when Harry came strutting into the Monroe Junior High gym, dressed, of course, in his navy blues. Chin and I always sat next to each other on the bench, and I nudged him when my brother walked in. Harry sat in the front row of the bleachers, floor level, and he could look right across the gym floor at me sitting on the bench. I looked at Coach Marsh as the game went on. I wanted him to know how badly I wanted to get into the game, wanted him to know my brother was there. The game began and ended, and we lost, and I never saw action. Harry left the gymnasium in silence, just stood up and walked right out the door. I felt ashamed. I hated Coach Marsh. I planned to quit the team.

The next morning I went to his office. I asked him how

come I hadn't played in the game — my brother was there, home from the navy, had expected to see me play. "How dare you ask me a question like that?" he said, then loudly reminded me we had lost the game. He slammed shut a desk drawer. Then he walked toward me; I had to back up quick to give him room to get by me. I feared the man more than ever. I forgot to quit.

We made the very top of the city's junior high basketball rankings despite our one loss. I started clipping stories and mentions of our team from the newspaper, just like Tiny. A lot of the grownups walking up and down Mt. Vernon Avenue, waiting in line at Tyler's Drugs for their prescriptions, had already started talking about a possible championship game between us and Champion Junior High. Then, halfway through our season, scandal struck our team. Worm and Aaron James and Tiny had been seen drinking liquor during a school lunch hour. Someone snitched on them, ran and told Mr. Wood, the roly-poly truant officer. You'd always see Mr. Wood walking around the schoolyard, sometimes outside the fence, looking for students playing hooky. Not a lot of kids decided to float out in the open and walk by Mr. Wood. Mr. Wood did an investigation, which meant he went around asking a lot of questions, asking who had actually seen Worm and Tiny and Aaron James drinking. He reported back to Coach Marsh that it was all true. The three players, our three stars, were kicked off the team. News of the scandal whipped through Columbus.

For several evenings after practice, as we were sweeping up the gymnasium, Chin and I debated the consequences of what had happened. We both felt pity for Aaron James and Worm and Tiny. But we also had hope for our own chances of getting to play more often in the games, even if that sounded selfish. I wanted to play; Chin wanted to play.

In the quiet of my bedroom, I prepared to play more often, going over the team's plays in my head, listening to professional basketball games on the FM station on my transistor. I had languished long enough. Only I didn't play more in the next game, or the game after that. In fact, I didn't play at all. Chin got most of the playing time, along with Gluesniffer. I decided again to quit. Earlier Chin had vowed that if I quit, we'd quit together. I told him it was time to step off the stage, to leave Coach Marsh behind. But now he didn't want to quit; he was getting playing time, he was happy. He cautioned me about having a "bad attitude."

We started losing games, by ten points, by twenty points. The losses were painful. Coach Marsh would turn red. Aaron James and Worm and Tiny would come to the games, sit up in the bleachers, laugh at us. They looked as lost as stowaways. But when Coach Marsh turned and scowled at them, they quieted down. You could tell they hurt.

Winter arrived in Bolivar Arms. The cold winds whipped around the housing project, rattling our windows. A lot of times I'd turn the heat up too high and the walls would sweat, little clear beads dripping down. Jimmy had always kept our house on the north side nice and hot in wintertime — "toasty," as Elvira liked to say. Mice were everywhere in our apartment, mostly hiding behind the washing machine in the pantry. Mousetraps set, I'd hustle upstairs into bed. The apartment would be warm.

By the time school had started for me at Monroe Junior High, my mother had been rehired at Yolando's, the Greek restaurant on the north side of town where my grandfather worked. She worked from four in the afternoon until midnight. She alternately worked as a waitress and in the kitchen — preparing fruit salads, tossed salads, BLT sandwiches, chicken sandwiches. Sometimes she would call Emily and recite all the different kinds of sandwiches she had prepared the day before. She'd talk about the cheesecake that everyone asked for, and the apple strudel, and the rice pudding that just flew off the shelf. My mother wanted her mother to be proud of her. Hard as I tried to, I could not fall asleep until she was home from work. It was as if a light bulb were on inside my chest and refused to switch off.

Late at night, outside our apartment, just below my window, I'd hear a car door slam. Then I'd hear my mother's voice and another voice, her girlfriend Bobbie's. Bobbie worked with my mother and drove her home from work every night. Their voices skipped across the darkened front yard. "I'll see you tomorrow, girl," Bobbie would say. She would wait for my mother to get safely inside the apartment, then she'd drive away in that noisy car of hers.

I liked it a lot when Bobbie drove away; only Bobbie more often than not did not drive away. She'd park her car and come inside the apartment with Elvira. They'd pull out a stack of old forty-fives: Nancy Wilson, Arthur Prysock, Joe Tex, Jackie Wilson. They'd turn on the stereo, and the voice that dominated the downstairs, that kept me from sleep, was not the stereo but Bobbie's voice. It was loud and untamed, a cabaret voice, a voice made to keep everyone from falling asleep. I'd go downstairs and, leaning on the stairway railing, beg Bobbie and my mother for quiet. Bobbie would look up at me, already tipsy, batting her big black fake eyelashes. She would turn toward my mother: "Elvira, turn the music down." And then my mother would roll her eyes at me, tell me to get off the railing, go to bed.

Sometimes my mother wore wigs. But Bobbie wore wigs all the time. Hers always looked theatrical. They were frosted. They were short. They were long. She had a variety of wigs, and a lot of them had reddish tints. She could bounce between Twiggy, Diana Ross, and Tina Turner like bouncing from Monday to Thursday. I'd be looking right at Bobbie's wig as I leaned against the railing; she'd look back at me as if I were crazy, as if at any moment she were going to ask me what the hell's my problem.

I'd go back upstairs, and after ten or fifteen minutes the music would be turned back up. I believe I hated Bobbie. My mother and Bobbie ignored my pleas, played their music, lived their lives: two waitresses on the edge of the 1960s, holding on.

Early one gauzy morning — I remember frost on the windows as I pulled back the curtains and looked out — the police brought my mother home. Something about her and Bobbie — too much drinking in a car, Bobbie behind the wheel. My mother was shaking when she came into the house. My sisters and I instinctively knew not to mention a word of this little episode to Jimmy and Emily. Elvira really didn't have to scream at us, warning us not to tell them, but she did anyway.

Yet there were times when Elvira went out and returned home early, as sober as a pilot. Her party had fallen through; the man she was to meet at the bar didn't show up; she had just felt tired and wanted to get home. I remember a Christmas Eve outing, my mother returning home early with snowflakes in her hair, on her coat collar — and stone sober. She fixed something to eat. She put some forty-fives on the record player. She put her hair up in rollers. Just me and her and my sisters. On those nights when I knew my mother was downstairs, sober, I could climb the stairs and fall asleep like a bird falling back into a nest.

Of course I did not know about grownups, that people need people. Men sometimes came home to spend the night with Elvira. I didn't like any of them. One man looked as old as my grandfather. Another man went by the initials S.T., wore granny glasses, dressed like a banker, and said hardly a word. Another had been a convict, bragged to me about it. I rolled my eyes. Sometimes my father came and slid into the house like a ghost; I'd see his car outside in the morning from my window. I didn't mind my father being around, brief as his visits were.

Emily, my grandmother, told me she'd buy my winter coat that year. I had seen a blue leather coat in the window at Lee's, up on Mt. Vernon Avenue. She told me if that's what I wanted, she'd buy it for me. It cost seventy-nine dollars. I had never had a coat so expensive. I wore it to school every day, double-checked my lock on my locker because I didn't want anyone to steal it. One night friends came over to our apartment to see my sister, Glenn Wilson among them. Glenn talked loudly, cheated at playground basketball, never carried books, and mostly made me nervous. He stole my leather coat from our hallway closet. Several friends told me they had seen him with the coat, trying to sell it. When I confronted him, he yelled in my face, cocked his fist, and turned and walked away. Glenn had three brothers at Monroe: a mini-tribe. I was a lone warrior and had to walk through the woods carefully.

I eagerly looked forward to our game with Indianola Junior High, my old school. I wouldn't play, no doubt, but at least I'd get to see my friends Bubbles and Tutu, Jesse and Dalton and Dan Hardesty. And they'd see me in my gold-and-green silk uniform. Elvira could never come see me play because she worked evenings. Sometimes she'd ask me the morning after whether we'd won, but not in any kind of tone where it would break her heart if we had lost. On game day, Mr. Wood would stand at the gym door, making sure no one sneaked in. We burst out of the locker room into the gymnasium, Gluesniffer now leading our charge. The gym was crowded and as warm as steam. I stared across our gym floor at Indianola and my friends. They looked tall; Dan and Jesse had gotten bigger. We all were growing like weeds. But they didn't wave at me. There were gentle nods of the head, no more: game faces.

Indianola raced out to a big lead, galloping up and down the court, playing with a ferocity we couldn't match, not now. I looked at the Indianola players, my friends, and wondered if I could have made that team. I guessed not, guessed I might have been thrown overboard, might have been walking home along the railroad tracks in our old neighborhood all by myself. They were up by eight, then by twelve. Then the referee called Indianola for a technical foul. That meant someone from our team would have to go to the free-throw line while the floor was cleared and shoot a foul shot. Probably Chin. Maybe Gluesniffer. Coach Marsh stood up, looked down the bench.

"Haygood!"

I looked up from the bench, startled. I was being sent in to shoot the free throw. Against my old junior high. Covered in silk, I tore off my warmup jacket, stripped off my warmup pants, ran and checked into the game. Then I hustled up to the free-throw line. My heart beat fast, and I felt that cold-hot sensation I always felt inside a gym when I first walked into it. My Indianola friends stared at me. Jesse Hunter, a fearless athlete, had his hands on his hips. He was looking at me as if he had never seen me before in his life. Tutu, my former fishing buddy, was behind me, and I could see him out of the corner of my eye. His face looked gentle. I bounced the ball until I got a rhythm, until the gym was quiet.

"Scarecrow, shoot the ball!" someone yelled. Then someone laughed. It sounded like Wanda Clark, who lived in Bolivar Arms, who was a smart-aleck, who smoked cigarettes, who I never liked. I wanted to kill her.

The ball arched from my hands. It rose high and spun cleanly. It sailed right through the net. I heard clapping, which sounded beautiful, like music. I had scored my first point of the year.

I hated Coach Marsh.

I loved Coach Marsh.

We lost the game, but the next morning my name was in the newspaper, in the box score. I cut it out. I couldn't afford a scrapbook. I kept my clippings in a large envelope, kept the envelope in my top dresser drawer. Nights before games I still scrubbed my socks on my mother's washboard, still polished my dress shoes, still touched up my sneakers with baby powder. I never scored another point all season.

I wanted my mother to come to our basketball banquet, but she couldn't: she had hundreds of BLT sandwiches she had to fix, hundreds of bowls of rice pudding she had to prepare. I received my varsity letter. The coach handed it to me in a little cellophane wrapper. I stood it up like a Bible on my dresser in my bedroom. It was often the last thing I looked at before I fell asleep. Sometimes when Elvira came into my room late at night to set my lunch money on the dresser, to philosophize, she'd accidentally knock my letter down. I'd just set it up the next morning, scoop up my lunch money — nickels, dimes, an occasional fifty-cent piece — and head off to school.

Spring came and the weather turned warm. The Goody Wagon, loaded with groceries and missing from our apartment complex during the winter, showed up, its bells ringing like a call to arms. Chin helped me get a job with him downtown at the police station, washing police cars. We made $1.25 per hour. The officers would drive their cars into the basement of police headquarters, climb out, and leave their cars in our care. They never said much, and they didn't seem friendly. I spent my money on magazines, hamburgers from Sandy's, silk socks. For some reason I had grown fond of silk socks.

Chin talked me into going out for the baseball team. We had to quit our jobs. Glenn Wilson also went out for the team. In tryouts Glenn played skillfully, scooping up line drives hit in practice by the coach, rah-rahing in a loud voice, his lips dry and chalky. Chin told me what had happened the year before: Glenn tried out, looked just fine, and days before the final cut the coach came to him and told him his grades were too low, sorry. Chin promised me the same thing would happen again this year. It did. We saw Glenn stomping around the practice field, cursing into the thin springtime air.

I had never played organized hardball in my life. I tried out for third base. To my surprise, I made the team. To my shock, I started. I was a horrible baseball player. Crouched low in a state of fear, I prayed balls would not come zooming down the third base line in my direction. They did, and I missed many of them; actually, more than many. But the coach kept me on the field. He had no choice. Not many boys were wild about baseball at Monroe. I crouched low at the plate at bat, my arms cocked at an upright angle, my helmet squeezed tight onto my large head. I went hitless the entire season. Chin played second base, wore white cleats, didn't miss many balls. But he couldn't hit a lick either. We lost every game and finished dead last in the league. Sometimes after games, when the May and June light was still good in the sky, Chin and I went to play basketball — swinging our cleats in our hands — and forgot all about our woes on the baseball diamond.

Rumors floated around school about who would be taking whom to the prom. Fatman would take Karen; Rodney would take the girl of my dreams, Toni; Aaron James would boycott it, as he boycotted all the school dances, since he was shy about dancing on his wooden leg. I got sweaty just thinking about the prom. I did not know whom to ask. Sally Barnes was pretty, too pretty for me. Lona, who had slapped me, was crazy. My sister Wonder saved me: she asked Doris Draper, her best friend, if she'd go to the prom with me. Doris had coppery skin, freckles, and nice-sized titties. She said yes. So there we were, shoved at each other. We shot each other glances in the hallway; no need to say a word, the asking already had been done, her yes already had been given, our little sailboat was ready to shove off. Gluesniffer asked my sister — Gluesniffer, who had pummeled me during my first days in Bolivar Arms. I demanded that she say no. She said yes.

My mother gave me money to rent my tuxedo. I rented it from O. P. Gallo, downtown, just behind the statehouse. It was a red jacket with black designs, a pair of black slacks with the silk stripe going up the sides, a black clip-on bow tie. I pulled my black silk socks up to my kneecaps, slipped on a pair of black patent leather shoes.

Gluesniffer came on foot to our apartment to pick Wonder up. He was wearing a yellow tuxedo and looked like a dirty canary. He sounded like an old man, with that raspy voice. We said little to each other.

Doris's brother, Earl, drove us all to the prom. Earl didn't have a date. He was afraid of girls, just like I was afraid of girls. Earl's eyes blinked a lot. Doris looked nice; her titties were as big as ever. She smiled at me but seemed to pay more attention to my sister. She sat up front with her brother. I squeezed in the back next to Gluesniffer, who was squeezed next to Wonder. Our prom was held in the gym of our school. Daylight was fading by the time we arrived and Earl got the

TONI *and me at the ninth-grade prom.*
I was not her date; I just begged her to be in
a snapshot with me. I rented the tux for
nineteen bucks — my mother's
waitressing tips.

car parked. Some students were hanging outside. Every time someone stepped out of a car, they'd start wolf-whistling, making jokes. Some of them couldn't go to the prom because they were not going to graduate on time. But they came and stood outside, as noisy as bees. Walking inside, we were all satin and silk, swishing together. Rhythm and blues drifted out of the gym as we drifted in. I was glad I wasn't alone, glad to be with Doris. Some of my friends inside the dark, warm gym didn't have dates. They looked as lonely as owls.

Doris and I danced. We sipped punch from paper cups. Mr. Wood walked around with a camera hanging from his fat neck. When I saw Toni, I stared. She was in a pink dress. It was above her knees. You could tell she had had her hair pressed and done up that very day. I asked her to pose for a picture with me. Doris got lost from me in the darkness and the music. I've kept the picture through the years. In it, I seem to be holding Toni too tight. She seems bored, preoccupied with her thoughts; I look to be swooning.

Wonder's friends were different from mine. My sister liked boys who smoked cigarettes and sniffed glue, boys who drove cars, boys who stole cars. My sister needed Elvira more than I needed Elvira. I roamed on my own, rubbed my basketball like a genie rubbing a crystal ball; the ball wouldn't let me down, would guide me straight. It lay beneath my bed at night. My sister had no crystal ball. So she bumped along with others, sailed on the itchy wind of others.

A week after prom night, seated with Wonder in the back of a car after a dance, I noticed her head bobbing. She began to slur her words. Inside our apartment she collapsed, just dropped like clothing. I yelled in her ear, slapped her face, pulled back her eyelids, carried her up to bed. Then I raced to the phone and called an ambulance. Then I called Elvira. The ambulance circled through the darkness of our apartment complex, came to a halt with lights flaring. I sat in the back and sped off to Grant Hospital with my sister. I remember the brittle lights of the hospital, the clean, smooth floors, the doctors and nurses huddled around Wonder's limp body. Tubes were pushed down her throat. Her stomach had to be pumped. They suspected a drug overdose. Wonder had taken some yellowjackets, tiny crazycolored pills that were easy to get in our neighborhood. I could see the liquid coming through her mouth and moving through the tubes. Her body convulsed, jerked upward and slammed back down. Elvira and Bobbie arrived. They had on their waitress uniforms, their wigs. I tried to explain. They crowded around the bed. I walked up and down the corridors, slapping my hands on the walls, scraping my knuckles. I felt I had let my mother down, my sister down.

Wonder came home the next day. For some reason, Elvira didn't make a big fuss about it. She told me in her stern voice that I'd better not say anything to Jimmy and Emily about my sister. Jack, our father, came by to check on Wonder. He had an uncanny ability to show up in times of crisis, like a night watchman with a flashlight.

Looking back now, I can see that that summer night, in the back of that car, marked the beginning of my sister's decline. When Wonder recovered, she climbed out of bed at home and walked straight ahead, thin as a wafer, into years and years of darkness. She would never again look as confident, as lovely, as she had looked while strolling into our prom on that fragrant night.

It is 1993. I am standing outside my sister's house in Columbus. I have come home to see about my niece. My family is worried; they haven't seen her in a week. My sister's phone has been disconnected. I knock hard on the front door. I circle the back yard, yelling for my sister, my little niece. I hear music inside. The curtains are drawn. Neighbors tell me that strangers have been coming and going. I call the police, stand at curbside, watch them enter the house. Two mean-looking dudes are brought out, one in handcuffs, wearing a holster strapped at his waist, the gun apparently pulled out by the police. I scold my sister, who is not arrested.

"I didn't know you had a twin sister," a friend said to me not long ago. Sometimes I'm quiet about Wonder.

It is 1994. I'm standing on the cool green lawn of Mary-haven Hospital in Columbus. My sister is in for treatment. Back again a year later. Back again months after that. On and on. Sometimes there is laughter, and we talk, sister and brother, the twins, laughing from our bellies. But I won't give an inch on my niece's safety. Jimmy and Emily didn't give an inch on their grandchildren. So sometimes I'm the cop.

I wanted to get a job in the summer of 1969, when I was fifteen. It would be good to have money to buy fishing and basketball magazines. The heels of my white straw shoes were wearing down. So I walked up to Mt. Vernon Avenue, to the offices of what was called Mini City Hall, a satellite city hall built a year earlier, the year of the first riots on the avenue, and applied for a job. Shirley Massey, who was in charge of hiring, had a dripping southern accent. She also was one of the sweetest ladies I ever met. She gave me and a lot of my friends jobs. I worked with a shovel on a cleaning detail, scooping up garbage and debris from the buildings being torn down on Mt. Vernon Avenue — the jazz clubs, the bars, the honky-tonks. I'd take lunch at the Chesapeake Bar & Grill, a fried pork chop sandwich. I got paid every two weeks. I'd give Elvira forty dollars out of every paycheck to help with the bills. Chin hated giving his mother money. He said she took too much.

I spent my money on clothes, buying them either at Lee's or Vernon Tailors — a sharkskin suit, pairs of black shoes, multi-colored shirts. I fished that summer. And I went to spend weekends with my grandparents. I'd walk across the St. Clair Avenue bridge, take shortcuts beneath viaducts. The journey would take me by Tiny's house. I'd bang on the door of that big brown boarding house; he was never home. I grew two inches. I shot baskets on empty playgrounds and let the sun set around me. I played checkers with my grandfather.

We listened to baseball games on the radio together. We rode to the racetrack in a taxi, the country trees green and thick. He was always asking me about my mother. I told him she was fine.

There was something mystical in our community about East High School. Boys who had walked its halls had turned into legends. It was at East that Bill Willis played, the first black football player signed by Paul Brown for his Cleveland Browns. It was East High that in 1968 won the state championships in both baseball and basketball, the all-black team beating the all-white teams as it mowed down competition in both sports across the state. It was East High that Mt. Vernon Avenue threw a parade for, those tall, muscular boys riding down the avenue in convertibles, smiling, wearing their orange-and-black letter jackets. I was both afraid of and excited about going to East. Maybe I'd get to ride in a convertible someday.

I decided I'd hit the ground running. I went out for football. I wanted to quarterback. In Bolivar Arms we had played football on the precious strips of grass that had been planted behind each of the apartment circles. I threw the ball hard and accurately. East High's football practice field, Harley Field, was an old stadium inside high fences. I trotted out on the first day of tryouts for the reserve team. On that field, on freshly cut grass, beneath blue sky, I felt confident. I lined up with the other quarterback hopefuls to take snaps. When it was my turn, when the coach had walked near me to focus on my technique, I leaned over the center's butt and took my snap. And another snap. Then another. Each time I stuttered. The big center started to laugh. The coach looked at me, right into my eyes, and I knew he knew what I knew: my stutter wasn't about to go away. I would not be the East High quarterback. Still, my dreams were free. I'd just dream other dreams. I walked home down Mt. Vernon Avenue the night I was cut. I passed brittle neon lights. I tromped across a grassy field and found the screen door to our apartment, not heartbroken, happy enough.

I could suffer the death of a football dream and not look back, but basketball was different. A basketball team was a crew of boys setting sail on unknown journeys, escaping school bells and long hallways to sweat and laugh and jump together. I vowed to myself I'd never be left behind on such a journey.

Scott Guiler was the East High reserve basketball coach. He smiled a lot, had a happy, light voice. Chin didn't go out for the basketball team. He needed to keep his after-school job. Chin needed money; I needed basketball. The coach cut me. Stunned, the next day I walked into the locker room, got dressed, and hustled back out onto the practice floor. I walked up to the coach and asked him for another chance, in front of everyone. I stuttered some of the words out. I felt a twinge of pity for myself. I could tell the coach was embarrassed, because there was silence. He looked at me, his lips tight. There were snickers. Then he told me to join the layup drills. I hustled more. I ran faster. I dove on the floor after loose balls. After practice I walked over to him.

"I'll see you tomorrow," he said.

Several days later he told me I was on the team. Word floated around school that I had begged my way onto the team. I didn't care. No one else from Bolivar Arms had made the reserve basketball team. I felt a little special. But I walked home alone into dark wintry nights. I pulled leftover hotel food from the refrigerator. I set my mousetraps, turned up the heat, climbed into bed, and listened for my mother's voice to scrape the outside of my closed window.

Then I started walking home with Nick. Nick was lanky

and neat. He had all kinds of lotions in his gym bag, and fragrant soaps, which he shared with me. When we walked home, sometimes we'd stop for burgers at a little burger shack that sat catty-cornered to his house. Nick loaned me money and never asked for it back. That made me want to give him money whenever I had it, which wasn't often. On occasion we'd sit in his apartment. He lived with his mother; Nick was an only child. He could look at a picture in a magazine and walk right over to his drawing desk and draw that very picture. He liked jazz and owned a whole assortment of jazz albums — Charlie Parker, Thelonious Monk, Miles Davis, music I knew nothing about, musicians I had never heard of. Nick would sit and listen and close his eyes and bob his head.

Saturday mornings when Woody Hayes's Ohio State football team was on the road, Nick and I would catch the city bus to Ohio Stadium. There were basketball courts beneath that gothic football stadium. It was kind of dark down there, and chilly, because the wind whipped through the stadium openings. But the rims had nets, and Nick and I could play all morning long. We'd choose sides with others who showed up. We'd play in the cold, our fingertips freezing, our noses running, the bounce of the ball echoing off the cement, our voices touching one another's voices like voices in a cave. When I'd pass the ball too hard to Nick, it would sting his hand, on account of the cold. He'd curse. "Damn," and you'd hear the echo: *damn damn damn*. We'd play six and seven hours, through hunger and without complaint, joy to the world and our basketball dreams. Sometimes when we came up out of the stadium, shadows would be falling across that huge campus, like giant lilies.

I rarely played during our reserve games. Then, a week before our last game, I had four days of wonderful practices. I threw blind passes, and players — especially Nick — caught them, caught them at the last possible moment. The coach smiled. In a scrimmage, he put me in with the first team, at the point guard position. I threw more blind passes. I made jump shots. I barked out plays to teammates, took control of the team. Coach Guiler walked up to me on the eve of our final game. "You're starting tomorrow," he said.

I had begged my way onto the team, but I had worked my way into the starting lineup. Nick was happy for me. I wished Elvira could come to see me start. I told Chin I was starting our last game of the season. He seemed not to care, looked at me as if I were bragging, changed the subject.

On game day I was nervous, but once the whistle blew, I calmed down. The opposing players seemed quicker, louder, more aggressive than I imagined they'd be. The light in the gym seemed blinding, as thick as glue. Then the whistle blew and the game was over and we had lost. It seemed a blur. I did not score a single point. I walked home with Nick in the cold, and I felt warm because I was a starter. Nick told me I had played fine, and I believed him.

We were not given team photographs or anything, so the week before we had to turn our uniforms in, I went to a photographer's studio and had a picture taken of myself in my basketball uniform. I had to pay for it myself; my grandmother had given me the money. I had to ride the bus all day to get to the photographer's, had to skip a half-day's worth of school. I was frightened that someone from school would see me on the bus. I framed the picture and set it atop my dresser, right beside the Monroe Junior High varsity letter.

At the end of my sophomore year I went and found Bob Hart, the varsity basketball coach. I needed to know things, to plan my future. I asked him if he thought I would make varsity the following year. Coach Hart was a short man, and chubby, and you would never have imagined that he had even played the game of basketball. But he had coached teams to state championships; the East High trophy case was lined with trophies with his name on them. He wore thick glasses. Behind them, it looked like his eyeballs were rolling around in a cup of gray water. He hemmed and hawed, and I pressed him. He said he didn't know; he said I had a fifty-fifty chance; he said there were some promising players coming from the junior high ranks; he said the competition would be fierce. A strange little smirk was working itself up at the corner of his mouth. I didn't trust him. I'd never trust him. Decisions had to be made, and I realized it.

I had to make a decision about how to tell Elvira I'd flunked algebra.

When my mother wasn't waitressing, or sitting around waiting for another call from another place of seasonal employment, like a racetrack, or leafing through her Frederick's of Hollywood magazines, or talking with Mrs. Erma on our front lawn about everything under — and over — the moon, she was in bed. There were times during the school year that the most I saw of her was a figure beneath a wool blanket in the morning, when I went into her room to tell her I was off to school. My mother never asked about my grades, and I didn't mind. When I told her I had flunked algebra, she shot me a vicious look. She stared at me in silence. "Close the door," she finally said, and I left her room.

My life, then, seemed ordained: I'd watch my sister Wonder out of the corner of my eye. I'd prepare my mother's grits. I'd walk across the St. Clair Avenue bridge to see my grandparents. I'd play basketball for coaches who were shortsighted men, who would never realize my worth until it was too late, like the last game of the season. I'd play college ball, then work my way onto a pro team — the New York Knicks, the Cincinnati Royals — and I'd sit on the bench, until a day would come when I'd jump over all my teammates, when I'd carry the team to victory, when the victories would pile up, reversing my hurt, crushing my past and all the slights.

Meanwhile, I had to take algebra all over again and pass it. I was as open as a floodgate to any ideas that might make that possible.

8

JAZZY JOE WADE was interesting to me. He got straight A's in math, and I could not imagine how anyone got straight A's in math. In addition to wearing patent leather shoes with no socks and never carrying books, he sold clothing from his mother's apartment: shirts, slacks, jackets, all brand-new. I'd gawk at the items, run my hands across them, tell Jazzy Joe I didn't have enough money to buy anything. He'd shrug his shoulders.

Jazzy Joe had gotten accepted into a summer scholarship program. He'd go away to a campus for three straight summers, prep to go to college. I also filled out an application for the program. It included a question about why I thought I should be accepted. I wrote, "Because after I was born I was placed in an incubator." (I spent four weeks in the glass box because of breathing problems; my mother's cesarean was difficult, apparently, for her and her twins.) The answer sounds rather strange to me now. I think, by way of explanation, that I thought I needed to catch up in the world; I felt behind.

I was summoned for an interview. It took place downtown, at the old Salesian Boys Club, in the basement. In the days of legal segregation, when the downtown Columbus YMCA would not allow blacks to play inside, the Salesian Boys Club went in the opposite direction, opening its doors, welcoming blacks. I noticed other students — and their parents — sitting on metal chairs. I was alone. I hadn't told Elvira I was going for the interview. I sat across from a square-jawed man who looked at me with an amused smile. His name was Roosevelt Carter. He took photographs all over town, a lot of society photographs of Mt. Vernon Avenue women. The pictures would show up in the *Call & Post*. In our town, men like Roosevelt Carter interviewed boys and girls for things like summer scholarship programs. Roosevelt Carter was what they called a respected member of the community.

I didn't think I'd get into the program. I had failed algebra. But I was accepted. I felt tingly; I'd be going away, on a kind of journey.

There was excitement in my family about my going away. Words were passed across telephone wires to relatives. It was like the excitement of a maiden voyage. Emily told her sisters, who lived all the way up in Detroit. She gave me a brown suitcase, one of the pieces of the four-piece luggage set that she always used when she went to visit her sisters. It was the first piece of luggage I could call my own. The insides of it smelled just like my grandmother's clothing — clean and flowery. I'd be away all summer, on the campus of Ohio Dominican College. Emily told me to be good; Jimmy told me to mind my manners and listen to the teachers. Elvira didn't give me any instructions.

Jack, my father, came to pick me up on the morning I was to

go away. Jack and Elvira sat in the front of the car, just like a regular married couple. We rode right down Leonard Avenue, past the stockyard, and down Sunbury Road to the campus. It was just a twenty-minute ride from our apartment, but it might as well have been a world away. A group of seventy or so of us kids arrived that summer, inner-city kids, desperate and desperate to learn. The campus was so green, and everything connected to it seemed to me willowy and leafy.

Some of the kids stayed in the only dorm on the small campus. I stayed in a house across Sunbury Road, a small white house with a screen door that slapped and a porch you could sit on. Actually, it was more a cottage than a house. Leonard was my roommate. He had monkeylike features — sunken eyes and real dark skin and pretty teeth. But of course you couldn't say that to Leonard, because he was black and there'd be a vicious fight. It didn't matter that I was black too. Enough people had called Leonard monkey that he had an immediate reaction, which was to charge you, his fists balled. So I called him monkey behind his back. Leonard was on probation from the Ohio Youth Services for attempting to steal a car. Claude Willis, the assistant director of the program, had pleaded with youth services to release Leonard into the custody of the college program. So here he was, walking around the campus with a limp, which he had been born with; it had slowed his getaway run, which is why the police had caught up with him when he jumped out of the stolen car and started to run.

The college had previously been known as St. Mary's of the Springs. It had been a Catholic girls' college. In the early 1960s it had sent one of its representatives, Sister Thomas Albert Corbett, down to Washington to plead for some money to host a summer scholarship program for inner-city students. Sister Thomas Albert was an old New Dealer; she had a certain antenna for such a program. But she practically had to beg: the powers that be in Washington thought that the campus was too small, that the administration didn't have the muscle, a strong enough army. But Sister Thomas Albert — and the school — got its money, its program, and us.

There was nothing I liked better in the summer of 1970 than walking across that college campus. I liked the quiet walk of the nuns, their determination to teach us, to settle us down in class, to discipline. Some of us were rebels; a few were tossed out that first summer. But many of us made it through. The nuns meant business. They could appear solemn, but they also smiled. That their smiles were rare made them all the more precious.

Sister Thomas Albert, whose hair protruded from her wimple like gray bubbles, was the director of the program. Her skin was albino white, and she had tiny eyes, smaller than marbles, and she squinted, raising anything written on paper to within inches of her eyes. She never forgot any of our names, which I thought amazing. But it was Claude Willis, the assistant director, whom we flocked around the most. Everyone called him Mr. Willis, and his name must have been uttered a million times a day on that campus. He was one of two legendary Willis brothers raised on the east side of Columbus. Both had been football stars at East High, bruising tacklers. Brother Bill had gone from East High to Ohio State to Paul Brown's Cleveland Browns to my grandfather Jimmy's lips on Sunday afternoons during radio broadcasts. Claude had gone to Claflin College, a tiny school in South Carolina. Even now, years and years after his football-playing days, Claude Willis had a hard body, as thick as an oak, and walked like a man who had just finished knocking someone over.

We studied, but we did other things too. We went horseback riding. Blacklick Woods was east of Columbus — hilly terrain, tall trees, riding trails. It had a rustic country-club feel. I'd heard about it but never been on its grounds. But there we were, a string of teenagers, boys and girls, on horseback. We rode as slow as a search party: we were city kids. One afternoon, however, my horse broke from the pack and galloped wildly into the woods. Dripping saliva, it made noises deep in its throat. Others in the party gave pursuit; I gripped the horn and howled. By the time my horse slowed and pulled up, my right arm was bloodied by a nasty licking from a branch. I still carry the scar.

Through the cafeteria windows we could see trees that rose up from the hillsides. In the early mornings, with dew on the grass, the campus buildings as quiet as church, we could smell the food in the cafeteria before we reached it. We could eat all we wanted. The cooks wore starched white, sweated, smiled, kept the big silver pans filled with food, and never said much. I gulped glasses and glasses of orange juice, went back for second helpings of food. The spaghetti with meatballs and lasagna were divine. We had steak, lamb chops, an assortment of desserts. I think my kitchen-working mother would have approved highly of the display of food. I made peanut butter and jelly sandwiches and folded napkins over them and walked across the green grass back to my little bungalow. At night I lay in bed, listening to Leonard tell tales about reform school and his basketball talent. We listened to crickets through the window's screen. We talked about girls. The moon looked swollen and far away.

J. R. Winchester had the coolest name in the program. You half expected him to sling a rifle. As the summer wore on, he became the most popular boy on the campus. J. R. came from the north side of Columbus, from the old Windsor Terrace housing projects. He was handsome, a high school football and baseball star. He didn't chase girls, though they chased him. Every night J. R. ironed the clothes he planned to wear the next day to class. We had to sit in his room and wait for him if we wanted him to go with us to shoot pool in the rec area. His ritual lasted at least thirty minutes. I had never met anyone so fastidious. J. R. refused to go anywhere in wrinkled clothes, but I snatched my clothes from a drawer, refused to iron anything — didn't have the time.

I liked Patty Taylor, but so did a lot of other boys. Patty had a small frame and big eyes. She talked in a high, chirpy voice. The voice seemed a put-on, a little theatrical, but no one cared. I slipped her notes, which she never answered. We got stipends every Wednesday, twelve dollars, two crisp five-dollar bills and two singles. It came in a little white envelope with your name scrawled on the outside. I bought Patty a gift with my stipend one weekend, an Al Green album. Sitting on a couch, fidgety, I handed it to her.

"Oh, thank you," she said, her wide eyes getting wider, her chirpy voice chirping away. I hoped for a kiss. I expected a kiss. We were alone. She stood, quickly and formally, and said, "But you shouldn't have."

I shrugged.

"Thank you again," she said, extending her hand for a handshake, then turning from me, walking away, scanning the album's liner notes.

There was no kiss.

One afternoon an older boy, twenty, maybe twenty-one — old enough to seem ancient to us — came to visit Patty. We found out he was her boyfriend. He had a car. They sat on a bench near angels and Jesus Christ; statues adorned the Ohio Dominican campus. We walked by, snickered. He snickered back. I could right away tell he was seddity. He was dressed up, wearing hard shoes. Sitting next to Mr. Seddity, Patty wasn't so girly anymore. She sat like a grownup, had a serious look on her face, looked at us as if we were children.

Fred Saunders, big, black, talkative, graceful, and kind, taught me how to shoot pool. Fred was a basketball star at Mohawk High. He was in the summer program but also on his way to college down in Louisiana, with a basketball scholarship in his hip pocket. He fretted about driving through the Deep South. I'd watch Fred shoot pool in the rec room, leaning his six-foot-eight frame over the pool green. He stroked the pool stick with two speeds: crushingly hard, scattering balls, or feathery. When he stroked it with his feathery touch, the ball he meant to go in the pocket would drift slowly, slower, then slower than that before dropping into the pocket like something tipped over. When Fred didn't have a shot on the table — or rather, when you thought he didn't have a shot on the table — he'd rise up, as tall as a stork, and circle the table, looking down on it as if he might eat something off it. "If you can't see it," he'd say about the results of a potential shot, "don't shoot it." I guess that was his version of wisdom. Then he would see a shot and position himself, bending like a boomerang. Whenever Fred was on the verge of making the winning shot, he'd break into that B. B. King song, "The Thrill Is Gone."

My coursework was challenging. I took political science. Jazzy Joe Wade sat beside me, his legs crossed, his ankles sockless, never cracking a book, answering every question thrown his way. After he answered, a smirk crossed his face, as gently as a shadow. I took advanced English lit. I took algebra, determined not to flunk it again. The nun who taught me algebra kept me after class, pounding equations and formulas into me. She was pretty and stout. She had black hair, though you couldn't see too much of it because she always wore her wimple. I asked and asked if I would pass algebra. I was desperate to pass.

I scooted around the campus. I groped for new things to do.

I took drama. Our teacher, Dave DuLong, was wiry and hyperactive. He had a beard and long hair. And he was more than just a drama teacher: he was an actor. He had starred in many of the campus productions, had had his pick of roles. He had played Tecumseh in a summer stock production. He had been all the way up to New York City to see plays on the New York stage! We were rowdy and he had to work hard to settle us down, to teach us stage movements and stage directions. Dave must have loved his job, because he worked for pennies. (Actually, the entire staff worked for pennies. Maybe they just wanted to be near inner-city kids, to spread some light.) For some reason Dave singled me out, pushed me harder. Onstage I'd hear his loud voice racing through the dark auditorium: "Make it real! Make it real!" I read my lines, acted out my roles; took easily, in fact, to the stage.

Mostly, however, my mind wandered, from class to the nearest basketball court. The college gym had wooden backboards. A lot of the gyms around the city had already installed glass backboards, but I liked the old wooden ones. You could almost feel the ball touching the wood. We played basketball in between classes, fifteen hot minutes of running and sweating. Jazzy Joe Wade played in his hard-soled shoes, scuffing up the floor. We played until Mr. Willis poked his huge head inside the door and shooed us off to class.

My mind wandered, and counselors took note of my wandering mind. One wrote of me, "Attention does not focus and maintain itself as it should." Another wrote, "If Wil's not continually prodded, he has a tendency to lose interest and his attention will wander." Still another wrote, "Slept through class every day." And this: "Would be very good in an advanced drama program."

Maybe, without my knowing it, my being on that college campus gave my family hope — for me, for all of us. I couldn't exactly see the hope, but I felt it, I knew it was there, like a pilot light inside an oven. No one in my family had ever slept a night on a college campus, but I looked up one afternoon and there they were, across the green grass, in the sunlight: Jack and Elvira and Diane and Wonder. I showed off the campus, the statues, the cafeteria. I pointed to friends, yelled their names. I said hi to monkeyface Leonard, who started talking to my family as if he'd known them all his life. Jack had on his dress shoes and waddled about like a bear.

Our end-of-summer dance was called the King and Queen Dance. Everyone talked about it, what they would wear. I didn't worry. Diane promised me she'd make me an outfit, and she did. Already she had started making outfits for my half-brother Macaroni. He strutted proudly around town in those outfits, pimping. My sister didn't let me down. My outfit was green and yellow. The pants rode high up to my waist and flared wide and wildly at the ankles. The jacket wasn't a jacket at all, but a three-quarter-length cape. It looked like something out of Shakespeare.

The dance was held in the rec room. The pool tables had been moved out of the way. I made a late entrance, on purpose, and watched as eyes landed on me and my caped outfit. I meant to act nonchalant, and I was elected that night to the King's Court. So were J. R. Winchester — who wore something commonsensical and quiet and neat — and three other boys. Leonard, my roommate, didn't make it, and hollered that the vote was fixed. We posed for photographs along with five girls — the queens. Then someone dimmed the lights and we danced. During one dance I slipped outside with a girl, Theresa, right behind me. I liked her, had been too shy to tell her so, but now summer was at an end and our boats would be rowing in different directions. She leaned into me by the side of Fitzpatrick Hall. I was surrounded by enough warm darkness to make me feel as if I were dreaming. Our tongues licked at each other furiously, as if a clock were ticking. She tasted good. I couldn't keep my tongue tight inside her mouth and keep my mouth closed at the same time. Saliva slipped out and formed a spot on her blouse. She pretended not to notice.

That summer passed — two more would pass in similar fashion — and I never forgot the books and the nuns, and Leonard yapping at me, and shooting pool for quarters and mostly winning because long tall Fred had taught me well. I never forgot the smell of the grass and Patty Taylor's eyes and the floor of the gymnasium, which was sky blue and certainly the most elegant gym floor I had ever seen or played on. I never forgot the boy who had epileptic seizures and the way Mr. Willis, down on one knee, would cradle his head in his hand, holding it like an apple, motioning to us with the other hand to go get the nurse, never raising his voice. I never forgot the white house I lived in, yards from the road, nestled against trees, and the good luck I felt in walking up into it, swinging books under my arm, the sun setting. I received the best actor trophy. Dave DuLong, the drama instructor, handed it to me and smiled. It wasn't as precious as a basketball trophy, but I appreciated it anyway.

The next day we all said 'bye to each other. The nuns stood before us in their penguin uniforms and wished us luck.

I passed algebra.

School bells rang across the city of Columbus. By the time they did, I had plotted a new plan. I would not return to East High. I feared that Coach Hart would cut me during basketball tryouts. I couldn't forget that weird little grin he had had on his face when I had asked him months earlier if he thought I'd make the team.

Mornings, preparing for school, I enjoyed the freedom of

an orphan. My sister Wonder was often moody, said little, went her own way. Elvira lay asleep most mornings, having worked late into the previous night. I did not bother her with my new plan. I just walked on over to Mt. Vernon Avenue and hopped on a city bus and rode clear to the west side to begin eleventh grade. I had once met some basketball players from West High School during a summer pickup game. They told me if I ever thought about transferring, I should come to West High. They were positive I'd make the team. I never forgot the sure sounds of their voices.

The west side was called the hilltop, because to get to it, you rode down West Broad Street and up a cresting hill. Once you crossed over the top of the hill, there it was, almost rolling into view. Churches sat on most corners. The west side was full of transplanted West Virginians; it was Appalachia all over. The houses sat close together. A lot of men walked out of them with pinched faces, happy to have jobs over at General Motors. The west side was mostly white and blue-collar. Not many people from the east side ventured over to the west side. Yet here I was, roaming like a nomad. In our town, the west side had a few image problems. It was where the juvenile boys' home was located, and, most wicked in our minds, it was where the mental institution sat — right next to the boys' home. There was one more thing: the town's remnants of the KKK held their meetings on the west side, which they considered friendly territory. It was common knowledge that the white boys from the west side were tough; they didn't back down from fights with black boys, as the suburban boys mostly did. If someone was going to visit a family member on the west side, you immediately assumed he or she was going to visit a child in reform school or someone in the mental hospital. The west side was as spooky as Transylvania.

I found the address of the school in the phone book. The

school itself sat right in the middle of a block full of houses. It was as if someone had uprooted several houses and plopped the school down; it startled you when you came upon it. I moved quickly through the hallways, wanting to be asked no questions, wanting to answer none. I sat alone in the cafeteria, ate my food fast, bolted. I squirreled my money, planning the next day's bus fare. Sometimes I had to skip lunch. In classes I listened, put my head down, studied, kept to myself. In the bathroom, boys smoked cigarettes and blew smoke rings and laughed when anyone trying to pee coughed from their cigarette smoke. Some of the smoking boys had tattoos, which looked like purple spots to me. Girls wore red lipstick — too much of it — and heart-sickened looks on their faces. The black kids ignored me. They didn't know where I was from, didn't know my family, didn't know my cousins, didn't know which Baptist church I attended, knew I was a stranger. I didn't feel fastened, but I knew I would as soon as basketball practice started.

But first I went out for cross-country. I'd never run cross-country in my life. But what was cross-country except a two-mile run? I wasn't afraid to run a focused two miles; hell, anybody could run. I arrived on the practice field. There was a nip in the air; the leaves on the trees were gold. Practice was held on a hilly golf course near the school. First day out, there was a practice run. Not full speed, just to loosen up. Still, you wanted to strut your stuff, just a little. The cross-country coach was a skinny guy who held a stopwatch in his hands. His face was unhandsome, his head shaped like an egg: Coach Huckaby. You never forget a name like Coach Huckaby. He casually blew a whistle and we ran off. I stayed near the front, then I finished in the top five. Just a practice run, but I felt like gloating; hee-hee-hee. Anybody could run. Then he blew the whistle again. This time a real run, full tilt. Everyone ran faster. The hills felt higher, my legs heavier. My chest began to burn. Runners blurred by, breathing easily; I fell back. I collapsed at the mile mark, fell to one knee, rested, caught my breath, felt dizzy. Then I finally rose. I finished the race dead last. The sky looked to be flying away, swirling. The cross-country coach looked at me and then right through me. His egg head swiveled just a little bit. The hell with cross-country; I was a basketball player anyway. I couldn't wait till basketball started.

Elvira would have been mighty angry if she had known I was way over on the west side, lying to school administrators, falsifying my address, forging yet another physical examination. Sometimes at home I feared the ring of the phone, feared it would be a school administrator tracking me down, my real address. But such a call never came. I simply scooped up the lunch money my mother had laid atop the dresser during the night and went away to school each morning while my mother slept.

The West High basketball coach had gray hair and wore plaid suits. He gave instructions with his head bowed, in a low voice. I had to scoot closer to hear. During tryouts he rarely smiled and stood stiffly on the sidelines. I couldn't see his eyes, to see if his eyes could see me, but I survived the first cut.

Evenings, after practice, I'd catch the bus back home to the east side. The bus rolled right past the mental hospital. In the distance, through the bus windows, I'd see people walking around on the hospital grounds. They were far away, like silhouettes. They were as foggy as museum pictures, and they walked obediently in lines, like prisoners. Their jackets seemed too thin against the rising cold. My grandmother Emily would never have let me wear the kinds of jackets they wore outdoors.

I did not survive the second cut. I read the roster of names attached to the coach's door, read it twice, a third time. The coach wasn't in his office, and I galloped off to find him. Surely a mistake had been made.

"I didn't make the team?"

He looked at me, then down. "I'm sorry." That's all he said. I felt dazed.

Walking away from him, my heart beating fast, my mind faster, I made up my mind what I'd do: I'd clear out my locker. I'd scram. I'd find another school, another team.

I went in search of another school through crisp mornings, the world suddenly full of strangers as I crisscrossed strange neighborhoods, riding buses in varying directions, flicking through telephone books inside stores, where I dashed to hide from the cold.

Farther west than West High School — clean out of the Columbus Public School District boundary, in fact — I found Franklin Heights High School. Franklin Heights was supposed to be pitiful; anybody could make its team. Riding the bus, without a team to fasten me down to life and time, I felt like anybody.

I caught the Sullivant Avenue bus after transferring downtown from the Mt. Vernon Avenue bus. At the end of the Sullivant Avenue bus line, I had to walk a mile down Demarest Road to the high school. I passed an old housing development — it looked southern, almost antebellum — and beyond that development, I passed rows of newer houses. The school sat in the middle of nowhere, flat fields all around. When I spotted it from the road, saw the silver lettering on its red brick, and was sure it was indeed the school, I backtracked to the houses I had passed and began my search for an address.

For some reason I was drawn to the old housing development; maybe it was its southern feel and look. I later learned the neighborbood was called Burnside. It was where I saw black faces on wooden porches looking down at me. I saw curtains being pulled back. I felt both at home and like a stranger. Burnside was its own segregated enclave, surrounded by all-white housing. A small neighborhood, a couple of roads; none of the roads were paved, most of the houses were one-floor buildings. I spotted a house that looked vacant and jotted down its address. Then I went jauntily on my way to my new school.

The principal's office was buzzing with activity. I filled out forms, was greeted and welcomed by administrators; I nodded and smiled. A day later I was given my course list.

Bob Cawley was the basketball coach. A thin man, he had blue eyes and a nose that ended in a point. There was a lilt to his walk, the kind of lilt men sometimes have when they are crossing a dance floor to ask a lady to dance. There was also a hillbillyish twang in the recesses of his voice. I told the man I was a basketball player. I told him I had starred on the reserve team at East High, had just moved to the neighborhood. He listened to my lies, his gaze strong. Tryouts had already begun, but the final cut hadn't been made, he said. I still had time.

The gym was huge, and handsome; well lighted, with glass backboards. When I first laid eyes on it, I stared across it like an explorer. I set my eyes to it as a match to fire. I wanted to hear the announcer call my name, wanted to lick out at the thick, sweet air on game day, wanted to spit on the tips of my fingers and walk to a spot on the corner during a tense game and stand alone, unbothered, wanting only the ball and my face to the basket.

A boy named Glenn was the first to ask me where I lived. "Burnside," I said.

"Burnside?"

He lived in Burnside. So he knew.

I begged him to keep quiet.

In practice I played hard, grunted, threw my elbows around, scored easily in scrimmages. But this coach didn't know me, didn't know my family, had never coached a relative of mine; had never shaken hands with my father, never smiled across a banquet room at my mother. I had no history, no accumulation of little moments, no trust. I sensed that some players were wary of me. I made the team anyway. The plank of a ship had been, at last, lowered. And I walked on board.

I was, of course, missing in action from the Columbus public school system. Who cared that I had transferred myself completely out of the city limits?

Elvira would care.

I fretted over how to tell her, sweated in my armpits. One morning I opened the door to her bedroom. She was sleeping. Her wig lay atop her dresser like a dead animal. Her makeup box lay open; her jewelry was jumbled together. I woke her, and as she heard my voice she began to move beneath the covers.

"Momma. Momma. I wanted to tell you that I'm not going to East anymore. I'm going to Franklin Heights High School. And I've made the basketball team."

The words must have circled her like birds, because there was only quiet. Then there was more than quiet. Elvira yanked the covers back from her head. Her eyes blinked open.

"Say what?"

I repeated myself. My mother rose up on one elbow in bed. She looked at me as if she had never seen me before, as if I were a burglar. I stiffened. She took a long time to say anything. She was thinking; the words were soaking in.

"You're the only one of my children who eats Jim Crow," she said.

That was a nasty phrase. Jim Crow summed up everything

that had gone wrong in the South for blacks. My mother was angry. She flung her Alabama at me. I had done something unthinkable: I had separated myself from her, I had eloped to a white school, set deep inside a white school district. She had no way to reach me way out there, to toss a life ring if I needed one. This frightened her.

I only wanted to play basketball.

My mother lay back down, covered her head with the blanket. Her voice rose from beneath the blanket in a whisper, and she told me to shut the door as I left her bedroom.

I packed my gym bag that morning and walked to Mt. Vernon Avenue to catch the bus to school. The October winds were howling, and it was cold.

Our basketball practices did not begin until seven in the evening, after both the girls' basketball team and the reserve boys' basketball team had practiced. School was out at 3:30, so I had three and a half hours to fill before practice. I could not go someplace and buy an early dinner, because I was already rationing my money, scrimping on lunches for bus fare. One morning, without telling me, my mother laid an extra dollar atop my dresser, in coins of course. And forever thereafter there was a dollar more. It wasn't enough for an after-school dinner, but it certainly helped. She must have known I needed more money.

I occupied myself between the end of school and the beginning of practice by walking along Sullivant Avenue. I'd sit inside fast-food restaurants, munch on snacks. I'd stare at strangers, look away when they stared back. Sometimes I'd roam the empty football stadium behind the school, kicking up dirt with my heels. Other times I walked the hallways of the school, sat in empty classrooms and took catnaps. I'd chat with the janitor, who never seemed to mind my walking the hallways.

The coach rarely spoke to me, kept a strange distance. Then, one evening before practice, he summoned me to his office. He was leaning over his desk. His blue eyes were cold.

"Do you or don't you live in the district?"

The question stunned me. Someone had ratted. I said yes. He stared harder. I said no. Then I looked away from him and those cold blue eyes.

He announced the punishment then and there: I could not practice anymore; I was ineligible to play on the team; I must leave the school and return to the school in my own district. But first, the next morning, I must report to the principal's office. There would be a formal disciplinary hearing. I tightened.

I dressed in the locker room to the sound of bouncing basketballs out on the gym floor. I wondered if the coach was telling the other players that I had been an imposter. I left the school, walked down Demarest Road — dark road, long walk — and caught the bus back to Bolivar Arms. Neon lights flickered against the windowpanes of the bus as it bumped down West Broad Street. I sat nearly balled up.

Word spread through Burnside, the little black housing settlement, and it spread like liquid rolling down a hill. The next morning when I returned to school, to the principal's office, an elderly black man was sitting in the office. I had never seen him before. It was Odell Wilson, father of my teammate Glenn. Odell had hatched a plan: he would become my legal guardian, which would allow me to remain on the team. I'd live in his house. He had, in fact, already discussed the plan with the principal.

I was surprised; the plan sounded far-fetched. I could not leave Elvira, my mother. The principal told me I had been wrong to lie but said he understood my passion to play basketball. If I agreed to a legal guardian, he would allow it. I did not want winter to roll over me without my having a basketball in my hands, so I agreed. I was given a form for Elvira to sign. I never showed it to her. I signed the form a day later myself, signed it with my left hand instead of my right. My left-hand writing was indecipherable — the perfect forgery. Legally, I had signed myself away from my mother, just as she had feared. But now I also had a team. Odell Wilson told me I did not have to sleep at his house, where he lived with his wife and son. I had no intention of sleeping at his house; Elvira would kill me. But I thanked him for signing me into his life.

I do not know how much the controversy hurt me, but I did not play very much in our games. I sat on the bench, and I sulked. When I got into games — only after we were winning by a large margin or losing by a large margin — I'd gun the ball up, shoot every time I touched it; I wished to score, to get my name in the papers.

Our team bus rolled through rural Ohio, through ash-colored late afternoons, around the edges of small towns with American flags snapping in the wind. The homes looked sturdy. Behind the doors of some of these homes sat the men who sipped martinis over at the Scioto Country Club, in the kitchen of which my mother worked during the out-door horse-racing season. The damp cold coming through the woods, across the flatlands, grabbed at us like claws. This was the Ohio envisioned by much of America — rural, flat, open, cold, and uncomplicated. Barns were everywhere, and near them, prizewinning cattle.

I wore my brother Harry's old navy peacoat. It drooped on me like a garment on a hanger, but it was mercifully warm. We played Teays Valley and Dublin and Olentangy, Hamilton Township and Grove City and Miami Trace. They were big country high schools with sparkling gymnasiums and marginal basketball players. Still, we lost as often as we won.

We stomped ourselves back onto our team bus when we lost, kicking snow from our boots, resting our duffel bags on our laps. When the bus rolled into the darkened high school parking lot, I'd dash down Demarest Road to Sullivant Avenue to catch the bus home. I knew by heart the bus schedule. The last bus left at 10:20. It got me downtown just in time to transfer to the last Mt. Vernon Avenue bus. Once I arrived at the bus stop at 10:30, late and out of breath, afraid my bus had gone. But the bus was there, with the familiar driver, a white man, small face, small eyes like pencil marks. I knocked on the window and he raised his head from reading a newspaper.

"Y'all win tonight?" he asked, with a smile.

Another time I made it to the corner at 10:45. I didn't have taxi fare home. I'd have to call my Uncle Ira. But how would he find this place, driving around the spooky west side late at night? I didn't need Uncle Ira. My bus was still there. I sat in the middle of it, rolling down dark quiet streets toward downtown, happy that the driver sped along, making up time so I wouldn't miss my Mt. Vernon Avenue connection. In more than a dozen close calls, my bus driver never left me. I think he knew how much I needed him.

Somehow I got a varsity letter. I treasured it, made a display for it. I didn't hang around my friend Chin much anymore, because I didn't see him much. I left home in morning darkness and returned in evening darkness. One day Chin came over. I hustled him upstairs. I showed him the awards atop my dresser, my Monroe varsity letter, my Franklin Heights varsity letter, a picture, framed, of me as an East High basketball player. I had a scrapbook, angled just so for all the world to see.

I could tell the next year, my senior year, that Coach Cawley wished I had not returned to Franklin Heights High School. He hardly ever spoke to me. He passed by me in the hallways in silence. But I would not go away. I had no place to go. I roamed the hallways again after school, waited for basketball practice to start, and when it did, I became joyful. No one in my family ever came to see me play. It was too far away, and we had no car.

Halfway through the season, when two of our players lost academic eligibility, the coach was forced to play me more often. Against Dublin High School, a school set deep in the countryside, I had a glorious night: I scored twelve points in one quarter, five consecutive jump shots. I seemed — as they say — on fire. My world seemed to open wide; the mornings practicing beneath the cold Ohio football stadium made sense; running to catch my bus late at night, falling asleep on the bus late at night, it all made sense. During my twelve-point night the coach sat on the bench, his legs crossed. His blue eyes looked glazed, his face pinched.

That night in my bed in my small bedroom, I could not sleep. I wanted dawn to come so I could rise and go get the morning newspaper, turn to the sports pages, see my name. It was all there: "Franklin Heights was led by three double-figure scorers, Doug Baer, Wil Haygood . . ."

Odell Wilson, my legal guardian, never missed a game. He'd sit up in the stands alone, a tough and quiet man, broad-shouldered and sleepy-eyed. I'd stop by his house now and then to visit. We'd sit in his basement and he'd talk about his daughter, Nancy Wilson, the great jazz singer. I wouldn't pay much attention, because I did not understand much about jazz. He'd pull out photographs of her, and I'd look at them curiously. Nancy had made her reputation at the Turf Club on Mt. Vernon Avenue in the 1950s. In the beginning, critics compared her to Dinah Washington. It didn't take her long to carve her own identity. She was too big for Mt. Vernon Avenue, too big for Columbus. Cannonball Adderley, swooping through Columbus for a gig one night, convinced her to try New York City. She fit right in in Manhattan; didn't look back.

We lost our first game in the end-of-season basketball tournament held at the fairgrounds. I played the last two minutes of the game, shot once — I was a right-hander but was forced to shoot a rather nifty (surprising myself) left-handed shot because of a gigantic defender — and missed. I wondered if there were any college scouts in the stands. I wondered if any of them had come to see me play.

Toward the end of my senior year my mother's sister, Aunt Creola, moved into our apartment. She had left Charles, her husband. There were supposed to be no other adults living in our apartment. That was one of the government rules for living in public housing. But Elvira didn't care about that rule. This was her sister, family.

It was nice having Aunt Creola around. She still worked downtown, at the big old Christopher Inn. She brought home Saran-wrapped goodies — fish steaks, lamb, shrimp, slices of turkey. She also had a car, a 1965 Buick. She parked it right in front of our apartment; it sat there proudly, like a spaceship. She'd take my mother up to Carl Brown's grocery on Mt. Vernon Avenue. They'd roam the aisles, as slow as rich people. They'd meet men they knew; they'd flirt over the baskets of vegetables, over the fresh chickens, over the sweet potatoes. Soon my aunt had a boyfriend. His name was Carter. Carter sometimes wore black dress pants and a formal shirt and a black cummerbund with shiny shoes — his sophisticated waiter outfit. He worked banquets with my aunt. He would come over some nights in his crisp banquet outfit, and when he left the next morning, his outfit was just as crisp. He must have hung it up in Aunt Creola's closet.

CREOLA *and* ELVIRA, *who is on the right:*
they were as skinny as sticks, as loud as roosters.
Creola played the older sister all her life,
with panache.

Aunt Creola dated a higher class of man than my mother. She could tolerate seddity men. My mother dated ex-cons, hustlers, fakes. Sometimes she and Aunt Creola would go up to Mt. Vernon Avenue to have a drink, to the Idle-a-While. And Aunt Creola seemed to have more self-control than my mother. Aunt Creola could drink all night long — she too was a bourbon lady — and stand as straight as a school principal and sound just as dignified. Her sister, my mother, drank and stumbled, slurred her words, made a commotion, refused to go to bed. It got worse over the years, until just one drink would send my mother reeling, ruining holiday dinners, her spittle flying in the faces of guests. And yet there would be her sober sister, my Aunt Creola, daring anyone to mock Elvira or ask her to leave. "Just leave her alone," Aunt Creola would say. She was fiercely defensive of Elvira.

I have a picture of my mother and her sister, taken in 1942. My mother at the time was ten, her sister twelve. Both are wearing white dresses with a bit of frill on the sleeves. Each clutches a little-girl purse. They had just reached the North from Alabama. There is a trace of smile on my mother's face, a quirky little smile that has a touch of mischief stamped on it. Creola's face and expression are flat, poised for the world ahead, all the things to come not yet imagined. There is something else quite revealing about the photo. Creola has her arm draped around her sister's shoulders. It is already evident who plans to protect whom in this world. A psychic could have drawn an outward line from the photo and figured rightly that Creola would be stronger than Elvira, that Creola would make the wise decisions in life. But there often is no allowance in photographs for that thing called fate.

With Aunt Creola in the apartment, my own fortunes improved: Aunt Creola gave me extra money for the school week, passing the money to me on the quiet.

Sometimes Aunt Creola's old Buick would not start — engine failure. But it started on the day of my high school graduation, and I was glad it did. I did not want to have to go to my graduation on the bus.

Public events made my mother nervous. A drink calmed her, but I was happy that she didn't sneak a drink from the pantry on graduation day. Aunt Creola had warned her. They both had taken the day off from work, which was a pretty big deal, for they wouldn't be paid. Aunt Creola drove to the west side, her face close to the steering wheel, looking for our destination. I only knew the bus route, which she didn't know. So she took her own roads; actually, she just steered westward. We looped around the city until we reached the mental hospital on the hilltop, because almost everyone knew where the mental hospital was. Then we swerved to our left and kept going until we reached Sullivant Avenue. Aunt Creola's eyes were as wide as an explorer's. We might as well have been on the high seas. My mother grew nervous; Creola calmed her. The scent of the perfume they both wore wafted from the front seat to the back seat. The car smelled like a garden.

Our ceremony was held outdoors, next to the school on an open field. The grass was freshly cut and shiny; the breeze was light. My mother and aunt sat on chairs in sunny weather making small talk with folks they had never seen before. It was June, and they were dressed in silk — reds, purples, greens — stockings and high heels; two still-slim ladies who looked good in dresses, with their good purses, the ones they kept at the top of the closets and used only on special occasions, swinging from their wrists. They beamed when I reached for my diploma.

The army tried to recruit me. A sergeant came by our apartment in Bolivar Arms, parking his shiny car out front, causing people to gawk. He took me downtown, out to dinner. I ordered steak. While I was eating the dinner, listening to him, wiping my mouth, ordering another soda, ordering and devouring dessert, having my fill, the army sounded good. When dinner was over and I was out the door, back in our apartment, the army sounded too far away.

I phoned basketball coaches at small colleges and inquired about scholarships. They said they'd never heard of me. I told them about the twelve points I had scored — in one quarter! — against Dublin High School. They said again they had never heard of me. They said they were not interested in a guard who averaged five points a game for a basketball team that had lost its first game in the state tournament.

I applied to two colleges. Otterbein was a small college just outside Columbus. I figured I could talk my way onto the basketball team at Otterbein. I called the athletic office and tried to get the basketball coach on the line. I aimed to tell him about my basketball-playing life, but the person who answered the phone always said he was busy. And I applied to Miami University, in Oxford, Ohio. I had never set foot on either campus.

A letter from Miami arrived. I took it out back, sat on the stoop facing the railroad tracks, smelled the manure from the nearby stockyard, and opened the letter. I was accepted; I felt good, warm, excited. I dashed and told Elvira. Standing there listening to me in her waitress uniform, my mother was obviously happy. Then a look of worry crossed her face. She mentioned money, reminded me that she had no money. I knew she had no money: on the financial aid form I had to fill out for college in 1972, she was listed as earning $3,100. But I told her I wanted to go to college. I told her I'd get loans and I'd work on campus. I was already hoping the nuns at Ohio Dominican College would give me a few extra stipends.

Before I left for college, I had to go get my draft card. Vietnam was still in the news. Everyone always told you that if you didn't get your draft card, someone could knock on your door any morning and haul you off to jail. I folded my card, tucked it securely in my wallet, didn't want to lose it, ever. Then I visited my grandparents. They were always passionate about school and books, about education. Jimmy, standing in front of Emily, gave me a little money. And Emily, standing out of sight of Jimmy, gave me a little more money. I could tell they were fiercely proud that I was going to college. I was more theirs than Elvira's. And now one of their own was going away — to read books.

My sister Diane bought me a three-piece set of luggage as my going-away gift. I found out she had been saving an entire month to buy the luggage. Then, without anyone noticing, she slipped a few ten-dollar bills into my hand. Then I hit the road — by bus.

The campus was set deep in the southwestern corner of Ohio, surrounded by tall woods, rich and lovely in early fall. The Greyhound let me off at the outskirts of the college. I lifted my three suitcases and began walking, carrying two and kicking one along with my feet, sweating in the early September warmth. The suitcases were heavy. A woman in a van stopped, told me to hop inside, and gave me a lift to my dorm. I told her I was a basketball player, told her to look for me during basketball season. Before I climbed out, she wished me luck with my college career.

I didn't know it, but eight years earlier some momentous history had whipped across the Miami University campus. A horde of brave and idealistic young civil rights workers had descended on this leafy campus for last-minute meetings before heading south. Three of those students — Andrew Goodman, James Chaney, and Michael Schwerner — never returned from Mississippi, at least not alive. They were finally found buried beneath some red dirt in a place called Philadelphia,

Mississippi. Klan murders. I wish someone had told me about Schwerner, Goodman, and Chaney during my years in Oxford, but no one ever did, not a single word.

My roommate, Doug, was a big strapping dude from Dayton. Doug snored, so I flicked rubber bands at him in the night; he rustled like a bear, swatted at the dark, quieted down. He studied more than I did, listened to music on his headphones, often left the room without saying goodbye or inviting me along. His major was communication. Soon I spotted him sitting on swatches of grass around campus, beneath trees, with the same blonde every time. She wished to unload her liberal angst on Doug, who was black, and he let her. Along with much romance. Several guys in the dorm were jealous. I hounded him for information about the romance, but Doug was skimpy with details.

Millet Hall, site of the basketball gymnasium, was huge and elegant, trimmed in red. I sneaked up on the varsity coach, badgered him with questions about tryouts, gave him my bio, verbally. Then I sneaked up on the reserve coach, told him I had spoken to the varsity coach, told him the varsity coach had told me they were always looking for good basketball players. I gave the reserve coach my bio, then I reported for reserve basketball tryouts.

Jerry Pierson was the coach, and Jerry Pierson cut me. I walked back out on the court the next day. Jerry Pierson was not amused. He pulled me to the side.

"Sir, I'd just like another chance," I said. Players nearby whispered together. "I know my name wasn't on the list, but please, I'd like another chance. I can play for you, sir."

He looked stunned. He said okay, quietly. I ran back out on the court, joined the drills. I asked Jerry Pierson if I could return the next day. He said yes. I kept returning. "I won't cut you again," he told me.

I begged my way onto so many basketball teams, including the
one at Miami University. The dream ended there. I'm in
the front row, wearing number 31.

I didn't blame Jerry Pierson. Other coaches at first blush
had missed my skills, had been shocked by my haranguing
them. So from class I hustled off to basketball practice and
after basketball practice, I studied, sleepy, tired.

There were many classes and many tests. When I performed badly on one midterm, on any midterm, I remained
calm. I told myself I'd bounce back on the final exam. At the
end of the first quarter I was placed on academic probation. I
was summoned to the office of an academic counselor, warned
that I was at the edge of the cliff, warned that a wind was at my
back. Another bad academic quarter and I'd be back in Bolivar
Arms, looking for that army sergeant. So I studied harder. I
hurried home from basketball practice. I pulled my grades up
the next quarter, saved myself.

I had no idea what I'd major in. I chose business. But I got an F on the economics midterm, so I majored in English, in literature: Hemingway, Baldwin, Fitzgerald, some Joyce. I'd lean on literature's door. I had no idea what I'd do with a literature degree. And I didn't have the nerve to ask Marian Musgrave. She was an English professor, the only black in the department. Students feared her; black students gravitated toward her, but black students feared her too. She was a big woman, and her hair was as wild as a witch's. She wore colorful clothes that billowed as she strutted into the classroom. I found out later that she was a Europhile, summered every year in the great capitals of Europe. She never married, traveled alone. She drummed into me words, literature, the timbre of short stories. Her diction was beautiful, loud, and words flew nonstop from her mouth as she leaned over her desk, her hands gripping the sides of the desk like a dog's paws. She'd stare right at me in class, finding what, I do not know.

There were times when I nodded off.

"Mr. Haygood!"

I'd open my eyes, look around like someone in the dark, feel embarrassed.

One day in class — we must have been discussing Baldwin — she began talking about the shame of black men conking their hair, straightening it with grease, trying to make it look like a white person's hair. She said the practice was undignified. She looked directly at me. I do not know why. I wore an Afro.

A counselor warned me of the folly of majoring in literature. Told me there were no jobs for literature majors. So I switched to urban studies, kept literature as a minor, took geography and sociology classes. In sociology class one day, the lights dimmed; we were looking at public housing developments across America on a screen. Then there clicked into view a photograph of some housing projects that looked familiar, brown brick apartments. I looked closer. It was where I lived. It was Bolivar Arms; the name was etched at the bottom of the screen. "I live there!" I shouted at the dimness, at everyone, at the professor. I was in that instant both ashamed and proud. We were studying where I lived; it seemed nosy, unfair. I suddenly felt a need to protect Bolivar Arms from the prying eyes of outsiders. The professor looked at me with a sorrowful look on his face.

I also had to take statistics. To pass statistics, I had to beg for correct programs and formulas from classmates over at the statistics lab. And I had to cheat.

My mother never wrote me letters. None had arrived when I went away to Boy Scout camp. None had arrived when I went to spend the summer at Ohio Dominican. When I was away at college that first year, away from her longer than I'd ever been, my mother must have missed me. A letter arrived, her scrawl in the upper lefthand corner surprising me. I could hardly read her handwriting. Her Deep South education, her hard times in the Columbus public school system — there had simply been little opportunity to master spelling. The letter was written on plain school notebook paper, and the last line said this: "We are all proud of you and I love you very much." I know my mother: she wrote that letter sitting at our dining room table in our Bolivar Arms apartment, facing the window that looked out onto the railroad tracks — and the open air that had taken her youngest boy away to get an education.

Sometimes opening my tiny campus mailbox, I'd be as surprised by what I found as if in fact I'd found a white rabbit inside. Every time my sister Diane sent me a ten-dollar or twenty-dollar check, I was surprised. In my sophomore year, my twin sister sent me three hundred dollars. It was her life savings. It was about three hundred dollars more than I had at the time. "Use this in case of an emergency," she said. There were plenty of emergencies.

The athletic department at Miami sent team pictures to every player's high school. So Miami, which had cut me in the beginning, sent a team picture with me in it to Franklin Heights, whose coach had also cut me. I felt proud.

Halfway through basketball season, in a game against Kent State, with a girl from Mansfield whom I liked watching me from the stands, I was hurt. I thought I had merely twisted my knee; it was worse, torn cartilage. I had, up to the point of injury, scored six points. I was carried off the court, then to the hospital. The next day's Cincinnati newspapers, which always carried stories about our games, did not report my injury. But they noted my six points in the box score, the clipping of which I scissored out to keep.

I had surgery. I was not on scholarship, and I was not doing well in school. I needed to study. I needed to move on, and away from basketball. I lay in bed in that hospital and let one dream — basketball — float out of me, so that I might grab ahold for keeps of another dream — education. I had crossed all of my basketball valleys; I had a decent enough scrapbook; Jimmy wouldn't like it if I flunked out of college. My brother Harry arrived at the hospital to pick me up following surgery. A comely lady was driving. I lay in the back seat. I had never seen the lady before. My brother told me he had only met her several days earlier himself. I writhed in pain.

My sister Diane had always been full of ideas to make money. She had yard sales. She baked and sold sweet potato pies. Once she even wrote a self-help manual on how to find the perfect romance. She placed ads in national tabloid publications. With a straight face I had to proofread the manual.

There weren't very many takers. Her profits from her ventures were always meager, but she was always generous in sharing them. My sister thought she could lift our family boat. She had a talent for sewing, could sew anything, make anything. She made heart-shaped pillows and sold them on Valentine's Day — to individuals, to downtown department stores. She hand-made suits for Macaroni, for other pimps. They looked like zoot suits. She made clothing for women.

When I returned home from college that first summer, Diane had put together a fashion revue. The group of models, men and women, were just acquaintances from my family's nightclub gallivanting. They included Harry, home from the navy, and my sister Wonder. The plan was to give fashion shows around Columbus, anywhere and everywhere, to make some money, maybe make Diane a designing star. Diane made all of the clothing: sequins and silks, lingerie; there was an obvious Frederick's of Hollywood influence. At one of the early rehearsals, held in a bar, I looked around and saw my family, saw them about to embark on something new, which looked exciting, and I did not wish to be left behind. At the rehearsal, Diane, trying to emcee, was constantly summoned backstage. Another garment needed adjusting; the models weren't moving quickly enough; woes and woes. Then she'd rush back to the stage and continue emceeing until she was called backstage yet again. My family needed an emcee. I stuttered, but I walked over to the microphone anyway and picked it up. Heads turned toward my voice. My words came out smoothly. I willed myself to talk right, not to stutter. I wanted my family to take me with them.

"Well," my sister said, "I guess we've found our emcee."

Shows were booked, posters were printed. "Ms. D.'s Fashion Revue," the project was dubbed.

It was — well, an interesting crew. Danny, our designated

driver, drove a brand-new gold Lincoln Continental, four-door. Danny was a Vietnam vet ("a Green Beret," he claimed) and had joined the show to be around the models. Diane teased him that he should be ready, on standby, as a reserve model in case one of the male models couldn't make an engagement. A muscular figure who did double duty as a bodyguard for the revue — lots of catcallers frequented the bars we performed in — Danny took Diane's teasing with glee. He had been a remarkable high school athlete in Columbus. But through the years, his stories were embellished: he talked about having played semipro football, semipro baseball, and semipro basketball after high school. It all seemed quite impossible. Danny told these tales with a straight face, tales about playing semipro baseball beneath the Carolina sun. We listened and smiled and felt a little sorry for him: his wife and children had died a year earlier in a fire. Danny had been compensated, bought himself a Lincoln, hit the road with us.

Harry, my brother, became the star of the show. Harry began billing himself as "H. Lee Haygood" — Lee is his middle name — and audiences began yelling for "H. Lee." I guess he thought the name had more of a theatrical sound. Women circled H. Lee. His hair was long and curly; he looked like a cast member from *Jesus Christ Superstar*. He began talking of going to Hollywood.

Marshall, a model whom Harry had recruited and who practiced Zen and had a Fu Manchu goatee, turned his modeling moments into a little schtick: he'd wave his walking stick at the crowd, twirl and swirl, and suddenly — at this point I'd say to the audience, "And for those rainy days . . ." — the walking stick would blossom open into an umbrella. Sometimes Marshall accidentally poked other models with the walking stick. The audience could never tell whether it was intentional.

We played bars and restaurants. I crossed my legs on a stool and emceed all the shows, without notes, ad-libbing all the way, forgetting I was a stutterer. In the bars, patrons sipped drinks, Elvira sipped drinks. Patrons oohed over the skimpily clad women, sipped some more drinks, got drunk, got loud. There was enough cigarette smoke to make a gray curtain.

"I don't smoke, drink, or chew," I would pronounce at every show, making for a light moment.

"And everything he don't do, I do," my brother Macaroni said, popping up from the audience at the High Chapparal, a nightclub on the city's west side. We later incorporated that little moment into all the shows.

Harry slept with two girls in the show. Both later became pregnant. Danny slept with a girl who hailed from Kentucky, who talked with a twang, who was buxom, whom I dreamed about. Diane shared the receipts. I slept with no one. Friends pleaded with me to introduce them to the models. When I approached the girls, told them I had friends who wanted to meet them, they looked at me as if I were their little brother — and they ignored me. During intermissions, Marshall, carrying the cane-umbrella, talked about Zen philosophy. Models would brusquely brush by him; Danny listened with a funny little grin on his face. Macaroni swooped backstage, watched girls undress, looked mischievously around, disappeared.

We did a show on the campus of Ohio State University, in the student union, accompanied by a jazz band. Both Harry and Marshall were attending Ohio State at the time and lingered onstage, highlighting themselves. In Marshall's case, the showboating was especially painful: his walking stick wouldn't open; he kept whipping it out until finally someone offstage yelled at him to move on. Alas, the show was sparsely attended. I think the people who peered inside thought it was burlesque.

*Ms. D's Fashion Revue, in 1973, when I had just gone off to college.
I thought we were going right to the top. Left to right:* HARRY,
WONDER, GERALDINE, MACARONI, *and* DIANE.

When I returned to college, I talked to the student activities council. I parlayed a gig for Ms. D's Fashion Revue. I hung posters around campus, bragged about my family. One evening my friend Doug even helped me hang some of them.

When they arrived, only Harry climbed from the van. "Where's the back entrance?" he asked. My brother did not wish to be seen by students. He did not wish to be seen until he crisscrossed the stage.

I was nervous, worried about the lighting, the stage set.

"Wil," Harry said, sternly, "we're the stars here. You don't lift another thing. Let Miami take care of it. Now, where can we get something to eat?"

We had steak dinners in the tiny town of Oxford. Danny laughed, Harry laughed, Diane laughed. Then we returned to the auditorium and put on Ms. D's Fashion Revue. There was wild clapping, especially at the sight of the sexy models. When we were on the road, Harry always jazzed up his performances a little more — lingered a little longer onstage, winked a little more to females in the audience, lolled a little more. The audience howled at Marshall's cane-to-umbrella moment. Marshall pranced offstage.

Always at the end of the show, I stood and introduced Diane. "And now, ladies and gentlemen, please give a round of applause to Ms. D herself!" My sister rose from her seat like a diva.

After the show, loading up, Harry slipped me some spending money. Then, behind one of the vans, Diane slipped me some spending money. I could tell they loved me, a lot. Then the female models kissed me on the cheek, told me to be good, to study hard. They rolled off into the dark woods, bound for home. Next morning I went around the campus removing Ms. D's. Fashion Revue posters.

There were do-gooders on the Miami campus, students

who fed the hungry, who tutored kids. One weekend I joined the do-gooders for a weekend journey. Rain had smacked the town of Peoria, Illinois, hard. There were floods, and families had been displaced. We were to take food and blankets to the impoverished. Personally, I felt pretty impoverished myself. It was still raining when we arrived. The town seemed dreary. We rode to a church that served as a makeshift shelter and started unloading food and supplies from our van. Everyone got soggy. Doug, my big, snoring roommate, had come along. A knot of folks, mostly black in that mostly black town, eyed us as if it were Christmas. I made eye contact with a girl from across the room. She returned the smile I gave. Then she vanished behind a line of bodies and through a door. She never returned, and for the rest of the day I felt blue.

I met Jim Vandervort the way I met a lot of people, shooting basketball in the dim light of Withrow gym. He was thin, with sideburns and a flat-footed jumpshot. Ten feet from the basket, however, he was deadly. Withrow was an ancient gym next to the ancient baseball field, which fronted the ancient football field. Miami was an old school. We'd shoot until we exhausted ourselves, then walk across that campus beneath the naked trees of wintertime. We'd scrounge for dinner, because we'd already missed dinner in the dining room.

It was extremely difficult for students to have cars on the Miami campus. You had to prove you absolutely needed one. Jim did not absolutely need a car, but he proved to the administration that he did. He had a well-off friend back east, a coin dealer. Jim had his friend write a letter to Miami saying that Jim was his midwestern representative and needed a car to tote those precious coins around. Jim never sold a coin during his Miami career, never attempted to sell a coin. In fact, there were no coins in his possession. He and I tooled around the Miami valley in his tiny red beatup car, along the rural roads, sometimes into Cincinnati, where we pooled our money and splurged on food.

When Wonder had her first baby, during my sophomore year, I casually mentioned it to Jim.

"Let's go," he said.

"Where?"

"Columbus," he said, reaching for his keys.

And there we were, zooming down the highway straight to Columbus, skipping class, straight to the hospital to see my sister and her newborn. I guess it's one of the mysteries of life that you never know when a friend might take the time to swing a gate open.

In the summer of 1974, Jim invited me to his home in New Jersey. I had never flown on an airplane, had never seen the ocean. Harry prepped me on flying: "You'll get the hang of it. Nothing to it. You won't even feel being up in the air." He was the sailor, the big Haygood world traveler.

Jim's New Jersey town, Little Silver, was small and elegant. It hugged the coastline. His family lived in a house surrounded by hedges and shade, with a huge screened-in porch to keep away pesky mosquitoes. Things inside the house were soft, rich, but not too rich. Noticeably lived-in. Jim's father had a big job with the state, told me that if I needed a job after college, I should look him up. I raised an eyebrow. He sat on a cushiony sofa, flipping the newspaper from page to page, looking at it over the top of his spectacles, which slipped on his nose. Jim and I spent lazy days at the Ship-Ahoy Beach Club, where he worked. The air smelled salty; the ocean waves lapped the beach. We sat under cabanas, ordered drinks that came in tall glasses, and felt the sea. We rode through coastal towns, walked the quiet campus of Princeton, hit tennis balls on grass courts. It seemed dreamy. I felt like a foreigner. So: this was life on the other side.

Jim mentioned the horses out at Monmouth Park race-track. I was familiar with racetracks from Jimmy, so we went and played the horses. I planned to dress up, and did: I wore a three-piece white suit to Monmouth. The vest, double-breasted, had Gatsby lapels. A silver-plated cigarette case, as thin as an empty wallet, lay inside my breast pocket, with the initials "WH" stenciled on it. I did not smoke. Smoking wasn't the point; the point was style. I had purchased the cigarette case at a pawnshop in Columbus, along with a money clip. I folded my money once over and eased it into the clip. I didn't really know horses, and I lost money; I slapped the racing form against the palm of my hand, just as I had seen Jimmy do. I thought the food at the concession stand was too expensive and told Jim I'd be damned if I was going to pay a buck and a quarter for a wiener.

I wanted more than anything to see New York City. I had heard so much about the tall buildings. In Columbus we only had one tall building downtown, the Lincoln Leveque Tower. Standing on a Manhattan street corner, I could not stop look-ing around, behind me, in front of me, at the colors and the noise and the mass of people. Jim walked around Manhattan in a white T-shirt and bib overalls. He looked like an Ohio hayseed. We walked and walked, tried chatting with girls, who all seemed to be in a rush. We spent a night in a hotel in the East Village. The desk clerk spoke broken English, charged us fifteen dollars each. I chained the door, jammed a chair be-neath the doorknob, heard car horns and screaming from the street all night long.

The spring quarter of my senior year at Miami, on the lip of graduation, I found myself struggling mightily through a bot-any course. I needed the course to graduate. The professor, a kind man with a hippie beard, led us into the woods that surrounded the campus, looking for plants on the ground that matched the plants in our course book. I found it difficult to match the plants, just as I found it difficult to pronounce their Latin names. I visited the professor in his plant-strewn office and told him that I was about to graduate, to go out in the world; I desperately needed to pass his course to do so. He seemed serenely uninterested in my worries, told me not to worry, he was sure I'd do fine. I worried too much; of course he wouldn't flunk me. He flunked me. Then he shook his bearded head with animation and told me there was nothing he could do; I had performed horribly on the final exam.

I felt walls collapse. My family was planning to come and see me graduate. I asked and received permission to participate in the graduation ceremony, to wear cap and gown. I'd fake my own graduation. I would have to remain on campus during the summer, however, to make up my science credit.

On graduation day, dressed in a black silk robe and cap, I waited in my room for Elvira and Jack and my sisters to arrive from Columbus. I wouldn't tell them about the failed botany course. I expected to hear their heels clicking down the hallway of my dorm, but I didn't. I stood on the edge of the road that snaked beside the assembly hall, looking for them, and looking. Friends ushered me on into the hall; the ceremony was about to begin. I convinced myself that they'd arrive any minute. Inside I craned my neck, looking for my family, letting the commencement speaker's words float right by me. At ceremony's end, dejected — didn't they care? — I walked back outside. I looked across an expanse of lawn and there they were, having just pulled up and climbed from the car: Jack, my father; Elvira, my mother; my sisters. Jack looked as if he had just stepped onto a remote island.

"Is it over?" Diane asked. "We got lost," she said. Then she shook her head. Then I shook my head. They felt sorry for me. I felt sorry for them. Elvira had that look on her face. My mother needed a drink.

We walked across the campus and we ate. I told them that I wouldn't be going back to Columbus with them. I explained that I wanted to remain on campus, to take a couple of courses, to relax and enjoy summer. They departed quietly and almost wordlessly. I stood holding my cap and gown under my arms.

That summer I took "The Physics of Sport" for my science requirement, the science course the jocks took; it was easy. The jocks sat on chairs that their bodies covered completely. On the first day of class the professor explained to us that he stuttered, and after he explained it to us, clearly and without stuttering, he proceeded to stutter, very badly, during every class. I felt for him. I said nothing in class. For some reason, being around a stutterer frees another stutterer to stutter; it sets off the emotions, it relaxes you into stuttering. I feared if I talked, the words wouldn't come out.

I got a C- on my midterm, so frightful a grade that I went to see the professor. I explained to him how much I needed to pass the course; the world, life, was waiting for me. When he stuttered, I wanted to finish his sentences for him. When I stuttered, he wanted to finish my sentences for me. We stuttered at and into each other. A spray of words, spittle, the catching of breath. A planned five-minute visit stretched into fifteen. Two stutterers, their words clashing like swords. Finally, after I felt I had explained myself, my desperation, I rose cheerily, caught my breath, shook his hand, and left.

The campus seemed mine that summer. I rose early, ate breakfast, gulped orange juice, went back to bed, rose again to go to classes. I also took an English course that summer, short story writing. The professor was a small man, nearly elfin. His voice cracked like a child's. We often sat outside, beneath the shade of trees, and talked in soft voices. The professor sat with his legs folded beneath him. We wrote short stories and talked about them, said unmerciful things about each other's work. I wrote a story about a boy who goes to New Jersey and hangs out by the ocean and gambles and offers cigarettes to ladies from a silver cigarette case. A boy who bets on the horses, loses money, dresses in white suits. Somehow I got a B. I got a C in my science course. I would graduate after all.

I wanted my degree, so I went to the registrar's office to get it. A smart lady behind a desk told me I would not be receiving my degree until I settled my remaining student bills. I told her I didn't have any money. She repeated herself, and I turned and walked back outside.

My college life ended quietly, among the trees, the shadows, the brick buildings. But I had things to be grateful for. I had bounced a basketball on this campus. I had made new friends. I had been taught — and scolded — by the great Marian Musgrave. And I had emceed Ms. D's Fashion Revue before a part of the student body. I packed my belongings, and I bummed a ride up 71 north, toward Columbus, toward home.

9

Aᴄᴄᴏʀᴅɪɴɢ ᴛᴏ ʟᴇɢᴇɴᴅ, fact, rumor, journals, ship's logs, and my teachers at Indianola Junior High, Christopher Columbus discovered America in 1492. (There is much about the explorer's life that still remains speculative and debatable.) The Italian seaman with the sleepy eyes and wide shoulders who had a fascination with gold, who had few close friends, who wore long silky robes and floppy hats, had been out looking for Asia and run smack into the Americas. It helped that fierce sea winds were pushing him. He was hardly the first sailor to benefit from serendipity. In the years to come, many places across America would be named after him. There's a Columbus, Georgia. There's a Columbus, Indiana. There's a Columbus in Kentucky; in 1862 the Johnny Rebs had to hightail it out of that Columbus — it was overrun by Union soldiers.

As for my Columbus, it was founded in 1812. It lies near the center of Ohio. It is often referred to as being in Middle

America, but actually it is more Appalachian-East than Midwest. Kansas lies in the Midwest, and Ohio is a long east-swinging jaunt from Kansas. Indians once ran through the woods of Columbus, Ohio, up along the banks of the Scioto and Olentangy rivers. That was eons ago, before the Revolutionary War, before the War of 1812. The Indians were forced from the region by the American government and sent west, to reservations; many went by railroad. In grade school we often took trips to the caves outside Columbus. Teachers would point at Indian markings, script scrawled in stone. I'd stare wide-eyed and listen to the gurgling water running beneath the shadows of the caves. We'd go to museums too, where we'd look at old tomahawks and hear teachers tell us that those tomahawks had once belonged to Indian warriors.

The turn of the century found my Columbus waving in immigrants — Germans, Irish, Italians, Poles. They worked on the railroads, shopped up and down Mt. Vernon Avenue when it was a railroaders' avenue, bought drinks at the Railroaders Club. The Railroaders was a members-only club; the proprietor had her fish delivered up from the Chesapeake Bay on the Pennsylvania and Western Railroad. My grandfather Jimmy didn't call the place the immigrants came from "Europe"; he called it "the old country." Joe Asmo, the bar owner my grandfather worked for, came from Greece, the old country.

Negroes didn't come to Columbus in appreciable waves until after World War II. Prior to that there had been enclaves of them near Columbus, mostly in and around Wilberforce and Oberlin: those were famous Underground Railroad locales. The great W.E.B. Du Bois once taught at Wilberforce University. I guess the Haygoods and the Burkes could have landed anywhere in America. As Oscar Handlin has written in *The Uprooted*, his classic study about immigration, "The place of landing was less often the outcome of an intention held at the outset of the journey than of blind drift along the routes of trade or of a sudden halt due to the accidents of the voyage." So Jack Haygood started out in Statham, Georgia, went to fight in the war, came home from the war, journeyed to Cincinnati to work in a hotel, left Cincinnati for Columbus. There was no map, just the will to voyage onward.

Columbus politics had been shaped by Cincinnati politics, and Cincinnati politics were shaped by the Taft family. The Tafts actually built a machine, and that machine leaned vigorously to the right. William Howard was the patriarch, the one who became the U.S. president, the huge man with the handlebar mustache. His boy, Robert, became a U.S. senator; a lot of people called him "Mr. Republican." Robert chased communists; the only -ism he believed in was conservatism. If Robert ever smiled, there were few witnesses to it. Someone once asked him what advice he'd give to families grappling with high meat prices. "Eat less," he said, straight-faced. Robert Taft hungered for the presidency; it was never in the cards. Truth be told, a lot of Washington Republicans thought he was a little kooky, too far gone to the right. He had spent much of his political capital going after and haranguing FDR. Of course, all of my school reports on Senator Taft just spoke of the highlights. I didn't know better; I was in the seventh grade. I seem to remember decent grades on those reports. "I can't think of a place where I get a warmer response — and fewer votes," Jack Kennedy said after he won the presidential election despite losing Ohio.

My town's straight-arrow politics followed a straight line of civic beliefs on other matters. Wrongdoers would be sent to the Ohio State Penitentiary in Columbus. The ACLU had best mind its own business and not Columbus's. The dope-smoking hippies and radicals who came gallivanting through town (town? city? that debate rages on too) in the sixties and seventies found quickly enough that the local police didn't tolerate tomfoolery and free expression; soon enough word went out on the grapevine that travelers heading east or west by way of Columbus would be smart to take Highway 71 around the city — or end up in the clink. Ohio State University was *the* school, which any decent kid would want to attend, where ag business was a hot major, always had been, always would be. "Millions for manure but not one cent for literature," complained an OSU professor. Nobody paid him any mind. And if you wanted to enjoy yourself, well, you'd just have to wait for the yearly Ohio State Fair to have an All-American good time.

The Columbus that my sisters and brothers and I grew up in in the 1960s and 1970s, however, had convulsed in small ways and large, and many of the convulsions soared past our eyes like flying pigeons. I didn't know or care anything about politics. Having Jimmy and Emily and Elvira all within my eyesight was the only yardstick of safety I needed and counted on; my politics was family politics. There were, however, two politicians who lay on the edge of my growing-up consciousness: Big Jim Rhodes and M. E. Sensenbrenner.

When my family bequeathed Columbus to us children — or you might say, gave us rein to go play and learn — M. E. Sensenbrenner was mayor. It seems strangely coincidental that he was the one politician, I'd later learn, who knew his way up and down Mt. Vernon Avenue. Sensenbrenner was Robert Penn Warren's Willie Stark, without the ruthlessness. He was the mayor, but unlike Big Jim Rhodes, he was also a Democrat. Republicans couldn't stomach M. E. Sensenbrenner — the same M. E. Sensenbrenner who used to sell Bibles out there on the west side of town. Republicans used to snicker about that, but they had to do it quietly, you see, because the ole Bible salesman (who had also once been a

Fuller Brush salesman) was the one mayoring over the city, not a Republican.

Maynard Sensenbrenner was born in Circleville, Ohio, in 1902. He bummed around in his youth, never attended college, spent time in California. Out on the coast he did some movie work as an extra; he sold some ads for the *Los Angeles Times*. Then he roamed back to Columbus. He got some civil service jobs, opened a little store on the west side where he sold Bibles. Inside the store, he also recited cornpone poetry — unsolicited — to his customers, and he took long strolls out into the sunshine wearing a straw skimmer that looked liked something left at a vaudeville party. He was a big Boy Scout booster; he handed out miniature flags everywhere he went; he was a big wheel in the local Kiwanis Club. Tall, bony, and dark-eyed, he was goofy, but in a goodhearted way. When he announced he was running for mayor, people laughed. His own son laughed. "My first reaction to my dad running for mayor was 'Jesus Christ, this just can't be,'" recalls Dick Sensenbrenner. In 1954, Columbus Republicans were bickering. While they were bickering, Maynard Sensenbrenner went on TV, which was still fairly new. He moved about like something that had been wound up. Members at his local church had taken up a collection to sponsor his TV time. He won by four hundred votes. Republicans were aghast: they'd been whipped by a Bible salesman. They thought M. E. Sensenbrenner was a lulu.

The new mayor celebrated all over town, and he didn't forget Mt. Vernon Avenue. He waltzed in and out of the clubs, glided onto bar stools, slapped backs. His claim to fame was grabbing land. M. E. Sensenbrenner watched the spread of suburbia, told suburban officials that if they wanted services from Columbus, they might as well annex. Then he'd twist arms and annex them. Call that cornpone if you must, but the city grew. And vice flourished. Sensenbrenner liked neon, liked a busy city at night, let bootleg joints flourish; he just winked.

He lost his reelection bid in 1959. There had been a flood; some said he reacted too slowly. Some news hacks got a kick out of writing that he was "washed out" of City Hall. He kept the flags handy, though, and came roaring back in 1964, with the crazy grin, the dark eyes flashing, the suit hanging loosely from his thin frame, the black hair swept cleanly back. He loved the sixties — at least in the beginning, because in the beginning there was money from Washington, FDR-style money, money for programs. Washington money built housing projects like Bolivar Arms. And there was Mayor Sensenbrenner, striding with the long legs, hugging the ladies who had just moved into those new apartments, handing out those miniature flags to the children, looking at the new apartments as if they'd been built with gold bricks, pausing, taking deep breaths, then looking around, looking for the new faces that had suddenly come up behind him, reaching into his pocket for more flags, grinning. Sometimes he'd stop over at George Pierce's house, the Mt. Vernon Avenue photographer's place, just to shoot the breeze, nothing more. The mayor liked going into George Caesar Berry's Chesapeake Bar & Grill, liked cackling up and down the aisles of Tyler Drugs, loved being inside Carl Brown's grocery store, smelling the fresh produce. He'd even attend some of the meetings of the Mt. Vernon Avenue District Improvement Association, when he had the time. Sometimes he'd ride up and down the avenue, leaning from the car window, handing out the flags.

M. E. Sensenbrenner liked the beginning but not the end of the sixties, because that's when the draft dodgers and the hippies and the radicals and the rioters came. Nixon was in office. His attorney general issued orders about wanted radicals and draft dodgers: hunt 'em down like dogs, he said. One fine May afternoon in 1970 on the Kent State University campus, some students started demonstrating against the Vietnam war. Some National Guardsmen massed. Someone threw rocks at some of the guardsmen. They opened fire: four students were killed. A lot of people called it murder. Crosby, Stills, Nash & Young sang a song, and one line of the song went like this: "Four dead in O-hi-O." (Big Jim Rhodes went to court twice, was acquitted. "I had some of the best brains trying to put me away," he told a reporter. "Lawyers right out of Ohio State, the ACLU.")

Highlighting civic boosterism, showboating up and down Mt. Vernon Avenue, snatching up land in the suburbs — who could blame M. E. Sensenbrenner if he didn't think that was enough? Who could blame him if he felt his love for the town should go unquestioned? But there was one blind spot, and it was fatal. You might even say it had long been the town's Rubicon, the river it couldn't quite get across: race. The police force and fire departments were nearly lily-white. And while Mt. Vernon Avenue existed in a kind of cocoon — it was one of those communities that you had to go through a back door to get to; it was out of the way, it was exotic — that didn't mean the shopowners couldn't feel the vibrations out there across America, the rumblings. Waldo Tyler, Jr., the soulful and tender (many believed too tender) pharmacist, had already started welcoming protesters into his pharmacy, giving them a meeting place.

The protesters on the Ohio State campus and the city's east side pained Sensenbrenner. He called them "kids," which they didn't appreciate. He saw a breakdown of law and order, and when the police in their black knee-high boots and helmets went to crush the demonstrations, he liked it, blinked happily, saluted the police. The kids weren't about to overrun him and his town. To him Columbus was the All-American city, and protests against authority didn't happen in the All-American city. At least, they were not supposed to happen.

The riot — actually, it was more a disturbance — came in September of 1967, right there on Mt. Vernon Avenue. It was really a people's protest. Afterward, some citizens would say things had been hemmed up for too long. It was about real estate: some protesters wanted Marvin Bonowitz, who was now operating Vernon Tailors on the avenue, to rent them an empty storefront. He said no; they massed the following evening. The first brick went through Spicer's furniture store. Ernest Mackey hustled to the back of the store, reached for the phone. Bricks were flying now. Raleigh Randolph — he used to be a jazzman on the avenue but now operated a newsstand — stuck a sign in his window: SOUL BROTHER ALL THE WAY. The soul brothers on the street hurled bricks at his window anyway. Randolph reached for a shotgun, fired in the air; the rioters moved on up the street. They settled in front of Bonowitz's place. Epithets were hurled. Bonowitz and Jim Jordan, a salesman, made their way to the back of the store, where they waited for the police.

Word raced up the street to Carl Brown's grocery store. Brown shooed customers out and locked up. He went outside and started walking as fast as he could, his barrel chest sticking out, looking back over his shoulder, unable to stop worrying about his store. But he kept walking forward, taking each block as if he were folding it up in his hands, walking hard. For three decades he had worked on this avenue. He had had a hand in building it up. When the Italian grocers were overcharging blacks, it was Carl Brown who climbed in his truck and drove all night down through the Carolinas, bought produce directly from farms, drove back up north to his store. He wouldn't let the avenue be torn apart. He walked past Tyler

Drugs (where Macaroni sometimes illegally signed for cough syrup) and he walked past George Pierce's photography studio. He walked past Arthelia Logan's beauty salon. He walked past the Chesapeake Bar & Grill.

Then Carl Brown crossed the street right in front of Vernon Tailors. Bonowitz saw him coming; he couldn't imagine why. Brown shoved his way past the rioters. He squared his thick shoulders at them, crossed his arms. "Go away! Now!" he yelled. "Leave this man alone!" he cried out. Many of them he recognized. He had given them summer jobs. He stared at those people especially hard and unforgivingly.

They finally turned away. Bonowitz wanted to reach out for Carl Brown, but Carl Brown was already walking away, seeing which other businesses he might be able to save. Mercifully, no one died. But there were four dozen arrests. The outside world had come to Mt. Vernon Avenue, shattering peace in M. E. Sensenbrenner's All-American city. The mayor rode around town in his official car, his dark eyes darker.

For days and months afterward, the mayor seemed haunted. The flags as gifts suddenly looked like a schtick. From 1969 to 1971 there was a wave of police brutality in Columbus, severe enough to bring forth federal civil rights investigators. Mayor Sensenbrenner pointed to the flag, pointed to the police, said the police must do their job, end of discussion.

On the eve of his reelection in 1971, Amos Lynch, the editor of the *Call & Post*, sat in the house that he rented to publish his weekly newspaper. Arrayed before him were black-and-white photographs of all the victims of police brutality in the past couple of years. Many of them he knew, like Dr. William Allen, former World War II flyer and doctor, who had an office on the avenue and who had been beaten in a downtown restaurant by police. It was a small town and all. Amos Lynch wasn't a big-time publisher; he was just the main publicity man for the Mt. Vernon Avenue District Improvement Association, just the little ole editor of a weekly east side newspaper. And he was the man who brought down M. E. Sensenbrenner's long reign as mayor. The day before election day, Lynch's *Call & Post* hit the stands, and there on a full page were the pictures of all the victims of police brutality, lined up next to one another: faces swollen, eyes closed, teeth knocked out. Grainy black-and-white photos. For a shining moment, Amos Lynch turned into the Citizen Kane of Columbus. As Kane said in that movie, "If I don't look after the interests of the underprivileged, maybe somebody else will — maybe somebody without any money or property."

After his loss, Sensenbrenner vanished from public life. When he went into a nursing home, he insisted that his boxes of miniature flags be moved along with him. During my interview with his son, Richard, I noticed that Richard had the same large head and dark green eyes as his late father. Before I left his office, he reached into his pocket and gave me a couple of those miniature flags his daddy had so loved.

By the early 1970s, many of the old-time merchants were gone from the avenue. Ernest Mackey, who managed Spicer's furniture store, never quite recovered from the disturbances. For so long his life had been simple, orderly. He read the Bible every morning at the kitchen table surrounded by his wife and daughters. Every morning he walked to work. On Sundays, after church, he drove his children around rural Ohio, sightseeing; sometimes they had picnics in cemeteries: it was quiet there. After the sixties he could cross over from "colored" to "Negro" easily enough, and further still, into being "black," but never so far as into black power. At mention of that phrase he'd rise up like a spooked horse. Sometimes he'd grumble to family members that he thought Dr. Martin Luther King was doing little but stirring up trouble.

Two Mt. Vernon Avenue lions: GEORGE CAESAR BERRY,
on the left, and ERNEST MACKEY, *from whom my mother
bought her first new set of furniture, on the right.*

Some new city health regulations drove George Caesar
Berry's Chesapeake Bar & Grill from Mt. Vernon Avenue.
The bureaucrats began showing Berry books and manuals
with new codes, said something about his stove being out-
dated. He didn't know what the hell they were talking about.
His customers — my mother, my Aunt Alice, my Uncle Ira —
never worried about codes and regulations, nor did he. Berry
abruptly left his grill — he just padlocked the place and left;
the waitresses didn't know what to think — and started a one-
man back-to-Africa crusade. He took all of his money out of
the bank right across the street. He visited Kenya and Nigeria
and Ghana and became an old black man hobbling on a
wooden leg — he had lost part of his leg while working on the
railroad — and writing long, rambling essays about his travels, which hardly anyone took the time to read; he kept mail-

ing them to friends anyway. Up to his dying day, he never shared his sweet potato pie recipe with anyone. There were many who thought he was just being churlish.

Marvin Bonowitz sold Vernon Tailors to Jim Jordan, the first black salesman the store had hired. Jordan scored a coup on opening night: he invited Muhammad Ali, who was in town for another event. Amos Lynch introduced Jordan to Ali, and Jordan immediately invited the champ to his grand opening. Ali begged off, complaining about not having enough clothes to spend an extra night in town. Jim Jordan told Ali there were plenty of clothes — silk, if he preferred silk — right inside the store, and he could have his pick. Ali dressed up and loved it. A few celebrity-watchers got carried away and snatched merchandise off the shelves and bolted for the door. Jordan liked having his own store on the avenue, but the joy didn't last. He got tired of being awakened at home at night by the police department. The break-ins were terrible, and he finally got out of the business. He went to work for Amos Lynch over at the *Call & Post*, selling ads.

George Pierce, my mother's favorite photographer, was still around, hustling for photo work, running twice as hard as the white photographers in town, who worked for the daily newspapers. Always fighting his way past the security people at events, always blushing when asked if he was with the *Dispatch* or the *Citizen-Journal*, because he was with neither; he was with the *Call & Post*. A lot of people wanted to pretend they'd never heard of the *Call & Post*, that racy tabloid, Mt. Vernon Avenue's newspaper. George Pierce, like my mother, was a native of Alabama. After a navy stint, he had hopped a train for Chicago. In Chicago he took a fancy to cameras, started hanging out at nightclubs, taking photos of couples. He got robbed one night, and that incident pushed him into Columbus. He worked the bars up and down the avenue, taking snapshots. And when he could, Amos Lynch kept him busy.

On the day President Lyndon B. Johnson himself was to come to Columbus, Pierce, who loved LBJ because he had signed all those civil rights bills, knew he had to get out to the airport by sunrise. When he got there, there was a mob. Pierce shook like a kid. He lolled until he saw the crowd turn, and then he saw LBJ and broke through the crowd, toward the president. He got closer, but some Secret Service men grabbed him, told him he could go no further. "Don't you understand?" George Pierce said, staring right at LBJ, who had now lumbered into his view. "I love that man as much as you do."

George Pierce got his photographs.

He continued to take pictures on Mt. Vernon Avenue, but he had to open another business, a flower shop, to make ends meet. To reach the photographer in the back, you had to step around the poinsettias and roses on the floor. The place smelled quite fragrant.

Waldo Tyler, of Tyler's Drugs, where I bought my fishing magazines and where my mother bought her nutmeg-brown face powder, grew even more eccentric. He was soft-voiced, gentle, an only child, quiet — had all the qualities, in fact, that might have made a person vulnerable to the rolling sixties. The sixties had in fact gotten hold of him and wouldn't let go. He became passionate — about politics, bohemia, the world, things. He sent missives to the White House complaining about cigarettes and cancer. Then he removed all the cigarettes from his store. When he tried explaining why to his customers, they shook their heads, walked away mumbling. They wanted cigarettes, not lectures. (The cigarette story got picked up by *Reader's Digest*, went all the way around the world; Tyler felt the sweet revenge of that.) He had always seemed torn between carrying on his father's legacy with the pharmacy and trying to save Mt. Vernon Avenue itself. Standing in a world on fire, he realized that he couldn't remain motionless behind a pharmacy counter, counting tiny pills all day long. So he used some of the profits to support progressive political candidates (not a lot of them won in Columbus) and to lobby for school desegregation.

The pharmaceutical chains blindsided him when they took over the wholesale companies. Tyler used to know the wholesalers. Many of them had known Waldo Senior, his father. So his word was good. And if he missed a payment — or two — no one screamed; he'd catch up the following week. But these new wholesalers demanded their payments on time. Some of their representatives — smart-aleck kids fresh out of college with their accounting degrees, he thought — sounded to him like robots. They never asked about the wife, the kids, the avenue. Now all of a sudden it was pharmacy by the book.

He began to miss payments. He had to let some staffers go. Carol, his wife, had seen this coming for years: the mystic on horseback tumbling to the ground. They'd stand staring at each other in long silences. Words just got in the way. They agreed to divorce. Some afternoons Tyler grabbed a bottle of wine, some verse, and some fresh flowers (George Pierce's flower shop was right next door) and went to the cemetery to visit his parents. He'd ask some of his parents' friends, people his parents had known, to go along. They would look at him, at the bottle of wine, say no thank you.

Police informed Tyler that some in the community were getting prescription drugs from his store and selling them on the street to those who wanted to get high, doped up. Pills mostly — uppers, downers. He couldn't believe it. He asked the police, once, twice, many times, if he could ride around with them, look at the people they thought were selling drugs. They agreed, and he'd sit in the back of the police car, head bowed, and he'd look out and see people he knew who'd be selling drugs. But he couldn't summon anger; actually, he'd get to feeling sorry for them. Then he'd start talking to the police officers in the front seat about police brutality, about ruined communities, about injustice. They stopped taking him on the rides. "I think there were people," says Carol, "who thought he was wacky."

Tyler began sleeping at the pharmacy, guarding it from break-ins. He'd tell people that the spirits of his mother and father still walked through the store. Eventually he lost the pharmacy, took a job with a community health organization, rode a bicycle to work, cried himself to sleep some nights.

Myrna Beatty closed the Novelty Food Bar. It had been the place where all the Mt. Vernon Avenue party crowd went to eat. Located a block from the avenue, it had the best lemon meringue pies in town, often baked by Mayme Moore, Myrna's mother, the same Mayme Moore who had been standing up there next to Dr. King himself at the 1963 March on Washington. Myrna rented the Novelty to a group of Muslims. They held their meetings in the place. One day, sitting in her home, she got a phone call. Someone reported that they were looking out the window of their home, watching the Muslims carry furniture out the door and down the street — her furniture. By the time Myrna reached the place, the Muslims and the furniture were gone.

So by the time my sisters and brothers and I came upon Mt. Vernon Avenue as young adults, it was not the Mt. Vernon Avenue of my mother, with its touches of glory and finery. It was an edgier Mt. Vernon Avenue, darker even. You might say we got the ashes. But if you hadn't known an earlier Mt. Vernon Avenue, how could you complain?

There was a bit of good news. Bobby Duncan, that little kid who used to slurp sundaes at old man Tyler's drugstore back in the 1940s, got himself appointed as a federal judge. It happened during the waning days of the Nixon White House, when the darkness of Watergate was turning the place inside out, when Nixon's guard was down, when William Saxbe could throw his weight around and get Bobby Duncan, his friend in Columbus, nominated. Nixon didn't exactly go around appointing a lot of black federal judges.

A few years after he was on the bench, however, in 1977, Bobby Duncan ruled on a landmark case and desegregated the entire Columbus public school system. The local school board had bitterly fought the case. It was a wordy decision with few memorable phrases. One, however, must have stuck in the craw of the board of education members. "But some firm action is needed when the horse won't drink the water," Duncan wrote.

Essayists and poets haven't written much about my Columbus by way of explaining its texture and mood. Perhaps it's a little too elusive. Maybe it's thought of too often as just a football-mad town. Maybe it's because sometimes it can seem otherworldly. A couple years back, Governor George Voinovich fired Billy Ray Inmon as manager of the Ohio State Fair. Being manager of the Ohio State Fair is a pretty powerful job in Columbus. Inmon didn't take the dismissal lightly. He fought back, staging a hunger strike on the statehouse lawn. One night a homeless man came inside his tent and peed on him. That story made the news wires. Lately there've been more Klan rallies in Columbus than in deepest Mississippi. Even if you understood the hate, you might be forced to wonder: why Columbus?

Someone might write a good sports biography about Woody Hayes someday, although those books do tend to have a limited appeal. There was drama in the life of Hayes, right up to the end of his coaching career, which came on a lovely day down at the Gator Bowl in Florida in 1978. The Buckeyes were playing Clemson. A streaking Clemson player was headed to his end zone, a clear path, running along the OSU sideline. Woody — and who knows what got into that man: dementia? — stepped out and coldcocked the player, right there on national TV. You could see he had strength in his upper torso — Woody, that is. Fans were startled. It was like watching some speeded-up moment from a loony Saturday morning cartoon. The Ohio State administration had to fire Woody, who had always said his only true hero was General Patton — had to show the legend the door. I remember calling Woody Hayes at home once. I wanted to do a profile for the newspaper I was writing for at the time. He listened to my appeal. Then, in a kind of lovely twang, he said, "Let's just leave it alone. If that's okay, let's just leave it alone."

On a pleasant June day in 1990, James Jackson, who had been rising through the police ranks for three decades, was appointed police chief — the first black to hold the position. It didn't take long for all hell to break loose. He launched investigations of police brutality. He turned the clock back and ordered officers to walk the beat. He clamped down. Officers (to tell the truth, mostly white) started complaining. Then a burglar broke into a house over on Franklin Avenue. It turned out to be the wrong house; it was Chief Jackson's house, and the chief — as big and strong as a stereotypical southern sheriff from a 1940s movie — was home. It was dark, but he found his revolver and let go with a round of bullets. The burglar fell but wasn't dead. Some officers called for an investigation of the shooting, implying that Jackson had shot recklessly. He was cleared; the burglar got prison time. Then Jackson was said to be soliciting the services of a prostitute. Again, some of his own officers initiated the investigation, said they did it out of civic duty; no, it hadn't been ordered from on high. Many thought the charges were trumped up; Jackson said it was all crazy and unbelievable. Eventually the prostitute-chasing allegation was dismissed, but not before laying a kind of tawdry gloss over the department. I remember sitting in an audience not long ago to watch some college students present Jackson with a community service award. He was under fire; the event seemed to give him a kind of balm. "I am in no way tired," he said on accepting the award. He's not what you'd call a gifted orator, but his words had the ring of an old Negro spiritual.

Political chroniclers have noted that of the three big cities in the state — Cleveland, Cincinnati, and Columbus — Columbus is the only one that has yet to have a black mayor. Oh, there was a chance in 1992. Ben Espy, black, and Greg Lashutka, white, went head to head, Espy the Democrat, Lashutka the Republican. Everyone delicately tried to keep race out of the contest. Both candidates were lawyers, and both had played football for Woody Hayes's Ohio State Buckeyes. Espy was the more animated candidate, the better speaker; many thought he was clearly more talented. A week before the vote, a poll showed the contest nearly neck and neck. Then Jesse Jackson came to town to support the Espy camp. That brought race right to the front of the campaign: that gave the contest a kind of outside threat and posture, a high-noonish quality. On the day of the shootout, Espy lost in a squeaker, and there are some around town who'll tell you today that if Jackson hadn't come to town, the outcome might have been different. Maybe that nudged the whites on the fence into a corner, and once in that corner they reached for Lashutka.

Actually, there was that book written by Philip Roth, *Goodbye, Columbus*. It had a catchy title, and there were a lot of people in Columbus who couldn't wait to get their hands on it, believing it was a novel about events in Columbus. They were disappointed; the book didn't have one thing to do with our Columbus.

I wouldn't be so presumptuous as to claim that something as simple as a grocery store — actually, two grocery stores — on a street in Columbus, Ohio, could even begin to tell the story of what has happened to urban America. And yet the rise, fall, and rise of Carl Brown's grocery store against the rise and fall of Rick Singletary's grocery store might serve as something of a parable for all the well-intentioned but flawed gambles that have gone whistling in the winds of our urban dreams.

This gamble began in the mind of William Potter, a World War II vet born and raised in the foothills of Kentucky. After his war service, Potter came to Columbus and began a career in real estate. In 1978 a shopping plaza rose on the avenue, right where the old Club Jamaica used to be. Potter had competently fast-talked Washington and city officials into footing the bill. If that sounds remarkable, consider that President Jimmy Carter himself came to the groundbreaking. So did Senator John Glenn, and so did Senator Howard Metzenbaum. (The pushy crowds gave my mother a headache.) When the shopping plaza's performance was below par, when the numbers just weren't coming up, Potter and city officials made another plan: they'd open a grocery store. The grocery store would bring people over to the avenue, and it would bring them because people had to eat. You might say William Potter and company were suddenly throwing good money after bad, or you might say they were trying to convince the citizenry that if the light on one dream was snuffed — as it looked like it would be — then another light was just being turned on.

Potter needed a grocer.

He stuffed some papers inside his briefcase and he went to

see the old lion himself, Carl Brown. Potter talked, and he talked about millions of dollars and about hundreds of feet of floor space. In fact, Potter talked about a grocery store that would have everything Carl Brown's grocery store did not have. Brown listened, kept the same serene expression on his honey-brown face. Carl Brown didn't fall off anyone's hayseed truck; he knew there had to be a catch. The catch was this: any potential owner would have to kick in $50,000 as seed money. Then the government would start kicking in loans. Before William Potter had a chance to unfold his slavery stories — his grandparents had been slaves, and he'd often go off on a tangent in business meetings, retelling their life stories — Carl Brown told him that he had been signing his own checks for decades now, that he trusted his own bank account, not the federal government's.

Brown toyed with the dice Potter had slid to him for a couple of weeks. He even listened to some federal government officials; their aggressiveness turned him off. And he thought the floor space was just too large for a store on Mt. Vernon Avenue. It sounded good; then again, as the grocer knew, good vegetables sometimes shielded rotten vegetables. William Potter grinned that little sad grin of his and thanked Carl Brown for his time.

Potter went looking for another grocer. He found Rick Singletary.

Singletary — short, boyish, energetic, also a dreamer — had worked as a manager for a Columbus grocery store for years. He had roots on Mt. Vernon Avenue: his father had been an electrician in the community; his mother still worked at Lee's Style Shop. Singletary sat listening to Potter for hours while Potter showed him drawings, floor plans. Singletary worried at first. He had never operated a store by himself. Chain stores provided comfort. You were surrounded by other managers; there was someone to watch your back, stop you from falling off the cliff's edge. There was great personal risk in having a store all your own. Every decision was a gamble, and every gamble affected every employee. And yet there were afternoons when Rick Singletary left his job early, rode over to Mt. Vernon Avenue, eyed the vacant land the supermarket would be built on. (Skurdy's, one of my mother's favorite bars — the jukebox that blared Fats Domino, the barstools that twirled — had been torn down to make room for it.) Rick would walk along the avenue, remembering when he used to run up and down it, reading the magazines inside Tyler's Drugs, buying fat fish sandwiches at the Chesapeake.

Sometimes, after looking at that vacant piece of land, Rick Singletary would walk across the street to the old Macon Bar. The paint was chipping on the Macon; some of the neon light bulbs were missing; the place still felt creaky. But that was fine, because the music, rhythm and blues and just plain blues, was still kind of sweet and intoxicating. Twirling on a bar stool, Rick Singletary would be greeted by old neighborhood friends. He'd start asking them what they felt about Carl Brown's supermarket, and they'd start complaining: it was too small, it didn't have enough of what they wanted, and it wasn't the cleanest place in town. Inside that dark bar, feeling warm and nostalgic, Rick Singletary felt a light coming on.

So William Potter had found his man.

Singletary raised his $50,000 — a bank loan, friends, family, and his life savings. He told himself he only wanted a classy store. There'd be a flower shop, a luncheonette, a cosmetics counter. And there'd be caviar. Caviar had never been sold on Mt. Vernon Avenue. Old people wouldn't have to walk from the nearby senior citizens' home to his supermarket; there'd be a shuttle bus. The market would be called simply Singletary's.

Down the street Carl Brown got by with a dozen employees and only ten thousand square feet of floor space. Rick Singletary had thirty thousand square feet of space. He hired 143 people. Carl Brown sat in his little store and had to listen to all the questions customers badgered him with. Would the new market cause him to relocate? He shrugged, checked his stock, his vegetables, ran his store, drove home to his wife in the evenings. He thought young Singletary might call him, ask him to come down, share some advice. He'd have gone. He didn't brag about it, but Carl Brown knew an awful lot about the grocery business, and he knew everything about Mt. Vernon Avenue. But the young grocer never called, and Carl Brown was just a little too proud to walk down there without an invitation.

Everyone was beginning to have faith in young Rick Singletary. Buck Rinehart, the mayor — a kind of low-rent version of Fiorello La Guardia, New York City's grandly hypnotic mayor of the thirties and forties — kicked himself up from his desk down at City Hall, rubbed his tiny hands together, and announced there'd be another city loan for Singletary. Then Buck, who took his name from Woody Hayes's football Bucks, bragged — after it was launched and over with — about Operation Summer Breeze, a drug sweep of Mt. Vernon Avenue: the dope pushers were arrested; those who weren't just scattered. Buck wanted them out of Rick Singletary's way. Buck was a kick-ass Republican in a Republican town.

Amos Lynch, the newspaper editor, went into action a week before Singletary's opening. He assigned lengthy articles, sent a hustling George Pierce out to take "exclusive" photos of the inside of the new store. Three days before the opening, the edition with the photos was published. It was grand treatment, a banner headline. Amos Lynch could put this kind of edition together in his sleep, but it still made him feel good to do it: his avenue was still alive.

The evening before his opening, Rick Singletary held a dress rehearsal, a walk-through inside the store. It was something he had learned from the chains: the preopening walk-through, get out any kinks before the doors swung open for good. His staff was outfitted in crisp red uniforms. Soft music floated. There were mounds of food, champagne, and the promised caviar. The store gleamed, and it was fragrant. Everyone kept whispering about how big it was: it now stood as the largest single building on Mt. Vernon Avenue. Before he went to bed that night, Singletary checked with his wholesalers out in Xenia, Ohio. He told them he might need a truckload of food on short notice the next day. He might be flooded with customers on opening day; he wanted a trucker ready to gun the engine and head to Columbus.

Sunday morning dawned beautifully on the avenue.

As he had been doing every Sunday morning for thirty years, Carl Brown left his home early, took Nelson Road to Mt. Vernon Avenue, and drove on up to his store. Churchgoers from Shiloh and Trinity Baptist, from Union Grove and Mt. Vernon AME would stop by after church — women mostly, hatted women — and begin wheeling carts down his tight aisles, looking for their collard greens and their chickens and their potatoes and chitterlings. When Carl Brown turned into his parking lot that Sunday morning, moving his heavy-lidded eyes from side to side, he was shocked: his parking lot was empty. He kept looking around. Then he realized why: everyone was two blocks away, at Singletary's grand opening. Had customers already switched their loyalties? After all these years? Didn't it mean anything that he had driven alone into the Deep South to get fresh produce and vegetables for his store, for them? He turned his head and noticed people walking right by his store as if it were not even there, headed to Rick Singletary's place.

A day after his store opened, Rick Singletary began sending

his buses to pick up senior citizens. The days were heady; he felt like a renaissance man. Carl Brown sat in his store down the street, his chest heaving, gazing at his empty aisles. He had not felt this fearful about losing his store since World War II, when all the capable males he employed had to go off to fight the Nazis.

Elvira, my mother, wouldn't set foot inside Rick Singletary's fancy new store. She had heard all about it — the fancy flower shop, the cosmetics counter, the seafood section (crabmeat, lobster) — but she had also heard about those high prices. High prices meant one thing to my mother: a seddity establishment had opened. My Aunt Creola wouldn't set foot inside the new market either. They just didn't chase after strange gods. Elvira had no intention of abandoning Carl Brown. Still living on the avenue itself, right across the street from his store, she walked proudly into Carl Brown's market every evening to do her shopping. Some evenings Aunt Creola would join her. The two of them would go to Carl Brown's and stroll down the aisles, squinting, both of them needing glasses and too vain to get them, turning cans sideways and looking at labels, brushing their hands over mounds of fruit. They looked for items on sale. Even if you forgot your coupons, Carl Brown's was the kind of market where the clerks would give you the items for the sale prices anyway. My mother and her sister wouldn't forget who sold the best chitterlings in town, the best liver, the best chicken. (Actually, by the time they finished doctoring their chicken, as my mother called it — dipping it in spices and herbs — they were convinced it was the chicken and not the doctoring that made it good, and so continued to brag about Carl Brown's chicken.) My mother's grocery shopping life had been reduced to what she could get on the shelves of Carl Brown's store. His melon, his tomatoes, his cabbage, his beer, his collard greens. Carl Brown would see her coming and smile, his chest would heave up just a bit.

Then other people began returning to Carl Brown's. Other people began complaining about those high prices in that seddity store down the street. The old lion sat in his store, smiled them back down the aisles.

Even before his store swung its doors open on that first day, Rick Singletary had begun punching numbers. He expected to do $250,000 in sales the first week. The total came to $172,000, 30 percent below his estimate. Right away he began to worry. There was something else he noticed as the weeks passed: his high-priced items — seafood, cosmetics — were not moving as quickly as he had hoped. Some customers who had stepped jauntily through the store during those first weeks, full of community pride, waving proudly at neighbors in the parking lot, showing off what was in their arms, were already waltzing back down to Carl Brown's market.

Some things he couldn't have realized until it was too late. He couldn't have known that some of his nighttime crew, while unloading the big trucks, would put some of the goods in their cars. And how was he to know that some of his salesclerks were motioning for their friends and family to come to their checkout line, and once they were there, sliding their goods across the counter without ringing them up? Grocery store owners call the practice collusion, and collusion got out of hand at Singletary's market. Singletary found himself interrogating clerks. Several were fired. He'd sit at home, his palms sweating, wondering why employees were taking advantage of him. Didn't they know what was at stake? Every time he thought he had fired the last crooked employee, there'd be another incident. He'd watch his workers. They'd watch him watching them. Tension built. One manager began carrying a gun; said it was for safety, told the boss the avenue was dangerous at night. Rick Singletary did not want his managers walking around the store holstered up like cowboys. He had to fire the manager.

Singletary forged ahead. He hired extra security, spent longer hours at the store. Then came the realization that he'd missed a wholesaler payment. Then he missed another. Many of his customers were on fixed incomes. He'd do hefty business at the beginning of the month, then taper off; the numbers by mid-month would look so low it'd be scary. Word swept the community after six months that Singletary's was in trouble.

It was traditional throughout the community to eat chitterlings on New Year's Eve. Eating chitterlings was a southern tradition. Chitterlings are hog guts, cleaned, boiled, and spiced up. Not a New Year's Eve passed in our house when my mother didn't boil a pot of chitterlings. She swore they were a delicacy; I cringed at the sight of them. As New Year's Eve 1985 approached, some local ministers urged their congregations to buy all their chitterlings at Singletary's. He sold $3,000 worth. It helped, but not enough.

Rick Singletary had to stop ordering certain goods and items. Elsie Singletary, his mother, showed up at the store one morning, dressed, as always, in dress and high heels. Elsie Singletary was a bookkeeper. She walked upstairs to her son's office, claimed a desk, pulled out a chair, and pronounced herself the new bookkeeper. She'd save her boy's store; if she had to do it alone, she'd save it.

The shelves grew barer and barer. Whispers about filing bankruptcy began. Ministers across town shook their heads: no, it must not be — they wouldn't allow it. A Solidarity Day was called for. Ministers in pulpits all over the city urged shoppers to get together on one single day and file into Rick Singletary's store. It was a very good day saleswise. But Rick

Singletary hated it when they all left; he felt he'd never see them again. Many he didn't. There were other wounds across the city, more pressing: the fate of the schools, juvenile delinquency, the crazy drug problem. Ladies would call him, tell him to hang in, to pray. "I was amazed at how many people thought if you prayed, everything would be all right," he said.

A year had passed. The sinking was now unstoppable. As the darkness circled, a city councilman tried to pass a bail-out plan for Singletary. Buck, the mayor, vetoed it. The blow was fatal. Rick Singletary filed for bankruptcy. One morning federal marshals showed up and seized some goods. The electric company turned off the lights. Then someone came and padlocked the front door.

There were significant differences between Carl Brown and Rick Singletary. To Carl Brown, a dime was a dime, and he had to feel that dime in the palm of his hand before he believed it was a dime. He counted dimes and he counted pennies. At the end of a given week, he could walk along the aisles of his store and estimate how much he had sold and be awfully close to the exact figures. The feel of his store had seeped into his bones. The rhythm of a chain store, which Rick Singletary had sprung from, couldn't seep into your bones. Everything at the chain store was shared. The money Rick Singletary had touched at the chain store wasn't his money. It was money that belonged to a corporation.

Maybe the essence of this urban parable is this: the people of Mt. Vernon Avenue went outside their avenue looking for answers and a savior, looking and hoping to remake a dream. The dream that had worked all these years was right under their noses. Inside Carl Brown's grocery store was where you'd find a grocer worth the risk, a grocer who knew a thing or two about penny wisdom.

10

M‌Y COLLEGE FRIENDS who had graduated went on to jobs with IBM, with Procter and Gamble, with large banks. My friend Jim Vandervort went to work for the state of New Jersey, the financial division, investments — his father; old connections. I wished him well.

I graduated with a 2.1 grade point average. No job awaited me.

For some reason, when I returned from college, I went straight to my grandparents' home, to Jimmy and Emily. I felt as if I had graduated beyond our housing project. I no longer wished to live near the smelly stockyard. I hurt my mother without knowing that I hurt her.

I applied for jobs and waited for the phone to ring. The phone in Jimmy and Emily's house did not ring for me. Jimmy wondered why. My grandfather thought men should work, not wait; should get their hands dirty, should bend their backs. Emily was patient; my dinner sat in pots atop the stove.

I took a cushy temporary job typing syllabuses in the sociology department at Ohio State University. The office was windowless and the work monotonous. I told friends I was thinking of grad school, which I wasn't; I couldn't have been admitted with a 2.1 anyway. After several months there was an offer of an interview with the Armstrong Company, a rug and tile company based in Cleveland. I'd applied for its management training program. I planned to take the bus to Cleveland on the morning of the interview, but it snowed, heavily. I feared a bus would be late, feared I'd miss the interview. Jimmy called his brother, my Uncle Henry. He did not ask Uncle Henry to come and drive me to Cleveland; he told him to. This was the eldest brother talking to the youngest brother. Uncle Henry pulled up, and Jimmy reached for his fedora and I reached for my coat. Burkes were not men to chat idly, so the drive was mostly silent, with some whistling, eyes scanning the flat landscape that rolled by. Uncle Henry looked bored. Jimmy had an unlit cigar in his mouth. My grandfather worried his brother about my being late, told him to watch for exits. Uncle Henry paid him no mind, whistled. Uncle Henry only had to stop once to find the exact location of the company. I loped off inside. Jimmy and Uncle Henry sat in the parking lot, remained in the car.

"What do you know about our company?" was one of the first questions the interviewer asked me.

I was speechless. I knew little or nothing about the company. All of this, of course, would change as soon as I was hired, as soon as I stepped into management. I remained speechless for too long, because I knew nothing about rugs or about tile. The interviewer's face tightened. He lowered his head, fingered anew my skimpy résumé, which lay on his desk. It was a fifteen-minute interview. It had started out bumpy, but I thought I redeemed myself toward the end, during those last five minutes, when the talk had turned to light banter, talk about Miami University, about the ride up from Columbus, about the city of Cleveland itself. I walked to the car optimistic. When Jimmy and Uncle Henry asked me how it had gone, I told them fine.

I never heard from the Armstrong Company again. And I never mentioned it again.

I continued working in the sociology department. My friends were driving cars, old Cadillacs with leather interiors, old Lincoln Continentals that were as long as hearses, cruising neighborhoods. I wanted a car. I went downtown to an auto loan office. A man with a wild grin and wild eyes told me he'd give me a loan — as soon as I got my driver's license. My brother Harry told me he'd teach me how to drive.

I had not been surprised to see Harry rise to become the star of Ms. D's Fashion Revue. He was the high flyer of our family, as handsome as our father Jack had been as a young sailor. Harry's track trophies sat on a stand in our grandparents' home, just below a picture of Jesus Christ nailed to a cross.

After he had finished his navy stint, Harry had entered Ohio State on the GI Bill. He met Renée, pretty and mysterious. Renée was one of the models in Ms. D's Fashion Revue whom Harry got pregnant. Together they moved north of the city, into a townhouse. They took on airs, became health-food freaks. Harry preached to me about the dangers of white bread, told me to eat brown bread; preached to me about pork. He insisted that if I absolutely had to eat sugar, I should eat brown sugar. Harry and Renée ate only fish and chicken, no red meat. A summer earlier I had witnessed them licking barbecue sauce from ribs; now they professed to hate the sight of red meat. They preached to my mother, Elvira, until she told them to leave her be, said she'd eat what she wished to eat, and she wished to eat pork chops, fried, with hot sauce, on white bread, with salt. They kept preaching; she kept rolling her eyes.

My brother and his girlfriend hopped from food concerns to medicine. Harry preached to us about home remedies. Herbs could cure everything, he believed, from the common cold to arthritis. Dick Gregory — the 1960s Dick Gregory, who had turned himself into a health-food freak — became my brother's guru. Harry shoved copies of Gregory's health book onto family members. My sister Wonder sometimes read her copy, a marijuana cigarette dangling from her lips. Harry also brought sacks of goldenseal to my grandmother Emily, said it would cure her of her ailments. She drank cups and cups of tea sprinkled with goldenseal.

When my brother arrived to teach me how to drive, he was behind the wheel of an almost-new Thunderbird. It was dark green with white leather seats, had kissing doors (the door handles kissed — were right next to each other) and white-walled tires. It gleamed. Harry scooted over, told me to get behind the wheel. I thought we'd drive around first so I could watch him, listen to his verbal instructions. I pulled off, and I was nervous. I kept checking the rearview mirror. I drove with a nervous foot, kept tapping the brakes. I'd slow down for no reason, then I'd hit the gas pedal. I pulled over, told my brother I wasn't up to learning how to drive right now, maybe another time.

"What are you? A punk? A punk motherfucker. Drive the goddamn car! And don't fuck my car up out here. Don't wreck my car. You hear? You hear me?"

I drove on. Then I stopped again on the side of the road, too frightened to go on.

"Drive the car, motherfucker. I'll be damned. You're a sissy. A sissy and a punk." My brother turned and looked out the back window for other cars. I wanted to leave — the car and Harry. I shook; my brother cursed. Finally we exchanged seats. Harry's face was red. I begged him to take me home, which he did. And I felt a little sad for having let him down.

Six months later, while Harry was visiting our grandparents, his green Thunderbird with the kissing doors — parked behind the garage, out of sight — was hauled off by the repo man. When Harry walked outside and noticed his car was gone, he cursed into thin air. One of Jimmy's major lectures about life had always been *Pay your bills*. My grandfather paid his bills the day they arrived.

My Bolivar Arms friends drifted from my life; I drifted from theirs. Chin joined the navy. His mother, at the age of forty-three, gave birth to twins: Elvira couldn't believe it. Wonder, my sister, moved in with Butch, an electrician. Butch drove a red Corvette and did not speak to anyone unless that person spoke to him first.

My mother received a letter from the Bolivar Arms management telling her she would have to vacate the apartment because she no longer had enough children living with her to remain there. She moved into a small apartment by herself on Mt. Vernon Avenue. It was no longer the old Mt. Vernon Avenue. A lot of the nightclubs were gone.

I spent more and more time with Jimmy and Emily. My grandfather sometimes asked to borrow money from me, ten or twenty dollars — racetrack money. He told me not to tell Emily. Sometimes Emily asked me if my grandfather asked me for money. I told her no.

I made two new friends, Olen and Flan. Flan was short for Flannigan, as in the Irish Flannigans, although my Flan was black. We became friends because of basketball. Basketball still connected me to things — happy times, sad times, life. Behind the bounce of a basketball there lay so many stories.

After high school Flan had talked the basketball coach at tiny St. Augustine College, in Raleigh, North Carolina, into giving him a scholarship. He returned from North Carolina wearing blood-red shoes, smoking a pipe, wearing a smoking jacket, and swinging a walking stick. Flan's blood-red shoes intrigued me. He told me he had purchased them in Washington, D.C. Olen had also gone away to play basketball and recently returned. He played for Ohio Valley Junior College, in the mountains of Parkersburg, West Virginia. Neither had played high school basketball; both had fast-talked their way into scholarships. They were not without talent. But now our basketball dreams were dying and we focused our interests elsewhere.

Flan wanted to become a con man, although the life of a pimp also caught his interest. For now, however, he passed himself off as a modeling agent. He had plenty of girlfriends and sometimes took me to meet them. He had pictures of them in various stages of undress. He toted the pictures around in an artist's leather portfolio case. Olen, who had taken to wearing knee-high riding boots and wraparound coats, wanted to get out of Columbus. In his mind he had adopted San Francisco as his home. Olen drove a four-door Lincoln Continental, read fat biographies, listened to music ranging from the obscure Shuggie Otis to Sly & the Family Stone, told women he hailed from San Francisco, and let me raid his mother's refrigerator for her delicious pound cake.

Flan also read books. In fact, he gave me two to keep. The first was *Players*, a book that chronicled the lives of California pimps. *The Con Game and Yellow Kid Weil* was the second, a book about a 1940s Chicago con man. The latter book I've held on to all these years. The copyright says 1948. There's a picture of Yellow Kid in the book. He looks like a harmless, slightly frail man. He conned millions of dollars out of the unsuspecting — horseracing schemes, land schemes, investment schemes. "Yellow Kid's authentic capers are both an education and a delight," the book jacket states, "the con man's fascinating art at its virtuoso height."

I carried the book about pimps in my back pocket, Yellow Kid's autobiography in my hand. Sometimes Flan, Olen, and I sat on Olen's front porch reading, the streetlight falling across the pages of our books. Neighborhood boys whom we knew, who were fascinated by cars, car engines, leaned beneath car hoods on the street below the porch. They laughed at us in our silk clothes, reading our books, though not nearly as bitterly as we laughed at them.

We walked the Ohio State University campus, striking up conversations with coeds. I lied that I was in grad school, Olen lied that he was from San Francisco, Flan lied that he was a modeling agent. We were widely believed. We wore silk shirts downtown in summertime and lounged at the bus station, eyeing girls who had just stepped off the bus from small Ohio towns, from Chillicothe and Elyria and Mansfield. We attended lectures around town given by scholars and high achievers and told ourselves that we were as smart, that our day would come.

We rode down Main Street and Mt. Vernon Avenue, watching the hookers. We wondered how much they made, wondered whom their pimps were, wondered where they lived. I sat in the back seat. Up front, behind the wheel, with Olen on his right, Flan narrated the passing scenes of our town; Flan was our Thornton Wilder. A couple years older than myself, he seemed to know everything I didn't know. I listened to him with rapt attention, as did Olen. I was fascinated with con games, but deep down I lacked the courage to participate in them. Olen did not. A forged check, a scam selling gold tooth fillings — the police did not find these transgressions humorous. The blades of real life cut sharper than any book. Olen took a judge's scolding, took probation.

We walked into nightclubs along Mt. Vernon Avenue — Larry's Ups and Downs, the Comeback Inn, the Batcave, the new clubs that had taken the place of my mother's clubs — and fanned out like spies. We sat inside all-night restaurants, ate, demanded separate checks, and kept talking about con artists, about girls, about pimps, and about leaving Columbus. We'd head toward the checkout counter when we noticed a knot of customers paying. The customers provided us with the perfect shield: one of us always stuffed a check inside his pocket, getting a free meal. We figured Yellow Kid would have been proud.

Some nights — warm, starry skies — we rode with Joe Eggleton. Joe drove a soft-top Bentley, quite beautiful. He never talked about what he did for a living. On the basketball court he tried hard, still played terribly, and was generous with compliments for other players. The police were always stopping him. Joe was the only black man in Columbus who drove a Bentley. The Bentley was candy-cane red, and Joe always had white women crowded inside. You'd see him rolling down High Street, grinning. The police gave Joe their best law-and-order looks. Joe didn't date black women, said they were too complicated. He had heard about my half-brother, Macaroni, the pimp. Olen and Flan desperately wanted to meet Macaroni. By now, Macaroni had roared into my family. He had grabbed ahold of us. I began taking my friends to Macaroni's speakeasies, introducing them to Macaroni's women.

11

Jᴀᴄᴋ ʜᴀʏɢᴏᴏᴅ, my father, began making babies just after World War II and fathered eleven children. He was handsome. Before he met my mother, he met another woman, Gladys. There was an affair. Three days after Christmas in 1948, Gladys gave birth to a baby boy and named him Gary. Gladys had a hard time caring for the baby; Jack was busy with another family. Something had to be done. In 1954 Jack and Gladys rode off to Statham, Georgia, to the Haygood family farm, with little Gary, six years old, in the back seat. When they left Georgia, rolling away on a scuffed dirt road, little Gary was left behind. Grandma Frances would raise the boy as if he were her own, which, of course, he was. Julius Haygood, my father's father, was, like all Haygood men, tall, bony, and rangy. He was a farmer, and he wrote out his grocery and feed store lists with a pencil, sitting beneath a tree on Haygood land, his knees as high as his chin. He pampered his grandson Gary.

Gary tried to escape his chores — plowing, picking cotton — but could not. He ran errands for white men who lived high on the hills around Statham and spent the money he earned at the country store. He ran Grandma Frances crazy; he was unable to keep still, hunting mischief. He did not miss his mother and father. "Grandma made everything all right," he says. There were, as well, aunts and uncles everywhere, men who looked like our father, women who looked like younger versions of Grandma Frances. Uncle Duke, my father's brother, became Gary's favorite uncle. Duke was handsome, drove cars fast down the Georgia roads, and liked playing with children.

The little country girls thought Gary was cute, and they adored him.

In 1959 a car pulled up to the farm. It was Gladys, Gary's mother, and her brother, Sammy Mattison. They had driven down from Columbus to get Gary, to take him back. Gary hugged his aunts and uncles, hugged Grandma Frances. There were tears, but Gary didn't drop a one. He left the South loud and rambunctious, a city boy who was already, at age eleven, outgrowing country living. In the years to come, he would travel to many parts of the country, but he would never return to Georgia or to the Statham farm.

Gary and his mother moved around Columbus, from the west side to the north side. In junior high he was the class clown. He was a slim kid, but also tough, wiry. He climbed onto the roofs of abandoned houses at night, alarming onlookers, and sang songs to the heavens, Sam Cooke love songs. He was fifteen when he had his first sexual experience — "with the neighborhood whore." He wore pointy-toed shoes and silk shirts, hung out with bad boys and with girls who wore too much makeup and dresses that were too tight. By the time he reached Linden McKinley High, he could be felt, like a wind at someone's back; he shook and he rattled. His high school career lasted two weeks. He was picked up in a stolen car. The Ohio Youth Commission sent him to the Fairfield School for Boys, in rural Ohio. The woods and tall trees reminded him of summer camp. He whistled five months by, came home, and enrolled at Eastmoor High. Eastmoor lasted a month. Gary left that school and pronounced himself finished with his formal education. "I was sharper and faster than anybody at school," he claims.

In the mid-1960s in Columbus, Ohio, a lot of young men wanted to be like Calvin Ferguson. Ferguson had grown up in the Mt. Vernon Avenue area, had been a pretty boy at East High, now drove fine automobiles, now was a notorious and highly successful pimp. Both state and federal authorities had files on him. Gary began trailing Ferguson, showing up at nightclubs he frequented. Ferguson had money, cars, and women. "At the time, that influenced me more than anything," he says. "Right then I knew what I wanted to do." Ferguson began noticing Gary around the east side. There were conversations, nods of admiration from both pimp and would-be pimp. Ferguson began sending Gary on errands, to pick up money, to drive his women around.

"Here comes the macaroni," a barber said one day as Gary strolled through the shop's door. Macaroni: Gary liked the name. It was odd, catchy, memorable. Pimps needed catchy names.

In the beginning, he was a petty criminal. A 1967 forgery charge drew only probation. He kept rolling. His ethics were simple: make money, have fun, avoid jail. He had never worked a nine-to-five in his young life and didn't plan to. There were schemes and schemes. For instance, there was the cough syrup caper.

In 1968 Robitussin cough syrup became the rage on the

streets of Columbus. It was a potent cough syrup; enough of it made you high, intoxicated. News of this particular side effect traveled fast and jubilantly through the city. As getting high went, it was cheap, which made it quite attractive. Health officials were not amused that Robitussin was being used for purposes other than lessening the effects of the common cold. Measures had to be adopted, and they were. All pharmacies were given instructions to sell only one bottle of Robitussin per customer and to threaten criminal penalties. Each customer had to sign a ledger upon purchase. However, addicts were willing to pay triple the drugstore price for a black-market bottle of the cough syrup.

Macaroni began waltzing in and out of pharmacies, signing for the cough syrup, using aliases all across town, making profits. He drank some of it himself, enjoyed the high. The police found out about his scheme. A warrant for his arrest was issued. On February 13, 1969, he was sentenced to the Mansfield State Penitentiary for sixteen months. His friends laughed at him. There was little macho pride in being sent to prison for selling Robitussin. He was twenty-one years old.

After charming and joking his way through prison, he walked out in mid-1970 with a glint in his eyes. Not long after his release, Macaroni was being hunted again by the police: forgery again. With the authorities closing in, Calvin Ferguson suggested that Macaroni leave Columbus, go to Dayton. Macaroni packed, bade farewell to no one, and disappeared. Ferguson had told him to get in touch with Flat-top in Dayton. Petty criminals; cartoon names.

If you were on the run in Dayton, Ohio, in 1971, you'd get over to the west side, around Stewart and Third. That was Dayton's mecca of vice, where hustlers and schemers plotted and planned. It wasn't difficult to disappear there. "Dayton was a wide-open town," Macaroni recalls. "Dayton didn't mind gambling and prostitution." He found himself a west side apartment and began frequenting nightclubs, mostly Peyton Place and Silver Dollar, dark places with the whiff of wickedness — exactly what he was looking for. In Columbus he had been more hustler than pimp. In Dayton he decided to go for broke; he would pimp. He met a woman on the west side. He was desperate, but she was more desperate. They both wanted to live well. Macaroni told her it took money to live well and explained about the streets, about sex, about suckers, about sex-starved men. The money started to come in. On Valentine's Day the woman gave Macaroni a Valentine's Day card with five-hundred dollars inside: "She paid me swell." Other girls paid him swell also. The Dayton police never harassed him. He began to like Dayton. "He was like a god over there," recalls Bob Kirkland, a friend of Macaroni's during those days.

Macaroni's reputation grew. It grew so much it attracted the attention of Emmett Washington and Creeton Ward, bounty hunters employed by the Columbus Police Department. When they found Macaroni, they slapped handcuffs on him and herded him into the car. As arrests go, it was easy, quick. On the ninety-minute ride back to Columbus, Macaroni tried to amuse the bounty hunters by making small talk. He prided himself on being a versatile conversationalist.

Calvin Ferguson posted Macaroni's bail. Macaroni, however, skipped his court date and fled back to Dayton. Ward and Washington got the assignment again. When they slapped the cuffs on him this time, Macaroni laughed: it seemed so preposterous. On the drive back to Columbus, the bounty hunters in the front seat, Macaroni in the back, the mood was light and relaxed. The flat land just unfolded all around them. In reality, they weren't very different from one another: three black men who knew some of the same people back in Columbus, who knew the nightclubs along Mt. Vernon Avenue and Long Street, who knew about the fried pork chops at the Chesapeake Bar & Grill, who knew the thin line between legal and illegal, the road of fate and the value of laughter. So they listened to one another, and the bounty hunters laughed along with Macaroni at his witty utterances.

Macaroni served less than a year on the bail-jumping charge. Shortly after he was released in 1975, he decided to become a businessman. He went into the speakeasy business. "You could rent a house for $240 a month and paint it dark inside," he explains. "There was always somebody to give you a jukebox and a pinball machine. The girls are going to come because of the music, the guys because of the girls." Indeed, the girls went to Macaroni's speakeasy, and the guys went, and I went, taking my friends along. You had to go around the back, knock on the side door. A man would come over, push back curtains. If he recognized you, he'd let you inside. If not, he'd summon Macaroni.

Macaroni's speakeasy was dark. My sisters flitted around the place, wiping tables, opening bottles of liquor, squinting through the red haze of the red light bulb. I was amazed at how easily my twin sister seemed to glide into Macaroni's circle. The darkness thrilled her. I wondered, often and nervously, if there was someplace in that darkness where I could fit in. My sisters put people at ease, everybody but me. I was never at ease. I stayed near the door, pulling the curtains back every five minutes or so. I expected the police to kick the door in at any moment. I did not wish to go to jail with my brothers and sisters. One night a friend of Macaroni's showed up. He immediately began an argument with Macaroni, something about missing money. Then he grabbed my half-brother around the neck, threw him down — like a movie gangster — and turned and left. Macaroni fixed his collar, rolled his shoulders, told us it was nothing.

I imagined that Macaroni's life was fascinating — speakeasies, silk clothes, women, thrills. It was, but it is only now that I realize how much of that life had a kind of two-bit quality to it. Macaroni was simply quite graceful. What could be fascinating and thrilling about driving to Kentucky, buying boxes of cigarettes on the cheap, driving back to Ohio, and hustling up and down Mt. Vernon Avenue and Long Street selling them to store owners? Or ducking the light of day because you owed people money on the east side of Columbus?

Macaroni bought a Lincoln Continental, four-door, cream-colored. "Paid cash for it." I leaned back in the passenger seat and asked him to turn up the air, to drive slower. He wore silk suits that were tailor-made for him downtown, at Frenchy's Tailors. He waltzed his Afghan dogs in sunlight across the lawn of the statehouse. No, he was not a dog lover; the dogs were wonderful conversation pieces with ladies. Women thought he was a schoolteacher, an entertainer, a salesman — anything but a pimp. He carried orange business cards in his pocket — "Members Only," they said, with a dollar bill and a champagne glass artistically drawn on them — that he handed out. Wonder always seemed to have an awful lot of the cards in her purse.

Sometimes he stayed at the St. Clair Hotel, a gaudy little establishment just off Mt. Vernon Avenue. "All the pimps had a room there," he recalls. His acquaintances — the dolls, the guys — had theatrical names: Too Sweet, Philly Red, Precious Herb, Scurve. On a street full of tall and handsome men, Macaroni seemed the tallest, the handsomest.

I'd watch him enter nightclubs. A nod here, a handshake there; he never lingered. He glided through doors, glided into his Lincoln Continental, just plain glided. He posed beside his Lincoln while admirers took snapshots with plastic cameras.

By the time I introduced my friends Olen and Flan to

WONDER, *at twenty-seven. There is*
plenty of light in her eyes. Her downward
spiral had yet to gather speed.

Macaroni, he was riding high with a reputation around Columbus. He had, in fact, given my family a certain cachet. Harry had been taken under Macaroni's wing. Diane adored our long-lost half-brother. I knew this: Macaroni avoided the men in our family, the old working men — my grandfather, my uncles. They couldn't see the ship he came in on. They saw smoke, mirrors, living that was too easy, and they grumbled. Emily, my grandmother, said little about him. She gave everyone the benefit of the doubt. Once, however, she pulled me aside. "Is your brother funny?" she asked. She put a little extra spin on the word "funny"; she meant homosexual. Elvira, my mother, conscious of her own meanderings through nighttime Columbus, was not so quick to dismiss him: "He's always treated me nicely."

My brother was more than just a pimp. He was also a thief,

a very good thief — as all thieves are, of course, until they are reeled in. Thieves have to possess nerves, and my brother had nerves. Macaroni's haven was downtown Columbus. He liked department stores, jewelry stores. His modus operandi rarely wavered: there'd be the casual stroll into the store, the idle chatter with the salesclerk, the words coming out of Macaroni's mouth smoothly, worldly. Items were laid on the counter, to view. One of Macaroni's working ladies, who had trailed him into the store and now stood at the far end of the counter, would summon the clerk. At the clerk's turning away — it took only a second — Macaroni would have just the time he needed to slip a piece of crystal beneath his long coat. Of course, there came a time when he grew desperate, when he no longer trusted the quickness of his hands, when he just walked into a Columbus department store, snatched a fur coat from the rack, and fled out the door, into the bright sunshine, clerks on his heels.

And yet there were moments, many of them, when I looked up to Macaroni, when I wished to be like him. Women did many things for him. I found the handing over of money to him — woman to man — unbelievable. He made it look easy, almost magical. So one day, after several days of wooing a girl — she knew Macaroni, knew I was his brother; she had a terribly long nose — and when I was feeling that I had gained her confidence, I asked her for money. Twenty dollars. I wanted to retrieve the words as soon as I spoke them. I was embarrassed. But she gave me the money, and when she did, I was no longer embarrassed. I put the money in my pocket, kissed her, felt the tip of her nose.

Two days later she arrived on the porch of my grandparents' home. It was late; we were asleep. She knocked on the door, hard, then harder, an I'm-not-going-away knock. I walked through darkness, hurrying downstairs, not wanting to wake my grandparents. I opened the door. The beam from the streetlight touched her face.

"Where's my money?" she said.

"What?"

"My money. You owe me twenty dollars." She crossed her arms. She aimed to stay put. Her lips were pressed together, tight.

I hustled upstairs, got twenty dollars, hustled back downstairs, and gave it to her.

I would not become a pimp.

My temporary job at Ohio State was coming to an end. I needed real work.

As a lark, I applied for a job at the *Call & Post*, the weekly newspaper headquartered a block from Mt. Vernon Avenue. I wished simply to fill out an application and keep moving, just as I had simply filled out an application at the gas company, at the electric company, at the telephone company, at Lazarus department store. I knew nothing about newspapering. I knew not one journalist.

The *Call & Post* was located in a two-story house catty-cornered to the Novelty Food Bar. There was no huge neon sign out front, just CALL & POST above the doorway in quiet black lettering, the lettering no larger than house numbers. It was a beige house, and the paint was peeling. Inside the foyer, on the left, was a window that looked like a telegraph office window. A secretary handed me an application, and I took a seat in the foyer and filled it out. Now and then the secretary, chatty and huge-faced, looked up at me and smiled. When I finished filling it out, I handed it back to her. She said the editor was in, I could meet him, I should sit still. I did not feel like sitting still. But just that quickly she stepped from her office into the foyer and opened the editor's office door — all in one motion, like a dance. And there I stood, staring at a strange bearlike man seated at his desk. Behind him was the mantel: I stood in the former living room of this house that had been turned into a newspaper office and wondered what the hell kind of newspaper office I had stumbled upon. Newspapers were everywhere, stacks of them.

The editor, the unsmiling man seated in the chair, was Amos Lynch. I had heard his name around Columbus, often in awed tones. Standing before him, I froze. He immediately asked me about my clips. His voice was hard, edgy.

"Clips?"

"Your stories. Didn't you work on your college newspaper?"

I told him I did not work for my college newspaper, and right then and there I wanted to leave. Then the phone rang. And when the editor hung up the phone, he explained to me that a housing grant was being announced downtown in two hours. I was to go cover it. This was my tryout. I'd better leave now, he said, and I did.

Things were spinning in my head. I did not have to embarrass myself. I could go home. I could go to other businesses, fill out more job applications. Instead, I went and purchased a notebook and a pen. I hopped on a city bus. I thought of how I'd write up the grant announcement. I decided I'd write it up like a short story. I knew short stories from Miami, from the writing course I had taken. I walked around the room inside city hall, heard speakers happily make the announcement, describe the benefit it would bring to those in need of housing. I introduced myself to men in suits, women in dresses, a roomful of people with sunny faces. I noticed the lovely gothic brick, the huge windows; I scribbled notes, notes about the styles of dress on the good people of Columbus who were about to dispense housing money. When I was sure I had enough, I bolted.

Back at the *Call & Post*, I climbed a flight of creaky wooden stairs. Upstairs there were three rooms, bedrooms that had been converted into tiny news offices. In the newsroom there were three desks, manual typewriters atop each one. I sat at a desk and started writing on the typewriter, banging the keys hard because they had to be banged hard. An old man sat across from me at another desk. He grumbled over a protruding lower lip when I introduced myself, smoked a pipe, and ignored the ash from the pipe that floated onto his clothes. He said not one word to me — John Combs, city editor. I wrote, and moon-shaped patches of sweat formed beneath my arms. I wrote about those people who had been at city hall, the clothes they wore, the types of chairs they sat on, the way they whispered and nodded. I wrote about the gloomy day outside and the sunshine in that room. Then I heard a voice rushing headlong, edgy still, up the stairs.

"Haygood!"

It was Amos Lynch, the editor.

I pulled the piece of paper I was typing on from the typewriter. Then I rushed downstairs.

Lynch took my story, began reading it. As he was reading it, he looked up at me, then went back to reading. I thought he had spotted something beautiful in the story, something unforgettable.

"Did you ask how much money the grant was for?"

I had not. I looked sheepish, and I felt sheepish.

He told me he had no openings. He said he liked my "energy." If anything should open, he said, he'd call. I left. I had performed badly; I had forgotten to ask about the dollar amount involved in the grant. I searched out other businesses. I filled out more applications.

Six weeks later, Amos Lynch called. "Young man, how would you like to come work for the *Call & Post* newspaper?"

He said it pridefully and explosively. He made it sound like the best job in America.

I showed up for work the first day of my new job as a reporter — warm outside, temperature in the eighties — in suit pants, bow tie, white shirt, and wool vest. I wanted to look and feel tweedy. I took a desk and dusted the typewriter. John Combs would be my editor. Combs talked slowly, walked slowly, and wrote slowly.

I wanted to meet the sports editor. John Combs informed me that *I* was the sports editor. I thought I had misunderstood him, as I misunderstood much of what he uttered, but that time I had not.

I titled my sports column "Wil Power on Sports." I had my sports column photo taken while in my vest. In addition to being sports editor, I was a general reporter. That meant I'd cover everything, and I did.

I covered Mt. Vernon Avenue, the businessmen and businesswomen trying to hold on. I wrote about murder — grisly crimes that had taken place in alleys, in broad daylight, in bedrooms. Combs liked murder stories, especially juicy murder stories, those being ones that involved sex and passion. Two decades earlier he had covered one of the most sensational crimes of passion in Ohio history. Betty Butler and her lover were lolling at a lake near Cincinnati. Butler was a strikingly beautiful black woman, and her lover was also a woman. An argument ensued on that lake — the newspapers reported that it was over sex — and Butler killed her lesbian lover. Old newspaper pros covered the story from every angle; Combs couldn't shake loose of it. Butler was sentenced to die in the electric chair at the Ohio State Penitentiary. Combs was there, notebook in hand, on the day she was to be executed. Two female guards escorted her to the chair. In the hallway they grabbed her arms for support; she might faint. "I can walk!" Betty Butler thundered. Combs saw the commotion, heard the comment, and the comment stunned him, the pride and arrogance of it. He talked his way into the coroner's office afterward. He peered at Betty Butler's naked, lifeless body. "Oh, she had a beautiful body," he said to me, the leer still in his voice. He wrote the hell out of the Betty Butler death scene, pulling a line from the poet William Cullen Bryant — "the majesty of her death." The boys in the daily newspapers around Columbus couldn't top that touch, and he knew it. John Combs informed me that I was not to sneer at crime-of-passion stories. "This is a weekly," he reminded me every time I handed in a story that disappointed him. "We want more than what the dailies give readers."

The staff of our newspaper was all black except for Mickey Seltzer, who was white. Mickey wore glasses, was thin, had a toothy grin and pale skin. She looked like Virginia Woolf. She could ingratiate herself in the black community better than anyone else at the paper. She wrote her stories quickly, never missed a deadline, was our best reporter. On Monday nights, the night we put the newspaper to bed — closed it out with that week's stories and prepared to ship it off to be printed — Mickey coolly finished her stories, handed them in, tidied up her desk, and walked down the creaky steps, out the door, home. I stayed late, rewriting my stories, watching John Combs watching me, watching him shaking his head at me. At two A.M. Combs and Lynch folded the newspaper sheets into long tubes and hustled them downtown to the bus station to be shipped off to Cleveland, where the paper would be printed.

I covered Ohio State football. "Columbus is a tremendous football town," the Frank Sinatra character says in *The Manchurian Candidate*. The Ohio State team, during the mid- to late 1970s, was brutal and ferocious, city boys and farm boys.

They always won, or always seemed to. Of course, every man, woman, and child in that town knew about Woody. The horseshoe-shaped stadium sat on the banks of the Olentangy, the river I had fished as a boy. The winds blew cold off that river, into that stadium. Hayes, who collected military paraphernalia, stalked the sidelines. He wore short-sleeved shirts in cold weather. He grinned as though it hurt his face. He had little teeth that looked like pieces of chalk rolling around in his constantly moving mouth. His players feared him; he wore granny glasses. The year I covered the big bruising Buckeyes was the year that Woody, you certainly might say, went around the bend, when he punched that opposing player on national TV.

I covered boxing events at the Fairgrounds Coliseum, watching going-nowhere pros punching each other, a knot of crazed fans screaming for blood. Some mornings I ran alongside Bill "Dynamite" Douglas over at Franklin Park. Douglas was training; I was trying to get a story. Douglas was one of the most feared knockout artists in America, but he had a difficult time getting fights. Higher-ranked fighters steered clear of him; Dynamite fought with abandon, feared no one, had rather bizarre habits in the ring. Sometimes he'd stand in the ring and take a vicious pounding — punch after punch, until he was bleeding. Then he'd start smiling, ever so slightly, and let fly a flurry of punches, knocking his opponent out. There were many around Columbus who thought there was something of the masochist in Dynamite Douglas. He drove himself to his out-of-town fights, returning with purple knots on his forehead, meager checks in his pocket, salving himself with Vaseline on the way home, mumbling through the dark, trying to heal the wounds before his wife, Bertha, saw them and started crying. A generation later, genuine glory came to Dynamite: his son, Buster Douglas, floored Mike

Tyson in a Tokyo ring, stunning the world. The old fighter got tears in his eyes. The young champ bought his daddy a fur coat, a big pretty Cadillac.

I sat in the gigantic RKO movie house downtown and wrote movie reviews in the dark. I wrote terrible movie reviews, but no one stopped me from writing them, so I kept writing them. We had a newspaper to put out.

I went and sat in criminal court, spotted friends from Bolivar Arms and friends from high school, dressed in orange jumpsuits, being paraded before judges. I'd wave, they'd nod; they wondered what I was doing in court. I also wrote a column called "Good Morning, Judge." The column chronicled the exploits of accused murderers, rapists, con artists, check forgers, pimps, prostitutes, thieves. Detectives, who liked getting their names in the paper, were helpful, jawboning with me until I grew bored, closed my notebook, and excused myself. "Good Morning, Judge" may well have been the most widely read column in town. I kept the names of friends out of the column — the least I could do. I feared coming across Macaroni's name, my brother Harry's name. Gossips and nosy people read the column religiously, hunched over their cabbage and liver and candied yams and cornbread, served on white plates across the street from the *Call & Post* office at the Novelty Food Bar.

Saturday mornings at the *Call & Post* were slow — opening mail, chattering on the phone, plotting ways to escape the editor's bark. On Saturdays we were still several days from our deadline. I leaned back, phoned girls, daydreamed. Visitors came by. The president of the Mt. Vernon Avenue District Improvement Association, Edna Bryce, a thin, frail lady with a beehive hairdo, always dressed up, would drop off announcements, news bulletins. She always looked at me as if she were seeing me for the first time, smiling out her curiosity.

The Mt. Vernon Avenue District Improvement Association at their 1955 swearing-in. AMOS LYNCH, *who gave me my first newspaper job, is second from left. He was the organization's publicity chairman. The members all look so proud; they meant to save that avenue.*

"Haygood. Haygood? I don't believe I know any Haygoods." Then her familiar question, the same one she had asked the previous week, and the week before that: "What church do you belong to?"

"Trinity Baptist," I'd say, more on behalf of my family than myself, since I rarely attended.

Mostly, though, old men from the neighborhood climbed those stairs. Some had previously worked there, had retired, couldn't let go. Hiram Tanner climbed the stairs like a wounded animal. He was the retired sports editor; I had taken his place. His hair was as stiff as copper wire and rose like a small houseplant. Hiram Tanner did not wish to be retired, so he'd bring me little stories he had done on his own, pulling them from his pocket, folded over twice, stories he had typed up at home. I tried to get as many of them into the newspaper as I could. There'd be heavy breathing as he pushed chairs aside, pulled out a chair for himself. When he finally settled, anchored himself, he sat there, catching his breath. You could tell he planned to sit a spell. He'd talk about Arkansas, where he was from; about his schoolteachers, whom he missed. He'd talk about segregation and horses and dirt roads and country food. He'd talk about Woody Hayes — "my friend Woody," he'd say — and about those "big colored boys" Woody brought to Ohio State. He'd talk about Jim Marshall, one of those who had played for East High, then gone on to play for Woody and from there to the Minnesota Vikings ("Of course, young Haygood don't know nothing about the great Jim Marshall"). He'd talk about the glory days of climbing aboard trains, his hat in one hand, typewriter inside a case in the other, going off to cover the big fights — Joe Louis, the Brown Bomber; Jersey Joe Walcott. Noon would come and I'd hop down the stairs and out the door and bring back pork chop sandwiches and small containers of peach cobbler from the Chesapeake Bar & Grill. (The food at the Novelty, across the street, was better, but by now it had closed.) Tanner's monologue would still be going, like an old newsreel. I listened, nodded, laughed, learned.

Every week, after I left the downtown police station and walked along Gay Street, I waltzed into the offices of *Hustler* magazine. It was sheer bravado for Larry Flynt to headquarter his pornographic magazine in our conservative Republican town — and a mere block from the police station! The building was small, dark brown brick with tinted windows. Inside the lobby there hung a photograph, life-sized, of a lady, naked. A snake slithered between her legs. I have no idea what kind of snake it was; the woman was Althea, Larry Flynt's wife. I had a reason for stopping in the offices of *Hustler*: I wanted to interview Larry Flynt. Every week the secretary said he wasn't available for an interview, and every week I came back. I bent my back and peered down hallways, hoping to see women, naked women. Bodies moved about, back and forth across the plush blue carpet, but they were fully clothed. The secretary, a comely brunette, always stared me out the door.

A picture of me in my wool vest took up the right half of my press card. I flashed my press card everywhere. I made $130 a week. Our pay was handed to us in a little white envelope, five twenty-dollar bills, two ten-dollar bills, and two five-dollar bills, the same combination every week. There were many missed stories on my part, and many missed deadlines. There were many photos that never got taken, because I was constantly leaving my camera at the office, atop my desk. I took many photos that were unusable or out of focus. Somehow the person I most badly wanted in the photograph would wind up on the outer edges of my developed film. This habit did not amuse Amos Lynch.

Elvira saved my stories, pointing them out to her waitress friends, who smiled as she did when looking at my picture at the top of my column.

I did not wish to continue to write stories about murder and mayhem, about love triangles. Yet I feared being fired. It would come any day, I knew. To blunt what I knew to be coming, after eleven months on the job, I walked into Amos Lynch's office and proceeded to tell him how I thought a weekly newspaper should be run. He had been in the business thirty years. I had been in the business eleven months. I did not know what I did not know. Still, I considered myself smart, believed in the potency of reverse psychology. Afraid to lose me, realizing that he had to change with the times, bend to the young reporter, perhaps he'd give me new assignments, a slight raise. He listened in cold silence. There would be no changes made, he said. He added that he was sorry to have to accept my resignation but he understood; reminded me that I had one more assignment, the Hall of Fame professional football game between the Cleveland Browns and the Cincinnati Bengals; warned me not to miss the bus to the game, because he needed the story. "Good luck, young man," he finally said.

I wished more than anything to start that meeting over, to walk back out of the office and come back in, but everything had been said, and the words that had been said could not be taken back. I had talked myself out of my job.

Jimmy, my grandfather, who had worked all his life, who judged others by their commitment to a nine-to-five job, to a work ethic, did not understand this, why I had quit. He shook his head; he rubbed his hands together. He asked me what I was going to do. I told him I did not know. I took odd jobs, temporary jobs, typing jobs. I ate what Emily placed on the stove for me.

Then I decided to become an actor.

I took an extension course in acting at Ohio State University, an evening class that consisted of dreamers, bored housewives, and myself. It would have been nice to have a stage to climb up on, or at least a classroom. But we had neither. We met in the far corner of the student union. We had to beg nearby knots of students to keep quiet. They shot us wicked looks. We formed a circle, dissected scripts, play-acted. We lavished praise on each other and left class feeling inspired. I bought books about the acting craft, Uta Hagen's classic book about acting. I read about Stanislavsky and his creation of the method approach to acting: you become the character you are playing. I had been a lifelong stutterer, still stuttered, in fact, but with a script in hand, while standing on a stage, I did not stutter. As long as my character did not stutter, I would not stutter. It was all very simple.

I chatted with my instructor about going away to study. All actors trained in New York City. Explaining myself, I slipped, got snagged on a word, badly snagged, with wind rushing backward up into my chest, stopping my breathing, stopping the word from coming out — a stutterer, and she knew it. Her eyes widened.

"Have you got a speech impediment?" she asked.

"No, not really."

"You'd better cure yourself of that before planning on an acting career," she said. There was nothing light about her tone of voice. I ignored her.

I watched, over and over, Marlon Brando in *One Eyed Jacks*. I watched it down in the basement of my friend Flan. (Flan's father wore a brown straw hat indoors. He never said hi.) I recited the lines Brando spoke in that movie. I broke his character, Rio, down. What drove Rio? What were Rio's motivations? What was Rio like as a child? I read a biography of Montgomery Clift, that gifted actor, that tortured man. I read a biography of Clark Gable, found out he had been born in Ohio. Did his big ears, much discussed in his biography, stop him from becoming an actor? As Elvira was fond of saying sometimes, no sir-ree bop. My stutter would not stop me from becoming an actor.

I flew on a cheap flight to Newark, took a train from there into New York City to see James Earl Jones onstage as Paul Robeson. It was a thrilling performance, Jones solo onstage, fluid and coltish, his heavy voice filling that theater. I stood in line backstage after the performance to meet him. He signed my program, looked into my eyes while he talked to me, seemed genuinely touched that I had flown all the way from Columbus, Ohio, to see him. When I later discovered that Jones himself had been a lifelong stutterer, I took it as an omen.

I told my grandfather that I was an actor. The tobacco rolled from one side of his jaw to the other. He said nothing.

My first role onstage in Columbus was in a production of *To Kill a Mockingbird*, Harper Lee's courtroom drama. The Players Theatre was a lovely little theater on the city's east side, on a tree-lined street with cobblestones. I studied the play for hours, bugged the wardrobe staff for just the right period clothing, just the right straw hat to carry in my hand as I entered the courtroom. I took my role seriously, took myself back to 1939 Mississippi. I showed up at the theater early every evening. I stretched. I did breathing exercises. I discussed acting tips with Dana Chatters, a friend I had made in the cast. I got dressed. My role was small, actually tiny; actually, I didn't have a line of dialogue. I was part of the crowd scene, in the gallery, the segregated gallery supporting the doomed black man. It did not matter that I had no lines to speak. I was in a play. Opening night was wonderful, the summer air outside clear and fragrant, the theater packed. Ed Graczyk, our director, was destined for bigger things than community theater. He would later take his play *Come Back to the Five and Dime, Jimmy Dean, Jimmy Dean* to Broadway, with Cher as the star.

My first speaking role came in *The Hot L Baltimore*. Then I got a part in a Neil Simon comedy at the Jewish Heritage Cultural Center. I rode the city bus everywhere, always with a hardback book in my hand, in and out of community theaters. I auditioned for Lonnie Elder's *Ceremonies in Dark Old Men* at the Sawyer Recreation Center, a mere block from the Bolivar Arms housing project. I wanted the role of the father, the elderly barber of the play. I put baby powder in my hair, aged myself, pulled on suspenders, slowed my gait, and rode a city bus to the audition — all in character. I was a method actor. People on the bus looked at me strangely. I looked back at them, but as an old man. I got the part, the lead role. The play ran for two weeks. I did an interview on TV. My photograph, along with those of the other cast members, appeared on the front page of the *Columbus Dispatch* entertainment section. I got stellar reviews. Harry, my brother — of all the Haygoods he had been the most comfortable and confident on a stage — came to see the play, dressed in a bone-white suit, and sat in the front row. After the play my brother, a lady on his arm, told me that I was too good for Columbus. "You should be in Hollywood," he said, looking around himself, waving.

Dave DuLong, my acting teacher from summer school, contacted me, asked me to come in and read for a role in *The Training of Pavlo Hummel.* Al Pacino had played the lead on Broadway. I'd play the second lead, the drill sergeant. After the audition, I was offered the part. One week into rehearsal I quit: creative differences. Additionally, I had asked about pay, money. I was impatient. I did not know what I did not know. Dave DuLong looked at me sadly as I walked out of the theater.

Flan, my friend, listened rapturously to me discussing acting. He still watched *One Eyed Jacks* with me, along with other movies, time and time again. He did not mock my passion. He told me he thought I should go to New York City. Broadway would be wiser than motion pictures, he said.

Driving around one night on the north side, coming to a stoplight, we were startled as half a dozen men hopped from the bushes on the sidewalk, rifles drawn and pointed at us.

"Don't move! Don't move!"

Police cars had wheeled in front and in back of Flan's car. Lights twirled. I was paralyzed; Flan went silent. We sat still.

"There's been a robbery," one of the officers yelled.

I feared being charged with a robbery I knew nothing about. Just then one of the officers who had his back to us turned from the darkness. I recognized the face; the officer recognized me. He walked over to the car. It was Ron Kenley. He had been one of the basketball players who had persuaded me to go to West High and try out for the basketball team. Now he was a police officer.

"These guys are okay," he said. "You guys can go. Take care, Haygood."

Again basketball had saved me.

Serious actors went to New York City. It was common knowledge. Serious actors studied with Stella Adler and with Uta Hagen. I announced plans to go to New York City. Right away! I'd study with Stella Adler! Flan's advice had sunk deep into me: Broadway over motion pictures. Train hard, respect the craft, starve a little. I had integrity. In the Clark Gable biography, which I had taken to toting around, it said that Gable had gotten his teeth fixed before embarking on his acting career. I got my teeth fixed.

I told a reporter at the *Call & Post* I was leaving to study acting in New York City. I was asked if I had a scholarship "or something." I indeed had something — the will to go, to leave, to get. But the reporter was fishing for a story. I gave him a story. Yes, I lied, I had a scholarship. I told myself, convinced myself, I'd get a scholarship as soon as I got there, proved myself, impressed the teachers, impressed Stella Adler herself. Then a story came out in the *Call & Post*: "Haygood to Study Acting in New York on Scholarship." I was ashamed of the story, and proud of it. I clipped it and saved it.

I wanted to make my family proud — Jimmy and Emily, Elvira, Aunt Creola. There were reasons why the family wasn't feeling so proud. Harry had been arrested for forgery. Jimmy used the house as collateral for bond. It hurt Elvira.

259 ❧ *The Haygoods of Columbus*

Harry received probation. My sister Wonder had taken to hanging out on Mt. Vernon Avenue. The drug addiction had started climbing up her back. "Macaroni used to come get me, tell me to get off Mt. Vernon Avenue," she remembers.

My mother's shoulders sagged at the news of my leaving. Then Harry announced with a flourish that he also was leaving. "You try the East Coast," my brother said to me, sounding like a gold prospector. "I'll try the West Coast." Harry was going to Hollywood. He was confident he'd find work once he got there. He packed his modeling photographs.

Then we were gone.

Goodbye, Columbus.

Harry was running west. I was running east. Macaroni also took off; I'd soon come to find out he was running from the long arm of the law.

Our mother remained in her apartment on Mt. Vernon Avenue. She decided to stand her ground — like Custer.

12

W<small>HEN I ARRIVED</small> in New York City, in the autumn of 1979, my head swiveled, my eyes blinked. I kept my money — five hundred dollars, all in cash — secure in my sock. I kept my socks pulled up high. I needed a place to stay and checked into the YMCA on Thirty-fourth Street and Seventh Avenue. Blue neon letters announced the outside of the Manhattan YMCA, just like the one in Columbus, Ohio. The lobby was busy, people coming and going, everything a blur to my eager eyes. I paid seventeen dollars per night, and I paid a week's rent in advance. The room was so small it shocked me. It was like one of the upstairs closets in my grandmother's house. I could stand in the center and touch both walls. I unpacked, laying my books on the dusty windowsill: *Building a Character*, by Constantin Stanislavsky, and *Technique of Acting*, by Stella Adler.

I walked the pavements of New York City that first day until I was bone tired. Up and around Times Square — lingering and circling around the huge theaters — then over to

Second Avenue, then down Park Avenue, then over to Madison Avenue, and from there over to Fifth Avenue, zigzagging; I walked and walked, until I couldn't walk anymore and stopped at the edge of the East River, facing river and sky. I felt glorious. I felt a million miles from Columbus, Ohio.

I retreated to my room. A bed with a thin mattress, a closet, four walls, now home. The shower and bathroom were down the hall. I saw men with vein-warped legs wearing flip-flops and men in bikini underwear walking to the shower; I saw men whose faces looked as cold as ice, and I even heard men coupled up, giggling in the stalls. There were many men at the Y who worked on ships, seamen whose ships had docked at the Hudson pier.

A man banged on my door one night. "You want to go have some fun?"

Apparently he had spied me in the bathroom, and his eyes had trailed me back to my room.

"No," I yelled. "Go away."

He went away. I feared going to the bathroom at night. If I had to pee, I'd hold it until morning.

There were sirens every night, all night long. One night an ambulance stopped at the Y. I looked through the small window of my small room, saw a figure on a gurney being wheeled away from the Y, into the ambulance, and felt strange. Someone had jumped. I felt spooked, so much so that I phoned my sister Diane a day later, told her perhaps I had made the wrong decision, the city was actually scary, there were strange men hanging out in the bathroom of the Y. I needed for her to tell me to come home. She loved me. Of course she'd tell me to pack right away, come home.

"You just got there," Diane said, almost clinically. "Give the place a chance. You don't want to give up before you get started."

I ate $1.99 chicken dinners that I purchased across the street from the Y at an all-night restaurant. The roasted chicken came in a little Styrofoam plate with a covering. I'd rub the juice from the plate with the cold dinner roll that came with the chicken. When I felt like splurging, I'd buy a slice of prepackaged pie.

Then I went to begin my acting lessons — the scholarship student without a scholarship.

The Stella Adler Studio was located at 419 Lafayette Street, in Greenwich Village. I noticed a crowd of people lounging on the sidewalk just outside the door, sitting along the brick wall — a lot of blond-haired folks, male and female, holding what looked to be scripts. They were acting students, and they were acting the part of acting students. Not one said hello. I almost laughed, but only because I felt slightly intimidated.

Inside, the lobby was crowded. The phones were ringing. I noticed a huge bulletin board to my right, and I scanned it, figuring what I'd do next, biding my time. Then I froze when I saw my name in bold letters: "Wil Haygood — Welcome to New York! I'm studying here too! Leave a message for me. Dana." The note was from Dana Chatters, whom I had acted with back in Columbus in the balcony scene of *To Kill a Mockingbird*. So he had seen the newspaper, and he knew: I had lied. No one here had offered me a scholarship, had even heard of me. I feared the story would get out to the administration of Stella Adler, and I feared I'd be arrested for fraud, for claiming to have a scholarship that I didn't have. I did not wish to see Dana. I turned, walked out of the Stella Adler Studio, and never returned.

I wished, for the time being, to be alone and unknown.

I convinced myself that I would find my own way to act. I would become an actor by reading, and by watching. So I went to all the plays I could. I saw Off-Off Broadway plays and I saw Off-Broadway plays. I sat in a small darkened theater and watched the famed Negro Ensemble Company perform play after play. I felt as light as a balloon. I cornered actors and actresses in hallways and badgered them with questions. I saw Broadway shows. I saw Meryl Streep in the lobby of Joseph Papp's Public Theatre, wearing a green pants outfit and red cowboy boots. I waved. She didn't. I saw a production of *Coriolanus* at the Public Theatre, starring the great — though at the time unknown — Morgan Freeman. I actually left that production before it ended; it was too long, and I couldn't quite get into Shakespeare.

I saw *First Monday in October* on Broadway, a play about Supreme Court justices. It starred Jane Alexander and Henry Fonda. After the performance, I lolled at the stage door, waiting on Henry Fonda. When he sauntered out, I introduced myself. He was wearing a hearing aid. He started walking to his waiting limo, long loping strides, that proud *Grapes of Wrath* walk. He looked at me warily. "What? What did you say?" I must have frightened him, that poor man. He bent uneasily and disappeared into his limo.

I spent hours at the Bleecker Street Cinema, watching movie retrospectives, foreign films, movies from Germany with lots of rain. Sometimes there'd be fewer than a dozen people at the weekday matinees. I'd stretch, watch the same movies back to back.

I bought copies of *Casting Call*, the bible for auditions, and laid them around my room at the Y until they stacked up. Their mere presence made me feel like an actor. They'd get dusty; I'd throw them away. I paid up several weeks in advance at the Y. I told the front desk clerks I was an actor. They looked at me blankly.

I had yet to go to one audition. I preached patience to myself; I'd get to the auditions in due time. Maybe I was fooling myself; certainly I was running out of money. In the beginning the Y rent seemed cheap, but it added up. Eating all my meals out added up. I hated the Y, hated the seedy characters who knocked on my door. And I hated standing in the line in the lobby to pay my bill.

Bob Haygood, my cousin, lived in the Bronx. My father had given me his number. Bob, as I had heard many, many times, was a Harvard man — "My nephew, now, Bob, well, he went to Harvard University, way up there in Boston." Bob had tried his hand at singing, folk singing. It was the sixties, Richie Havens, Woodstock. Bob wanted to be an entertainer. He even got himself on a national variety show, strumming his guitar. But singing didn't work out, and he eventually became a salesman. We met in midtown, for dinner. Bob had my father's grin, my father's chin, and he had the lanky Haygood body. I told him I was a struggling actor, in need of work. He grinned. Maybe he'd offer me a job, lead me to a job, hand over a little money. He picked up the dinner tab, waved good-bye. "Call me sometime," he said. He didn't sound as if he meant it, and I never saw him again in New York City.

I began my search for a job. I felt strange when I wrote "YMCA" for place of residence on applications. I did not imagine that anyone would phone me at the YMCA. But finally I landed a job — delivering hamburgers, BLTs, slices of coconut cake. The manager of the Prime Burger, on Fifty-third, just off Fifth Avenue and across the street from St. Patrick's Cathedral, hired me on the spot, pointed me at the kitchen. The kitchen manager explained my job: hustling out the door with deliveries to area businesses. I was a running waiter. The pay was meager; mostly I earned my money on tips. I delivered a lot of food, all of it in brown paper bags and much of it to the women buyers at Saks Fifth Avenue, where there was a little side door. You just gave the security guard a nod and raised your bag of food to his eye level and he'd let you in. The buyers all had lovely hairdos, all dressed stylishly, and most tipped quite well. They rarely established eye contact; they seemed very formal. I wore a long brown tweed coat, dress slacks, dress shirt, leather loafers. I would not be mistaken for a bum. I was a struggling actor delivering sandwiches around Manhattan.

"You don't look like you should be doing this type of work," a lady said to me one afternoon, gazing at my clothing.

"I'm an actor," I explained. A pinched look overtook her face. She shook her head and walked away before I could ask for her phone number.

I had never eaten poached eggs, but I ate them every morning at Prime Burger. Breakfast was free; so was lunch. The cook was a surly man with a coconut-brown face, and sometimes you had to lean over the counter and yell your order through the steam. He'd look at you as if you were crazy. But he never forgot exactly what you ordered: two poached eggs, bacon, home fries, wheat toast.

On my days off, when I wasn't going to the theater, I walked around Queens and Brooklyn like a surveyor, looking for an apartment. A referral service sent me to a house in Queens. There was a room its owner was looking to rent — "nice one-room studio in back of house; quiet, clean." The owner was a large man in work clothes, unshaven, with large hands. There was a perpetual gleam in his eyes — a little too much gleam. He led me to the room, which was tiny, like my YMCA room. It was not clean. The room was actually just off the kitchen; it resembled a large pantry. The man told me he lived alone, smiled when he said it. I immediately left, fled back to the referral agency, demanded my thirty-five-dollar fee back. The skinny man to whom I had given my fee cupped his hand to the telephone, held it back from his ear, smiled wickedly as I hustled through the door.

"You didn't like it? Too small? Ah, have a seat, I'll be off in a minute."

He talked standing up. There was much shifting of his feet. He talked and talked, and I left.

Some evenings I called home, back to Columbus, collect, from phone booths on unfamiliar street corners. Emily would hand the phone to Jimmy, who wanted to know when the last time I talked to Elvira was.

At the Y, going up on the elevator one evening, I met Ted Geislinger. Ted was as small as a Civil War bugle boy. He had bad acne, squinted when he talked, came from Iowa, was looking for someone to share an apartment with, was studying to be an actor. We talked about Stanislavsky for hours. We rifled through *Casting Call*. We decided we'd share an apartment in Brooklyn.

Ted and I strolled around Brooklyn Heights, which looked lovely, green, and quiet but was already, by 1979, getting pricey. Clinton Heights was a different tale: gritty and funky, it also looked safe enough. We found a two-room walkup, top floor of a triple-decker, and left the Y together on the same day, hauling our belongings through the coolish fall air onto subway platforms, into the subway cars themselves. The landlady was stout, short, talked extremely fast, and wore thick eyeglasses. She looked like a black Shelley Winters. I wondered what she thought of us: tall black guy, short white guy; black guy from Ohio, white guy from Iowa; two actors. Maybe she thought nothing at all. Maybe she had seen it all. The apartment was tiny; the ceilings in the main room slanted downward and I had to duck when going over to the window. The wood floors creaked; there was only a shower, no tub, and the walls were peeling blue paint. There was a refrigerator, but no oven. There was, however, a skylight, and that was a novelty to my eyes.

Some days, walking around Manhattan with a rolled-up

copy of *Casting Call* in my back pocket, I felt like an actor. I whiled away hours in cafés, picked at greasy food, hoped to come upon an audition notice that struck my fancy. I didn't do auditions for musicals. I also steered clear of auditions for road shows. I wanted to act in New York, on the New York stage. Many an afternoon I whiled away at the New York pier, reading *Casting Call*, reading a novel, daydreaming, the river rolling by.

The owner of Tony's Restaurant, an Italian restaurant in Brooklyn, needed a dishwasher. Tony was owner and, along with his wife, chef. He chain-smoked, had a tough lined face, wore a sauce-stained apron. When I told him I was studying to be an actor, he nodded just a little, almost a *heh-heh* rising in his voice. I worked from six in the evening until one A.M. At the end of my first night, Tony came into the kitchen, lifted up the floor mat, saw that I had swept beneath the mat. He told me it was his secret test: if a dishwasher swept dirt under the mat to hide it, he knew he wouldn't keep the person. I was grateful I had passed Tony's little test; he never checked under the mat again.

After work, Tony or his wife prepared huge Italian meals for me — spaghetti, mussels marinara, ravioli, veal cutlets smothered in red sauce, rigatoni. I could have anything on the menu. I ate in a plush wood-paneled booth, all alone, a white napkin lying across my crotch, hogging food like a mafioso. Tony paid me cash, from his pockets. Every day I showed up he seemed a little surprised. I guess good dishwashing help was hard to find.

Ted, my roommate, read *Casting Call* with a vengeance. He hustled out to auditions. He told me stories of waiting around in crowded rooms to read a script for two minutes, then being ruthlessly dismissed. He ate cereal late at night, letting milk drop from his lips onto his mattress. Ted wore clothes that devoured him. His shirtsleeves fell past his wrists, nearly down to his fingertips. I asked him more than once where he purchased those shirts; he wondered what business it was of mine. "Are you going on auditions?" he'd ask me, a tone of indictment in his whiny voice. I told him that all I was seeing in the trades — the term used to describe the casting periodicals — were musical auditions, and I didn't audition for musicals. I wanted straight drama, James Earl Jones–type roles. Sometimes I came home and as I was climbing the stairs I would hear Ted screaming at the top of his lungs. I'd find him seated on his mattress, in a Buddha-like pose: vocal exercises, he explained. He told me he had much angered his father by bolting from Iowa and coming to New York to become an actor.

Ted and I went to Greenwich Village when our first Thanksgiving rolled around. The restaurant was dreary. We sat on rickety wooden chairs. I complained about the food; Ted devoured his and said it was delicious. It was the first Thanksgiving in my life that I wasn't seated at the dinner table at home, eating my grandmother's dressing, my grandfather's peach cobbler — the first Thanksgiving I hadn't crowded into the kitchen to grab Aunt Creola's sweet potato pie.

Ted liked New York City, didn't mind being mostly broke, didn't mind auditions with a thousand other hopefuls, didn't mind our roach-infested apartment. One night, when we were talking about girls — actually, I was talking, Ted was listening — Ted told me he wasn't really sure he was interested in girls. I thought nothing of his comment, but minutes later a bell rang. "Are you a homosexual?" I rushed the words out. I waited for an answer, as tense as someone waiting to be shoved from the door of an airplane on a parachute plunge. "I don't quite know," Ted answered. "Probably." I wondered, quickly and shamelessly, if he looked at me naked, dashing from the shower. There had always been a rather alert look in Ted's eyes when I stepped from the shower. "I'm not attracted to you, if that's what you want to know," he said. We both went silent.

A short while later Ted announced he was moving; he had found a place in Manhattan, where he'd be closer to auditions, he said. I helped him move his few belongings, struggling down three flights of stairs and up the street to the subway, heaving and sweating and dragging. On the subway platform, while we were seated on benches, waiting for the train to arrive, a man yelled at us from across the tracks: "Hey! You two fucking fags!" Ted looked at me. I looked at Ted. "Yes, you two. Faggots!"

Sometimes I missed Columbus, Ohio.

Ted's new apartment, located down a semilit hallway in a rundown building on West Twenty-third, was small, but it was his very own, and I complimented him on it. It was on one of those New York City blocks crowded with women in tight clothes, salesmen with their goods draped across their arms, unsupervised children, evangelists, junkies, noise. Ted and I shook hands on the curb. Standing there, looking at him, looking around him, I felt sorry for him. He seemed the tiniest person in view. Of course he wasn't, he just seemed to be; already the surroundings had appeared to reduce him in size. I wondered about his safety. But he genuinely seemed at ease, looked to be at peace. Ted was actually fearless, and perhaps braver than I'd ever be. Now and then I'd find myself scanning cast listings for Off-Broadway shows. I was sure Ted's name would come up sooner or later. He seemed so committed. But I never came across it.

That winter, alone in my Brooklyn apartment, I froze. Snowflakes floated through a crack in my skylight. Ms. Black Shelley Winters refused to fix it. I'd wake up mornings and see snowflakes on my bed, see cockroaches scampering across those snowflakes. I'd pray for the snow to stop. I argued with my landlady. Not only did she refuse to fix the skylight, she controlled the heat and refused to turn it up. I would stand outside her door, her door chained but open, her eyes peering at me through the three inches between chain and door.

"The heat's up. You mean you don't feel it?"

I wondered if she was being sarcastic. She'd close her door, painted red, in my face. I couldn't complain too often, because too often my rent was late, sometimes two weeks late. I missed Ted's half of the rent. At night, with the snow falling through the skylight, the wind whistling, I lay awake, staring up at the beautiful starry sky.

Some nights it was the landlady's daughter and her common-law husband who kept me awake. They lived below me. The fights, which usually began around two A.M., were nasty affairs. Items were thrown, bodies bounced off walls, voices shrieked. I'd toss and turn, then I'd march downstairs, barefoot, and knock on their door. They refused to answer. Some days I'd see them on the street, hand in hand, as calm as Sunday. They'd smirk, keep walking.

With Ted gone, my acting consciousness evaporated. What I desperately wanted was a better job than washing dishes.

Striding through the glittery first floor of Macy's one afternoon, my mind drifted to my sister, to Ms. D's Fashion Revue. I knew a thing or two about fashion. I looked around the store and wondered if my fashion revue experience might fetch me a job at Macy's; I sent away for information about the executive training program. I knew nothing about business or management, certainly not about retailing, and the store's executive training literature informed me that it didn't matter: Macy's wanted liberal arts graduates, well-rounded people. I walked over to the Pratt Institute of Art, near my apartment, found a typist's name on a bulletin board, paid her too much to type out my résumé. Macy's wrote back, summoning me for an interview.

I intended to be prepared. I subwayed into Manhattan, went into the New York Public Library, and checked the references on everything ever written about Macy's department store. I pored over books and documents at a small desk in the reading room. I liked the fluorescent lamp atop the table.

The Macy's personnel director — clean-shaven, smart suit, businesslike but with a cheery smile — asked me a few questions about Ohio. Then he asked me why I wished to work at Macy's. "Well, sir, when Mr. R. H. Macy founded this store in 1858, I think he had people like Wil Haygood in mind to work for it." The quoting of that date got the personnel manager's attention. His eyes widened, and they widened more as I unleashed a stream of facts, figures, dates, all about Macy's, about retailing history in New York City, what it would mean to me to beat Gimbel's every quarterly retailing season.

I was invited back for a second round of interviews. These interviews would last all day, and those who survived the cut would be invited to join the executive training program.

Twenty-five of us marched into Macy's that morning, prepared to stay throughout the day. There would be mock situations — mock business conferences, mock business problems on the sales floor. A tall blond lady walked in, wearing a fur coat. She even smelled rich. Several interviewees carried briefcases; I wondered what in the world they had inside them. I had no briefcase. Many were from Ivy League backgrounds. The day was grueling, long, sweaty. The Ivy Leaguers looked to be under severe pressure. I relaxed. I was careful not to stutter.

At day's end we were told that twelve of the twenty-five would be invited to join the training program. "You will be informed by Monday by telephone," one of our interviewers told us.

I stiffened: I had no phone. I rushed over to the interviewer, explained that I had no phone. "I wouldn't worry about that if I were you," he said. So I wouldn't be chosen. So I really didn't care. I went to work that evening in my Brooklyn restaurant, stuffed myself with Italian food, stared out the windows, watched the darkness.

Early Monday morning my doorbell rang. I imagined someone had the wrong apartment, but it kept ringing, so I hustled downstairs. A Western Union telegram. Had something happened at home, in Columbus? I started worrying and ripped it open: "Macy's Department Store would like to extend an offer to you to join our executive training program. Please contact at your earliest." I raced across the street and phoned home. Jimmy was excited, as were Emily and Elvira. I walked to my job at the restaurant and proudly announced to Tony and his wife that I'd be quitting in a week, would be joining Macy's, would soon become a Macy's executive. Tony smiled, his wife smiled.

On my last night at the restaurant, Tony prepared my meal, heaps of Italian food, so much that I wrapped a great deal of it and took it home, walking through a Brooklyn night that finally held something beyond the coming morning that would prove prosperous for me: a job.

We trained for nine weeks, a disparate group of chosen executives-in-training. More than a few were Ivy Leaguers. Bert was a Jamaican. Mona was the blonde with the fur coat. She spoke with a clipped accent — Scandinavian, it turned out — which I thought was a put-on, and she called me Willie, which I detested. I counted myself the only midwesterner out of the dozen. We met every day in small rooms and talked about moving stock from store to store. We talked about seasonal changes in merchandise, about the dangers of letting a stockroom become too cluttered. We talked about comparing sales figures from year to year, and we talked about how to manage a staff of salesclerks. We talked about statistics, which sailed right over my head. Everything sounded exciting. I purchased a briefcase, swung it passionately while walking up and down the streets of Manhattan.

One afternoon I spotted a girl in the cafeteria, smiled across tables at her. She smiled back. We finally met on the elevator. She had hazel eyes, creamy skin, perfect little teeth. She was lovely. Gloria hailed from, of all places, Springfield, Ohio, a mere fifty miles west of Columbus. I felt the twitch of destiny. She worked on the first floor of Macy's, in cosmetics. It took several days to wangle a date. I laid a white rose on her cosmetics counter; her back was turned. She turned, saw the rose, saw me, said yes to a date. Hot chocolate at a small diner near Macy's; it was freezing outside. Sitting there, talking about Columbus, about Springfield, she glowed; maybe we both glowed. Time passed, and sweetly. She invited me back to her apartment. It was small but well furnished, on the West Side. I slept over, fell in love, visited often. I hung around the cosmetics section at Macy's, often enough for the silly store dicks to take notice of me. They did not know I was an executive in training, ensconced upstairs, high upstairs, in the corporate offices. I chuckled.

I began asking Gloria questions. I wanted to know how she could afford a West Side apartment working on commission in cosmetics at Macy's. It did not add up, and I wanted things to add up. Gloria confessed: she was being kept; the man who was keeping her actually lived in Europe, bopped into New York City now and then. The confession pained me, and we drifted apart. I grew lonely, missed her.

As our Macy's training came to an end, we braced to learn which store we'd be sent to. Everyone wanted Herald Square, the flagship store. Those thought to be future stars got Herald Square. Edward Finklestein, the Macy's guru, the man who had jazzed up Macy's, bringing in music and mirrors and glitz, was known to march through the Herald Square store, dispensing his eclectic takes on merchandise and managers. To be based at Herald Square was priceless, but the Queens Macy's was nothing to scoff at: volume was high, the store was busy. I wanted Herald Square; I'd settle for Queens; Long Island was my final choice.

No one wanted Flatbush, the Macy's in Brooklyn, known to be a dead-end posting, rumored to be soon closing, a kind of Siberia.

We gathered on the last day of our training program. We looked chipper, felt anxious. Only one of us — due to stress, we were told — had dropped out. Names were called, store assignments right after the names.

"Haygood, Flatbush."

I craned my neck, pretended I didn't hear what I heard, saw everyone in the class look at me. The assignments ended. I was the only one assigned to Flatbush. This was not the way to launch a promising Macy's career.

The Flatbush store was small and unattractive. The store manager, as bony as Abe Lincoln, ignored me. He sloped through the aisles of the store looking as if he did not have a care in the world. It was common knowledge that if you did not stick with a store after two eight-week trial periods, you were damaged goods, damaged beyond repair. I couldn't get liftoff from the runway at a store like Flatbush, and I knew it. The store was quiet, almost spooky. Brooklynites had lost their passion for their store. I stood around, stared. I wondered why the lights were so dim; I wondered about my career.

The Flatbush manager told me I would not be kept. "Don't take this hard," he said, his voice serene. I took it hard.

Days later, I was told I'd be transferred to the Macy's in Queens. I hoped, in heading out to the Queens store, to be placed in the Oriental rug department. Men's fashions would do as a second choice. The Queens Macy's was a large-volume store. It was also bright, sunny from the sunlight streaming in off Queens Boulevard.

I was told I could not have Oriental rugs because someone was already managing that department, and someone was also managing men's fashions. I was given the children's clothing department. Little jumpsuits, little knickers, little dresses.

Other executives told me of executives who had risen high at Macy's and whose careers had begun in children's. I wondered. Children's was located on the second floor. The salesclerks whom I managed were pleasant, matronly Queens ladies who often inquired about my personal life: Married? Single? Eating enough vegetables? How's Ohio? I liked the light in that store, the way it streamed in through the large windows. I went to work bouncily, a briefcase in one hand, a hardback copy of *The Stories of John Cheever* in the other. I read Cheever's short stories — "The Swimmer," "The Sorrows of Gin," "The Enormous Radio," "The Sutton Place Story" — more often than I read Macy's weekly reports of sales figures.

One morning, in a chipper mood, I instructed the salesclerks to put pink clothing on every child mannequin. Then I told them to move all the mannequins into the aisles, forcing shoppers to notice them. My department was wild with pink. For days it remained that way. I fussed with the mannequins, looking busy when I needed to look busy. A week later the store manager summoned me to his office. The previous week's sales figures, he said, were astounding. He sat at his desk, eyeing me, eyeing the sales figures and the very sales report I had not even bothered to look at. I had no idea what he was talking about. He told me I had found a home, a store. I would not be transferred again; I was being promoted to domestics — fine linens, towels, sheets, a much larger-volume area than children's. Puzzled, I could only smile and thank him. We shook hands, a confident and cocky handshake, a go-out-and-sell-a-million-towels handshake. I walked from his office, proud of the click of my own shoes.

After three weeks, I knew I was lost. In too deep. Semi-weekly reports were due, to be handed in to buyers in Manhattan, zipped through interoffice pouches. I was late with my reports. Buyers screamed at me over the phone; I stuttered back; they interpreted my stuttering as an attempt to hide the truth, to hide what I didn't know. Elizabeth Calderone, a fellow manager, came to my rescue. She helped me with my reports, explained the statistics to me. Elizabeth wore flat-soled shoes, had a short-cropped flapper hairdo from the 1920s, eschewed makeup, and was no-nonsense. She loved retailing, took easily to the hurly-burly, the long hours, the shoppers, the jing of the cash register, the semiweekly reports. On days when our reports were due, or days when the store manager was on one of his walking rounds through my department, Elizabeth would come looking for me. Often she'd find me in my stockroom, at my little desk, beneath a naked light bulb, reading not sales reports but the stories of John Cheever. I'd rise up like a grunt soldier at boot camp eyeing a colonel. Once it was a buyer from Manhattan who showed up. He saw my stockroom, a mess, but I tried to explain — the mess had been there before I arrived. He screamed anyway, said it was now my responsibility. I stuttered. And this he did not like. And so he kept screaming.

A new store manager, Janet, arrived. I was happy. With a new manager there would be a grace period. I planned to buckle down, learn statistics, clear my stockroom. Janet smiled quietly, was forever twirling a piece of jewelry around her neck as she stood making mental notes. She had a New

England accent and a lisp. Her lips were thin and lifeless. She began asking me for reports, began badgering me with questions that I did not have answers for. She wanted to know about "projections," about "gross," about "net."

Janet summoned me to her office after work one day. She closed the door. She said she wasn't happy with my work, wondered if I understood the weekly buyer reports, questioned whether I wanted to rise to be a Macy's buyer. I told her there was nothing in the world I wanted more than to be a Macy's buyer.

"No you don't," she said, too quick for comfort, her tight lips tightening, a shark's grin surfacing.

Janet said she wanted me to start thinking about what I wanted to do in life. She told me to go home and write it out, give it to her. And she told me my Macy's career was over. Twirling her necklace, grinning her tight little New England grin; I did not like her at all. Then she said that she liked me; many people in the store liked me, she said. I would not be fired right away, I would be given two months to look for another job. I asked for another chance. She shook her head in silence.

That night, alone in my Brooklyn apartment, I stopped fooling myself. I genuinely wondered what I wanted to do. I could not latch on to retailing. The only thing I had liked, had enjoyed doing, since college, was writing: people, stories, the gathering up of life's moments. I wanted to write, and I wrote that down on lined paper and fell asleep.

I applied for jobs at Lord & Taylor, at Saks. But they had my number and didn't plan to hire me. The eight weeks passed in a blur, and then I was out of a job. I walked the streets of Manhattan, went to jazz clubs, saw movies, told not a soul back in Columbus that I had been fired.

I lolled around; days flicked by. One Saturday afternoon

a man approached me in Greenwich Village. He asked me where I was from; before I could answer, he said I could make some money; before I could say I was busy, would be on my way, a woman joined us. The talk was fast, silky. He wanted me to hold a wad of money; she didn't want me to trust him; she told me to give her my wallet, so she could show me how to conceal it. This was the moment when I decided to unspool my own thin line of larceny. I smelled them and their little game. I was nobody's hick. I was Macaroni's brother, not some rube from the sticks. I'd play their little con game and make off with their money. I watched every move they made, the exchange of wallets, the shifty eyes. Giddiness entered my body. I looked around. We were to meet in twenty minutes at a bar they pointed out, across the street, a bar I had no intention of ever entering. They flitted away. When they were out of sight, I checked my wallet, pulled the crisp dollar bills out — only they were not dollar bills, they were fake, any fool could see, and I howled, turned on my heels, needed a policeman, slumped on a stoop, realized I could not tell a policeman. What exactly would I say? I shook my head, studied my hands, felt ashamed. I called my friend Elizabeth, my Macy's colleague. Elizabeth taxied to the Village, sat down, consoled me, then told me I knew better, asked me why in the world I had trusted strangers, told me it would be all right, gave me money to get home to Brooklyn.

The days stretched out, long and sad. My rent was late, and I crept past my landlady's first-floor apartment. She'd open the door just a crack, the chain still hooked, and harangue me about my late rent. I called Columbus, my friend Flan, and told him of my miseries, wondered what I'd do. Two days later Flan was at my front door, having driven all through a single night. He said he had come to take me home: more than a friend. I left the crate and dining table and mattress in my apartment. Flan and I lifted only what we could carry in one long-strided dash to his car. He gunned the engine, and I escaped from Manhattan without saying goodbye to a soul.

We drove around mountains and through tunnels. Then came the flat earth of Ohio, the land and place I knew.

Back home in Columbus, everyone wondered what had happened to my acting career, to my Macy's job. I ignored them mostly. Jimmy, my grandfather, scolded me: "Pay your bills," he said. Creditors had been looking for me.

I took a job working nights, a kind of twenty-four-hour social service hotline. Men and women called searching for food; battered women called looking for emergency shelter. The offices were in the basement of an apartment building. But I wanted to write. I wanted to flee Columbus again. When I told my mother I wanted to bolt, she stared at me in silence. She wanted me to stay put. Jimmy simply wished for me to keep working. He never wanted to see me unemployed again.

I wrote to the editor of the *Charleston Gazette* in West Virginia, begging for a job. I had never set foot in West Virginia. The editor wrote back, invited me for an interview. I boarded a Trailways bus that smelled like urine. The bus zoomed across the Appalachian border, over the Ohio border, and into West Virginia. The hills were steep, the wind strong — it was late autumn. A huge chandelier hung in the lobby of the *Charleston Gazette* building. An elderly woman sat behind the reception desk, her hair as silver as new dimes. The antique chairs looked like ornaments. Glass climbed the walls, and a wide staircase led upstairs. It all reeked of antebellum. This was quite different from the creaky stairs of the *Call & Post*.

During the interview, the editor, smoking a cigarette, bespectacled, full of good cheer, told me there were no writing jobs open. There might, however, be an opening soon for a copy editor — someone to edit reporters' stories. I took the copy editing test. The editor graded it while I waited outside his office. I performed well, and he told me that if any openings occurred soon, he'd hire me. Spelling seemed to be a crucial part of the test. Back at Weinland Park Elementary, I had won a couple spelling bees.

Don Marsh, the editor, called me two months later.

Seven months after dragging myself home to Columbus, I bolted again. Elvira and Jimmy and Emily did not know quite what to make of me: I came, I went; they just kept loving me, wishing me well.

When I reached Charleston — again by bus — I took a room downtown, at the Daniel Boone Hotel. It was roomy, and full of faded glamour and elegance. The Kennedy campaign had been headquartered there during the tense 1960 Kennedy-Nixon contest. That was the contest in which West Virginians — old newsreels showed grainy faces, hollow cheeks, soulful looks — kicked the old Catholic taboo in the teeth, giving Kennedy his victory. He later repaid the debt by sending scores of antipoverty workers and programs into the state. The hallways of the Daniel Boone were noiseless and spooky.

In the newsroom I sat at the copy desk, surrounded by a bitter woman, a recovering alcoholic, three bitter men, a hippie who rode an expensive bicycle down a mountain to work, and Moo, who was thin, mean, pinched, and our boss. Everyone hated him except the bitter woman, who professed to understand him. These were wordsmiths, fact-checkers, trivia buffs, and they welcomed me.

After a week at the Daniel Boone, paying my own expenses, worrying about going broke before I received my first paycheck, I moved out and rented a room in a large Victorian home on Quarrier Street. The owner, a gray-haired lady, had fallen on hard times. Her husband had died; her son had lost his job; the sky had fallen. She explained this to me in a hushed voice, her hands clasped together like magnets. Her house was full of antique furniture, mirrors, porcelain, real silverware. My bed, framed in a lovely burnished red wood, was too small, though the quilts that covered it were warm and cozy. After two weeks she asked me to leave, said I was too noisy, said I came in too late, said I had had company and she did not want her rooming guests to have company. She said all of this to me in a hushed voice.

I finally found my own apartment, located in an old World War II building just off the Kanawha River. It was a studio apartment equipped with a Murphy bed, the kind you pull down from the wall, the kind you see in Three Stooges movies. The springs creaked furiously.

Each morning I walked three blocks to the lovely old gold-domed capitol. The cafeteria was supposed to be for state employees, but no one ever bothered you if you went there. The biscuits and cooked apples were delicious.

The man walking fast through the *Gazette* newsroom, blue-eyed and sockless, thin and wired, loud of voice, was Ned Chilton, the publisher — and the town's best-known eccentric and liberal. Chilton had made his name in the 1950s, writing scathing editorials against J. Edgar Hoover and his FBI. (Chilton convinced me to write scathing editorials; I wrote mine against Ronald Reagan.) Hoover kept a file on the newspaper. Chilton, who looked either completely Gatsbyesque or completely Abbie Hoffmanish, had attended Yale, where one of his closest friends had been William F. Buckley, Jr. After Yale, Buckley went right, Chilton left.

Edward Peeks, the business editor of the *Gazette* and also

the only other black on the staff, introduced himself shortly after my arrival. A courtly man who spoke in a Georgian drawl, he invited me to his home for dinner. His home was small and elegant; his wife, Yankee, busied herself in the kitchen, where food simmered on the stove. The house smelled southern, rich, like Sunday. Peeks was the kind of man who wore a hat outdoors, opened doors for men and women alike, and had a shot of bourbon before dinner. The meal was delicious, served in candlelight. Afterward, Peeks and I sauntered to his study, which was full of books, a manual typewriter. He lit a cigar and offered me one: no thanks. He had taken a graduate degree from Northwestern, had come up on southern black newspapers, where he had covered the civil rights movement with distinction. He rose and pulled a book from his bookshelf, a book he had written. I'd never met an author before, and was genuinely awed. The old reporter spoke fondly of Martin and Malcolm and the marches he had trailed and covered in those jittery starlit southern towns. When Chilton hired Peeks, some KKK ruffians had threatened to march on the newspaper. It roiled the publisher's blood; he let the anti-KKK editorials fly. Peeks, seated in his study, his voice marinated by bourbon, the memories warm, offered me a drink. Sometimes I wished I drank, at least had a taste for it, especially that evening, but drinking scared me the way the dark scares a child.

David Lieber became my best friend at the *Gazette*. He was a New Yorker who had come to Charleston by way of Fort Myers, Florida, where he had been fired for threatening to beat up the managing editor of a newspaper he worked for. There was a parting of the ways, and David drove his skyblue Volkswagen to Charleston. He was short and as tough as a hammer. He fancied himself an investigative reporter, hit Charleston in full stride, and proceeded to write exposés that brought down civic officials and errant politicians. The more politicians hated him, the better he liked it. As an undergraduate at the University of Pennsylvania, he had gotten city officials in trouble from his perch as a columnist for the student newspaper. In Charleston, David argued with his editors, worked on his days off, and saved every story he wrote.

David loaned me a hundred dollars to buy a stereo at a downtown pawnshop. Together we listened to Sinatra, Harry James, Tommy Dorsey. When Harry James, on his last leg as a bandleader, swung through Charleston, I was there, in a huge ballroom with dark floors, to write about it. James, his neck like chicken skin, was suave and snapped his fingers coolly, directing his band. There was a lush redhead on vocals, as in some jazzy movie. After the gig, James gave me an interview. He seemed indifferent, bored.

My friends and I sat inside Fitzgerald's, a bar overlooking the Kanawha River, and listened to Mike Fowler, a huge white man who sang like a black man. We tried picking up actresses traveling through town on the dinner-theater circuit. Jack McCarthy struck gold one night: the actress stood six feet, wore a red wig (Jack told us the next morning), had a man's voice and a sexy body. I dated a temperamental schoolteacher. I liked her more than she liked me. We spent a weekend at the publisher's log cabin, high in the West Virginia mountains. It was rustic, and not without elegance. We made love, argued about little things, suffered through some of our meals in absolute silence.

David and I drove around West Virginia through winter and spring in his VW Beetle, looking for stories. We drove through mountains and hollows, along riverbeds and creeks, down through gullies, in and out of towns where darkness came quickly in the evening and the locals stared at us as though we were aliens.

David convinced me to ride with him to the Moundsville State Penitentiary. He had a story to do, suggested I write about an inmate's lawsuit. I wore a bow tie. In the car on the way to the state pen, David suggested I take the bow tie off, said it would send the wrong signal to inmates. He meant to say the bow tie was a little effete. I did not want trouble with any of the Moundsville inmates, so I removed my tie. When we got there, Warden Bordenkircher leaned across his desk and offered both of us a bit of helpful information. "Don't get too close to the bars," he said. "There's inmates in here who'll snatch your eyeballs out for a pack of cigarettes." His voice was hard, full of cigarette smoke. His guards took us down to death row. A German shepherd came along. The death row cons looked like albinos: no sun. They whispered words I couldn't quite make out; they stared, pitiful stares, evil stares, sad stares.

I wrote enough stories at the *Gazette* to land me a job in Pittsburgh, at the *Post-Gazette*, as a full-time writer. On the eve of my moving from Charleston to Pittsburgh, my twin sister showed up at my apartment to help me. She had rumbled from Columbus to Charleston in a bulky white truck driven by her boyfriend, James Brown, some two-bit soul singer from Columbus (and no relation to the real singing James Brown) who I never liked. But I had a new job; she wanted me to get to Pittsburgh; we loaded my belongings in the truck that James Brown used to travel in with his band and rode onward. I asked them not to smoke dope while driving, because it made me nervous. "That's cool," James Brown said, almost singing the two words out. I wanted to give him some money for moving me. My sister stopped me: "No, you don't. Save your money."

In Pittsburgh I covered collapsing steel towns, murders, fires. I broke some stories and itched for a job at the *Boston*

Globe. It was a writer's paper; writers bragged about the space they got. I sent money home to Jimmy, my grandfather. Later, my grandmother told me he had bragged on me, had also spent that very money on the horses, on the dogs when dog racing was in season. Harry also bragged on me, wrongly telling folks that I had had a "tryout" at the *Wall Street Journal.* Right metaphor, wrong team: in 1985 I landed a job with the *Globe.* It was actually a three-month trial, tightrope walking, but I survived. There were many stories, many trips across America, writing about farmers, the Deep South, passions along the Mississippi River, crime and punishment in L.A. There were travels abroad to write of foreign places. I had found a vocation. I hoped to stay put, to rein in my animal instinct to cut and run. I sat and wrote a book.

Then the calls began from my brother Harry, now out in Los Angeles. He needed money — no, not by mail, mail would take too long, use Western Union. There had been arguments between Macaroni and Harry, arguments over money, failure to keep promises, trickery. There were more calls, from San Francisco, from my sister Geraldine, who had also left Columbus to join Macaroni, to take part in his schemes. Geraldine suffered badly in San Francisco — she was too soft, too weak — and called crying for money to go home. I'd walk to the Western Union in Boston and wire my brother money. I'd walk again to wire my sister money.

Then the calls ceased. I went back to trying to finish a book, my second. But my sister Diane phoned, worried about Harry and Macaroni. Had I heard from them recently? No, I had not, and was grateful not to. Diane called again. She had not heard from either in eight months, then a year. I told her they were grown men, they would get in touch when they wanted to get in touch. She did not believe it, feared something was wrong — "For all I know, Macaroni could be dead out in

California, under a bridge someplace." My sister didn't say it, she merely hinted it: if Macaroni, tough, wily, shrewd, was dead, then worse could be imagined for Harry. She hinted that I should go west, look for both Harry and Macaroni. But I wanted to stay put. At night I tossed and turned in bed, felt my stomach tighten, blamed my family for bothering me, for making me lose concentration as I tried to bring my book across the finish line. I cursed. Then I bought a plane ticket and flew west to look for my brothers.

I needed help in that land of palm trees and desperadoes and dreamers. Marty Berg and Jerry Roberts, newspaper friends living in Los Angeles, helped me find Harry. We had no luck with probation officers, L.A. County jail officials, ex-girlfriends, former drinking buddies. Homeless shelters were plastered with notices: "Harry Haygood. Please call home. Wil, your brother." It turned out that Harry, with the killer smile, the wonderful wardrobe, whom I had last seen at the L.A. airport in a sunny suit and a pair of sunglasses sixteen months earlier, was now living on Skid Row, sleeping in a huge carton, the kind refrigerators are packaged in. On chilly nights, he kept warm by a bonfire. He spoke bitterly of Macaroni, had no idea where he was. It turned out that Macaroni was further north, on San Francisco Bay. He had, in fact, a beautiful view from the Marin County hills. He could see the rise of the ocean every morning; he could hear foghorns from the ferry — all that from the west wing cellblock of San Quentin Penitentiary. But how happy my family was: the brothers Haygood were at least alive.

Still, I couldn't help but wonder how the things done in the dark had finally caught up with my two brothers, as my grandmother Emily had always warned they would — and finally came to light.

13

I LOOK BACK and realize that of all my family members, only one was always chipper, constantly up, the heartiest of the hearty. You could hear Macaroni's voice, his laugh, rumbling from behind the bar of his speakeasies. He meant to be heard, he meant to play to the back of the auditorium, and he did. On cloudy days even, Macaroni was ever so sunny. He had reasons — more than anyone else in my family, perhaps — to become bitter. Being alone in the world can scar a soul, and he had become accustomed to being alone — first in the Georgia woods, then in Columbus, then in the boys' reformatory, then in prison. But he never looked back, never entertained self-pity, so it was full throttle ahead.

He was not always brave, but more often than not he was fearless. And he learned how to take care of himself, to turn doubters into believers. On his probation reports, in the space where he was always asked what kind of job he was holding or planned to get, he'd write one thing: salesman. What kind of salesman? Used clothing. Albums. Jewelry. All lies, but his probation officers could picture him as a salesman, so they would take him at his word and believe him. "Your brother is suave," a probation officer who was befuddled by yet another one of Macaroni's schemes told me, "but also pathetic." The word "pathetic" made me wince.

In another time he might well have been a haberdasher. He also had the gift of gab, and there were many who told him he should have gone into politics, a subject that he often held intelligent discussions about. "So, what do you think about Ross Perot?" he blindly asked me one day. I thought there might be more pressing matters to discuss, inasmuch as he had just been released from a prison camp. But before Macaroni had a chance to follow the straight and narrow, the zigzagging had already begun, and he found it impossible to turn back, more rewarding to soldier onward.

Macaroni did not head straight for California in 1977 when he fled Columbus. He first surfaced in New York City. Calvin Ferguson, the pimp who considered Macaroni his protégé and who had been run out of Columbus by the feds, promised to help him get a start in Manhattan. Ferguson had an apartment near Madison Square Garden. He had women, and he gave each of them a Mustang to scoot around the city in. Ferguson also gave Macaroni the use of a Mustang — and a twenty-dollar bill whenever he needed it.

Manhattan was noisy and crowded; Macaroni felt right at home, a smart hustler in an ever hustling city. He walked around the city, leaning on telephone poles, his hands mischievously clasped behind his back as if he were handcuffed: "I was out on the street, I was sharp, I was looking around." He spotted a young lady hanging around Madison Square Garden, realized she was a pickpocket, introduced himself by letting her know he knew she was a pickpocket. He wanted to know if she'd be interested in a partner. After talking things over, after learning that Macaroni was from Ohio (did she think him a hayseed? a rube?), after deciding there was nothing this strange man from Ohio could do for her that she couldn't do for herself, she told Macaroni no thanks. That was always the given in his line of work: on some, his silky words worked; others thought them ludicrous and stopped themselves just short of laughter. He kept his feet to the pavement, hustling through the darkness.

Parts of the city reminded him of Mt. Vernon Avenue. But the women he met didn't wish to join his personal crusade. It was risky stealing another man's women: you could get slashed, you could get shot. Macaroni never wanted to get hurt. He was lucky to have a place, for the time being, rent-free. Vera belonged to Calvin, and Calvin told Vera to let Macaroni stay with her for a while. It was strictly platonic. Vera found him funny, a charmer. "He was amusing," she told me. But she said that Macaroni made the mistake of believing he could live off his Columbus reputation in New York City. He was a midnight cowboy in a town that ate up midnight cowboys from the Midwest. "He lacked fortitude," said Vera.

One day Vera's rent money came up missing. She looked around. Macaroni was the only suspect. There were arguments. She wanted her money back. He said he didn't take it. The smile and the jokes and the charm no longer worked. It was agreed that Macaroni should leave Manhattan.

He boarded a bus at the Port Authority Terminal — would have preferred flying, but he had to watch his money, never knew where the next twenty-dollar bill might come from — and rolled toward Columbus, his broad shoulders hunched against the glass windows, his spirits as high as ever — no, higher. The joy was always in the rebound, the comeback, the reappearance from the dark tunnel. There was plenty of

The gallant MACARONI. *He took these two ladies
to Los Angeles to sell, among other things,
fried ice cream.*

America out there to enjoy and explore. He remained in Columbus long enough to pack. Then he vanished again.

This time he wasn't traveling alone. Never again would he go into a strange town without women, without a team. Their names were Linda and Jamie, and they held to Macaroni like weak shipmates holding on to their strong sea captain. This time he was flying. Everyone was giddy: plenty of money out there in California.

When Macaroni stepped off the plane in L.A. in 1978, it was he, Linda, Jamie, and his Afghan, well coifed as always. In photographs I have of their arrival, they look as loose as gypsies. Macaroni didn't want anything to do with Watts. Politically astute, he knew Watts had been shell-shocked. There was no money flowing through Watts. He took his entourage over to Wilshire Boulevard, Hollywood. "When you go to a strange town," he says, "you just check into a hotel and act like you been there all your life." He immediately liked the smell of Hollywood, the scent.

They found a cozy motel, the kind of place where the desk clerk didn't ask too many questions and didn't give a damn about the dog. Macaroni paid in advance, cash. Jamie and Linda went to work right away, strolling La Cienega Boulevard near the Wilshire district, disappearing into cheap motel rooms with men who had potbellies, men who had dirt rings around their shirt collars, lonely men. In case there was trouble, Macaroni waited out of sight, leaning on a palm tree, shaded. He looked up old friends from Columbus, slapped backs, flashed his money and smile. Before long, there was a lot of laughter. And the money started to roll in, plenty of it. Macaroni found California easy. "I used to tell people I could sell fried ice cream in California," he says.

He figured it was best to move every couple months, and so they did, from motel to motel, the dog barking and prancing. They'd stay a while in Westwood, then they'd pack up on the spur of the moment and head over to Culver City, staying in forgettable motels, cheap curtains but central air, eating their meals in fast-food restaurants, and looking over their shoulders. Once, flush with money from a scam — the john had been robbed — they moved to a motel out in Marina del Ray, "so I could be by the water," Macaroni says.

The scams worked well. Wallets were lifted; johns were

hustled; checks were forged; stolen goods were fenced; then there they would be — Macaroni, Linda, Jamie — collapsing on a bed, laughing, howling, counting their money in the land of fried ice cream. They zoomed up and down and around the Los Angeles hills, sucking in the long fragrant nights. Macaroni loved basketball, so they'd go see the Los Angeles Lakers at the Forum. He didn't want to sit just anyplace in that cavernous place; he had his eye on ringside seats. Dwight Lamar had played basketball at East High School in Columbus; now he was a member of the Lakers. Lamar knew Macaroni from Columbus. In Columbus the athletes respected the hustlers and the hustlers respected the athletes, often showing up at their games in memorable outfits, with women, waving. Macaroni contacted Lamar, asked for tickets. My brother expected people to be kind to him, and they were. Lamar would leave the tickets at the box office window, and Macaroni would strut around the Forum like a rooster, taking a seat, crossing his legs, checking out the crowd for any potential marks. He liked this: the crowd, the coliseum, the good seats, the television lights, his own rootlessness, every day an adventure.

Things were going so well that Macaroni encouraged our brother Harry to join him on the West Coast. Harry wanted to get out of Ohio, and Macaroni told him of the easy money to be made in L.A. Harry flew west with no promises of a job of any kind. His two suitcases were full of elegant dresswear. And there they were, under the sun, two thin Ohio bulls scratching at the California dirt.

What was there to do in the beginning but feel the warmth of the California sun and make jokes about the cold Columbus winters? And that is just what Harry and Macaroni did together. But they were different, and they had always been different. Macaroni had reached his fork in the road years back. He knew as much as he would ever know about human nature, about making easy money, about taking risks. He was already full of a thief's courage, a gambler's instincts, a gentleman's honed table manners, an intellectual's curiosity. Harry was intrigued with the fanciful life, but also a little frightened by its danger. He had not yet been pushed to the fork in the road, the do-or-die equation. Harry wished, in the beginning, to stay on the right side of the law. He wished to get into the entertainment business. So he marched right to the seaside home of our cousin, the Academy Award–winning actor Louis Gossett.

Helen Gossett, Louis's mother, and my father, Jack, were first cousins. Eddie Bee Ray, Helen's mother, was my grandfather Julius's sister. Though Lou was raised mostly in New York City after his family left Georgia, his mother often took him back to Georgia, where he played as a child with my aunts and uncles, his cousins. He starred on the New York stage, did episodic television, won an Emmy for his sterling work in *Roots*, then an Oscar for *An Officer and a Gentleman*. Harry, always itchy, always full of animation, thought nothing of approaching him, despite our sister Diane's urgings toward caution and good manners. "He's family!" Harry would thunder back.

As it turned out, Lou liked hearing from extended family members. He invited Harry out to his mansion in Malibu. Harry liked the mansion, the art and decorations, the wide windows, the ocean beyond the windows, the drinks he lifted from the tray held by Lou's maid. Soon enough, Harry was running errands for Lou. When Lou moved from one swell home to another, always by the water, Harry helped him. Harry also introduced Lou to Macaroni. While Harry looked up to Lou, Macaroni looked sideways at him, believing that little separated him and the Oscar-winning actor except luck and chance. "I didn't need his hundred-dollar bills," Macaroni says.

Harry told Lou he also wanted to act. My brother had no theatrical training. He wanted to slide easily into the business. Lou's long climb — stage, TV, the cutthroat world of getting movie roles, the sacrifice — fazed Harry not at all. Lou's Oscar gleamed; Lou was starring in his own television series, *The Lazarus Syndrome*. Lou told Harry he'd arrange for an audition. Harry was thrilled, imagined playing third or fourth banana to Lou, good money, the coveted Screen Actors Guild card. Lou meant an audition as an extra — a figure in a crowd scene, a classroom, someone hustling across the street. My brother complained that he didn't have time to go stand in a cattle-call line all day for a role where he wouldn't even have a speaking part. Distraught, he forgot about acting. (He did get his photograph in a national entertainment magazine, though. It was a movie premiere, and there's my brother, just over Lou's shoulder, nearly out of sight, smiling a movie star smile, happy.)

Harry got a job for a stationery company in Los Angeles. He drifted back into Macaroni's world. The competition between the brothers continued. Macaroni wanted to lead, Harry refused to follow. Scams were plotted, only to go awry, each blaming the other. Fists were balled, angry words exchanged, threats made. So they stopped seeing each other, went their separate ways. Both began to drift from the family radar.

Macaroni began to lose his focus, his sharpness, for heroin had entered the picture. With a heroin habit, he needed more money. The scams became riskier. More pressure was put on Linda and Jamie. Linda was the first to balk, to complain. Finally she left and returned to Ohio. And Jamie had to take more chances. The motels were seedier and seedier; now any john would do. The credit card scams — ordering credit cards to be sent to a particular post office box, then making off with them — began to backfire. Using the post office was a federal offense, and the FBI began snooping. Macaroni barely eluded the FBI's knock at one motel door. That was enough for Jamie; she too fled back to Ohio. The Afghan was turned loose to roam the streets of Los Angeles. Things were going bad. Time for Macaroni to hit the road: "I'm not one to stick around when somebody's looking for me."

He thought of places to go. Columbus was out of the question: too many ghosts, not to mention an old arrest warrant. He thought of Phoenix, but he had gone there briefly once, had a bad time, had to bolt. He had always heard San Francisco was a city of opportunity. "It's where the degenerates go, thieves, pimps. And the homosexuals are a liberal group. It's sin city," he explains. So he headed north, up the rocky coast.

Macaroni arrived in San Francisco in the winter of 1985. He liked the town right away, its hills, the bohemians, the trust in the eyes of so many people. He moved from cheap motel to cheap motel. He tracked down Bob Kirkland, a friend from Columbus, borrowed money from him, and kept moving, waltzing around the city like a tourist. He'd case jewelry stores, stroll through the lobbies of the fancy hotels up on Nob Hill, peer into the windows of clothing stores and make mental notes of the distance between door, shirt case, and security guard. In Los Angeles he had considered himself too classy for Watts, the grittier slice of that city. Here, in San Francisco, low on money, high on humility, he made his way to Haight-Ashbury, home to hippies, poets, crooks, socialists, dreamers, fascists, writers. "But it was that beautiful cut of clouds I could always see above the little S.P. alley, puffs floating by from Oakland or the Gate of Marin to the north or San

Jose south, the clarity of Cal to break your heart. It was the fantastic drowse and drum hum of lum mum afternoon nathin' to do, ole Frisco with end of land sadness — the people — the alley full of trucks and cars of businesses nearabouts and nobody knew or far from cared who I was all my life three thousand five hundred miles birth-O opened up and at last belonged to me in Great America": these are the words and the missed commas of the rootless Jack Kerouac, meant, maybe, for all the Macaronis in the world.

There was something else about Haight-Ashbury that appealed to Macaroni. It was the kind of place where a wanted man, a man on the run looking to make some quick cash without doing anything that involved brawn, might try his chances. Macaroni realized what he had become: a pimp without a car or women who believed in his gospel. That was the down side. The up side was, he was a man standing above a twinkling city unfolding before him.

The gentleman loping into the Cable Car Museum, stuffing items for later sale into his pockets; the gentleman going into the import and export shops over on Post Avenue — noticed, but never as a thief, only as a gentleman — and slipping silky things beneath his long coat; the gentleman waltzing into the first-class Fairmont Hotel, picking up unattended suitcases and walking out the door with them, as calm as a bellhop, then vanishing around a corner; the gentleman streaking down a side street over in Pacific Heights, a shopkeeper on his heels — the shopkeeper yelling for the police, cursing, but never catching up with him because his long legs were quick as a deer's: Macaroni.

Soon my sister Geraldine joined Macaroni. They schemed together. Of my family members, Geraldine at times has struck me as the most difficult to gauge. In Columbus, after high school, she worked, learned computers, married a good man — a factory worker — furnished her house with white furniture and sky-blue carpet. Not my style, but I was happy she was happy. Socially astute, she befriended lawyers, doctors, nurses, movers and shakers. She wrote jingles for radio commercials. She could quote passages from the Pulitzer Prize–winning poet Gwendolyn Brooks's "Annie Allen."

Then she changed, grew bored with her lifestyle, grew bored with her job, skipped work, popped pills. Eventually she lost her job and her husband. Some of the movers and shakers she befriended were mere frauds, some of the doctors quacks. The quacks supplied her with pills. Her hubris forced her from Columbus; Macaroni welcomed her to San Francisco. For a while their schemes worked well — forging checks, selling prescription pills, thievery. But there were arguments, there was too much scuffling. It ended one night when Geraldine called me in Boston, crying to me to wire her money to get back to Columbus. She had had enough of Macaroni, and she had had enough of San Francisco. Macaroni had had enough of Geraldine. Macaroni could survive out in the cold world. Geraldine could not.

The weak and soft-hearted found it easy to listen to Macaroni about life, his wanderings. He worked a few months in a low-class bar in the Hunter's Point section of the city, near Candlestick Park. He hung around the Hayes-Valley housing project in Haight-Ashbury. He was just the kind of man Lavonne Larry's father had warned her about all her life: a man who didn't work, who talked about a lot of things he didn't have, who appeared cheerful even as the storm circled. Which is why she had married a good working man, the kind of man who was not going to disrupt her sleep with errant behavior. She first saw Macaroni from her porch, walking down the street. He didn't look desperate, on the run, wanted by the law. "You know Mac liked to go first class," she says. "First time I saw him, he was in a long black coat, leather pants." It wasn't a romantic attraction. Lavonne was honest in her marriage, though truth be told, the waters surrounding her and her husband had been roiling of late; but they were still on the same boat. Lavonne Larry was a church lady, gave people the benefit of the doubt. She sat and listened to strangers, as long as they realized she was a city lady and nobody's fool.

It was not long before she was snared by Macaroni, she and her husband both, listening to him, laughing at his tales, his life, appreciating his generosity. He'd bring things by, goodies for them, toys for the kids. He'd stay for supper. He'd empty his pockets, and bills would just fall out, and he'd ask if anyone at the table needed any money. "Take some," he'd say. He had a soft spot for kids, talked to them with clarity, talked up to them, which they adored. "The kids loved him," says Lavonne.

Macaroni found a little apartment down the street from Lavonne Larry and her husband. When her husband needed a pair of sneakers, hemmed and hawed about the high price of sneakers, Macaroni told him not to worry. He left and returned hours later with various shoe selections, sold them to the Larrys for a third of the retail price. He'd go over to "Japantown," and he'd steal silk dresses, silk scarves, sell some to Lavonne and throw in something for free. He'd show up with Harley-Davidson leather jackets, holding them up to the light, pulling Lavonne or her sons out of their chairs, forcing them to try the jackets on, telling them before the final sleeve had been slipped on how good they looked in that jacket. Once he called Lavonne from the Fairmont Hotel. He was in a room with a girl, had paid $125 for the room, was just now leaving the room, heading downstairs to see James Brown — the real James Brown — perform. He looked good and he felt good — Macaroni, not James Brown. Of course, it took nerve to show back at the Fairmont, the very hotel he sometimes stole luggage from. "He was bold," says Brenda, Lavonne's sister.

It was Brenda — whose antennae had responded more quickly than her sister's — who began suspecting that Macaroni was feeding a drug habit. Then he confessed about the heroin. They had had a family member suffer from drugs. They empathized, told him to pray. He said he would, then went in search of the next fix.

"Did he tell you I used to cook for him?" Lavonne asks me. We're sitting at her dining room table in her San Francisco home. There's a Mahalia Jackson CD atop a TV stand. "I'd make sure he would eat."

Lavonne tells me that sometimes Macaroni would come to her house and begin looking for a scarf, a rag, anything to tie his arm in a sling. It hurt from shooting up the heroin. Then he'd show up a day later, looking like a different man, cleaned up, his vowels easy to understand. He'd have stuffed animals for the kids. He'd have football hats for Lavonne and her husband, and tubes of fragrant body lotions — stuff he'd picked up on the way out of the drugstore, easy stuff to steal, especially the lotions. Then there were times when he would ring Lavonne's door at two in the morning. He'd have scarves draped over his arms, and he'd be standing there asking her in a rushed voice if she wanted to buy some silk scarves, any price. She'd fuss with him; her husband would be calling from the back room; lamplight from the street would lie through the doorway, straight as a snake. "Macaroni, why you coming here so late?" she'd ask, positioning the scarves nearer to the light. He'd start to smile, at her and against the darkness, and he'd ask about the kids, knowing full well they were asleep, had been asleep for hours, but he always asked about the kids. "One Christmas," says Lavonne, "we didn't have to buy anything." Macaroni bought all the toys. A merry Macaroni Christmas.

There were times when he'd lie on the floor, high, dreamy, and get to talking about his family back in Columbus. "He'd talk about his sister Diane, always about Diane, and about the brother who was a writer," says Lavonne. They could never tell if he was telling the truth, she says, if there actually was a family in some faraway place called Columbus. Why, when he told them he used to be a big-time pimp, they laughed; when he told them he used to drive a brand-new Lincoln Continental, they laughed. They laughed, in fact, at all of his memories and loved him just as he was.

Once the police stopped him a block from a drugstore and pulled stolen goods from his pockets. Nickel-and-dime thievery, so they shoved him around, told him to beat it, didn't even run a check on him. They'd have found little or nothing; he was traveling under several aliases. The more desperate he grew, the more mistakes he made. Then the arrests began. He found himself downtown, at the local jail, awaiting a possible prison sentence for stealing and forgery. Lavonne had a brother in the police department. She pleaded with him to check up on Macaroni. Macaroni was fine, was writing letters to the judge, begging not to be sent to San Quentin. The judge dispatched social workers from the renowned Delancey Street Drug Rehabilitation Center to interview him for possible admittance to the program.

The Delancey Street drug center had a national reputation. It gave ex-cons and struggling drug addicts another chance, albeit just one. Its motto was trust. There were businesses run by those staying at the Delancey Street facilities — a restaurant, a store. There were no bars at the drug center, no gnawing sense of confinement. Macaroni charmed the social workers, found himself two weeks later at Delancey Street, noticed there were no bars, were lax rules. In three weeks he was gone, having fled into the darkness one evening. When the police found him, he was quickly whisked back to the San Francisco County Jail on Bryant Avenue and was finally on his way to San Quentin to serve a one-year sentence.

He did not like San Quentin, especially West Block. Prisoners in West Block are let out of their cells only one hour a day. Macaroni counted time by the Larkspur ferry, which left the San Francisco pier on the hour — a wooden ferry taking passengers home across the chilly waters below the Marin County hills, directly past the beige-colored buildings of San Quentin Penitentiary. (I took that same ferry once, passing San Quentin, noticing it as the ferry approached. In that California way of things, San Quentin, from the outside, did not look like a frightening place. Still, I could not have imagined myself inside.) Macaroni always bragged about the view from his cell, remembering the beauty.

Macaroni minded his business inside San Quentin, ran errands for the guards, was trusted. He got an early release, was placed on probation, then broke probation, drugging, stealing. This time he was sent to Soledad Prison for two years. For nearly a year of his Soledad sentence, he was sent into the hills of California to fight fires. The Mount Holmes Fire Camp was located just outside Fresno. Macaroni did not look lightly on the possibility of getting his flesh burned by raging brushfires, so he talked himself out of the actual running and climbing fire detail and became the fire camp cook. He'd go at any new task like a man possessed — until the boredom set in. And he cooked up a storm, drawing raves, making suggestions to guards on duty about how to save food, which food cooked better outside. After he had finished cooking for the day, he'd sit on the ground smoking cigarettes, relaxing, eating as much as he wanted while fires raged in the distance and other cons stormed the hills after them like free men. He'd write letters to Diane, and she'd send money. She'd send sneakers so he could shoot hoops.

Macaroni was released from Soledad into a halfway house in Oakland, near the Oakland Naval Shipyard. One evening, craving drugs, he walked up to the roof, one story up, and jumped. Gray had started to show in his hair, but he still had spring in his legs. He ran as fast as he could and disappeared. Then it all was put into yet another computer, and the search was on. In the old days, back in Columbus and Dayton, there had been no computers. Now everyone had computers, and he didn't have eyes in the back of his head. A month later Macaroni was on a bus, being sent back to prison, back to harsh San Quentin.

Inside San Quentin again, dodging the quick-tempered gang members, Macaroni talked himself into a job — shining the warden's shoes, running errands for the warden. His gentlemanly manners had always brought him extra favors, even in the most ruthless places. There were times, however, when he took his gift of gab further than it could go, and there were repercussions. He tried to serve as an intermediary between rival Mexican and black gangs during his second San Quentin stint. When a fracas broke out, an inmate lunged at Macaroni, stabbing him in the arm. He healed, sleeping the wound away by the rhythm and horn of the Larkspur ferry rolling by his cell.

His friends never totally abandoned him. Bob Kirkland, his best San Francisco friend, thought he knew why Macaroni was not able to make it there: "You have to be vicious to make it on the streets. Deep down inside, Mac's a nice guy. And people like him. In the penitentiary he'd stay out of trouble by talking all day long. He's always had the ability to charm people."

Before I left Lavonne and Brenda in San Francisco, I couldn't help but ask them why they had tolerated Macaroni, why they had made such allowances for him.

"He had class," said Lavonne.

"He'd share anything he had with you," said Brenda.

"He was crazy about the children, and the children were crazy about him," said Lavonne.

"He respected us as a family," said Brenda.

"He was always trying to lift your spirits up," said Lavonne.

"And Macaroni was just so much fun," said Brenda. "We really miss him. You had fun with Macaroni."

It pleased me no end to hear such good things about my half-brother. I had forgotten, myself, what fun he could be, had in fact always been; how he had sometimes made our family feel more like a family. Brenda and Lavonne rounded up pictures of their children before I left. "Give these to Macaroni when you see him," Brenda said.

Macaroni's fall seemed headlong, inevitable. The world he emerged from, he simply returned to. It was the fall of our brother Harry that shocked, that stunned. Macaroni had come to our family dining table late in my life; Harry had been there from the beginning.

There is not a shy soul among the Haygoods. And it is beyond debate that Harry has long been the most exuberant of these shy-less souls, the chief limelight-pursuer. It was Harry who yelled into Lou Gossett's outside intercom, and it was Harry who wouldn't go away. It was Harry who fell in love with Los Angeles, a city with so many delicacies — trapdoors? — that he lost himself in them. He liked the unbelievability of the city, cruising down the freeway heading for Beverly Hills, the palm trees swaying, the sun's glare kept from his eyes by sunglasses. Harry felt on top of himself, of Macaroni, of life. I

HARRY, ELVIRA, *and* JACK *in* 1987. *Harry was*
traveling cross-country with a rhythm-and-blues
group; when they hit Columbus, he gave
our parents first-class treatment.

slapped him on the back when visiting, sucked in by those
delicacies, my big brother, his surroundings.

I first visited Harry in Los Angeles in 1985. At the airport
he was in sunglasses, he was wearing linen, he was smiling, he
looked good. It was my first visit to California. Harry lived off
Martin Luther King Boulevard, on Harvard Street, where he
rented half of a double house. It was full of wicker; a fishnet
separated the front room from the bedroom; sunlight soaked
the place in daytime. We picked lemons from nearby trees and

made lemonade. I wondered if we were not stealing the lemons; Harry told me not to worry — "just keep walking." We ate large amounts of food for breakfast in diners, read the morning newspaper together. I was surprised how well my brother knew Los Angeles, the sidestreets, the freeway exits. He pulled up to a yellow-and-white house one morning, not more than five miles from his own house. Tall hedges circled it. The neighborhood was quiet. "That's where Marvin Gaye lived, where his father shot him," he said. We sat there, the engine idling, paying homage. (My cousins from Cincinnati told me that Harry gave them the same tour when they visited: Marvin's home, Lou Gossett's mansion, the Venice beach.) We drove up to Oxnard, to the beach, and ran in the water, laughed, splashed, laughed an afternoon away. I was proud of my brother.

A year later I visited again. Harry was late to the airport; one hour turned to two. When he arrived, he looked harried. He hugged me tight, as always, and he laughed hard, slipping the sunglasses back on.

I had come to the city for the *Boston Globe*, to do a story about a serial killer on the loose in the grittier sections of Los Angeles. John St. John, the detective working the case, was near retirement, had worked L.A. all his life. Nothing new anymore, just life's same miseries: he missed big band music, he missed Jackie Robinson and the L.A. Dodgers, he missed Bogart on the screen. He grabbed a drink at a dark bar. Inside the bar he pulled a three-inch stack of business cards from his jacket pocket. They were held together by a rubber band. He asked me for a business card, slipped the thing in the pile, put the stack back in his pocket. Then we rolled in his sedan through back alleys. He pointed out places the serial killer had struck. "Murder is murder," St. John said, "and blood still runs red." It sounded almost lyrical; it sounded like Raymond Chandler. I jotted it down.

Later that night, I told my brother I had to return to the places St. John had taken me. I needed to get a nighttime feel for the area. Since the killer had been killing prostitutes, I needed to interview prostitutes. Harry insisted on coming along. He stopped his car and I walked through the darkness, notebook in hand, near neon-lit motels, my brother edging the car slowly along, just out of view. When I was interviewing a stranger and the stranger's questions to me came faster than my questions to him, when his voice suddenly turned jumpy, my big brother jumped out of the car with the baseball bat he had insisted on bringing along. "Hey, he don't mean no harm," Harry said to the man, referring to me. His voice was even, and it also had an edge to it. "He's my brother. A reporter for the *Boston Globe*. He's just out here to do a story on this crazy motherfucking serial killer on the loose." Indeed.

Always my brother has been full of familial pride, ready bravado. And always he has been generous with family. But his generosity came at a price. The lovely stationery he sent me, those two dozen boxes? Of course they were a gift, from him to me. I was his brother; he knew how much I liked to write letters. But: "If you could spot me a hundred dollars, I'd appreciate it. I'll pay you back my next paycheck, two weeks. Hope you liked the stationery. Beautiful, ain't it?" It was thus with Harry: a gift today, a favor tomorrow.

In the fall of 1987 Harry made frantic phone calls to me at all hours of the night. He needed money. "I told you, I need it to pay some bills, then I'll be on my feet." I walked through rainy Boston nights, found Western Union, wired money, cursed at him through the rain and the dark. The calls didn't stop. Once he asked for five hundred dollars. I said no. Then four hundred dollars. By then I knew better. Harry was drinking. Harry was taking drugs. Harry was finally fired.

He lost his apartment. Then he was arrested — drunken driving. While he had been driving, drunk, he had smashed another car up. There were hordes of outstanding traffic tickets also. I reached him by letter at the Los Angeles County Jail, scolded him, told him he was throwing his life away. He never wrote back. The judge sentenced him to a prison camp, six months. I felt sorry for him.

While in Long Beach in 1988, visiting friends, trying not to think of my brother, I could not think of anyone else. I contacted Harry at the prison camp. I told him I'd drive up in a few days, visit. He sounded chipper, gave me instructions, said the drive would be hilly and take about three hours but I'd find the place as long as I had a map. On the day before the scheduled trip, driving around Long Beach with my friend Marty Berg, with the window down, the salty sea drifting into the car, feeling comfortable, I suddenly realized I did not wish to drive three hours into the mountains, searching for some prison camp. I wished to loll along the Long Beach coastline with my friends, eat grilled fish. I phoned Harry and told him I wouldn't be making the trip, told him I was heading back east. He cursed at me, then hung up the phone on me.

When Harry was released, he had nothing — no apartment and no car and no job. All the pretty clothes, gone. All the girlfriends, gone. Lou Gossett — well, Lou did not want anything to do with Harry. Harry had worn out his welcome with Cousin Lou. So Harry went downtown, past the beautiful Biltmore Hotel, past City Hall, to claim a place on Skid Row. Harry slept on grates. On chilly nights he built bonfires in trashcans and stared into the flames. He carried a pocketknife. He dropped from sight. One day he spotted the poster we had stapled at various shelters, seeking his whereabouts. Harry called home. Elvira, my mother, told him to come back to Columbus. But Harry had too much pride to return to Columbus. What would that have said about his California dreams?

My brother, a navy veteran, walked over to the Veterans Administration in downtown Los Angeles and turned his life over to them. And the navy tossed him a life preserver. He was enrolled in a special drug and alcohol rehabilitation program for vets. Then he got admitted to a program to train to be a nurse's aide. He did well in the program. He studied anatomy, physiology, charts and diagrams. He asked a million questions. The directors wanted to make my brother their poster boy: they'd point to Harry as a success story. A local TV news show had heard about the vets program. Harry, who had always been enamored of Hollywood, escorted a television crew down to Skid Row, showed them where he had once slept, waved to fellow bums, smiled at the camera with an actor's timing. He was featured on the six o'clock news. Harry insisted that the TV station make him a copy of the tape, and it did. When I first saw the tape — my brother's triumphant return to Skid Row — I stood tottering, caught between laughter and tears. I watched it alongside my sister Diane, and she blinked, kept blinking, hard.

After he completed his training, my brother was hired by the veterans hospital as a nurse's aide.

In 1993, when Los Angeles erupted in riot and violence and fire after the acquittal of the policemen who beat Rodney King, I was sent out to report on it. Before boarding the flight, we were told that once we were near Los Angeles, the plane would be rerouted to a nearby airport, because smoke from the fires made it impossible to land in Los Angeles. Already the National Guard was moving in, cutting off streets. I needed my brother Harry, and called him before taking off. He told me he'd get near the Orange County airport and gave me an address where I could meet him — a female friend's in Compton.

Upon landing, I rented a car, gunned the engine toward

Compton and my brother. A woman answered the door, disappeared to the back of the house, and rousted Harry from sleep. He gave me a tight back-breaking hug, as always. "Don't worry," he promised, zipping his pants, grabbing a hat, rushing for the door, motioning for me to follow him, "we'll get into Watts." My big brother was my big brother. We sped along into Los Angeles. My brother knew how to avoid the roadblocks, knew how to take back alleys to get to Watts. I'd see a dead end, he'd see another route out of the corner of his eye. "Turn here, a right, go, go, go!" Harry got excited. He took the wheel while I took notes about burning buildings, looting, National Guard soldiers hopping from trucks. We parked the car, and he watched it while I interviewed. I could tell that my brother would protect me with every atom of his body.

Interviews finished for that first day, we raced back to the hotel. I had a story to write and send back east; I was on deadline. Harry insisted that we stop. He needed a beer. Actually, a six-pack. He was tired. Reporting is exhausting. Did I have any money for beer? He almost whined the request out. I bought my brother a six-pack. He drank on the hotel bed while I wrote. Before I finished my story, I turned, and there he lay on the bed, asleep like a baby; I'd exhausted him. I noticed three empty beer cans.

The next day we did the same thing, driving fast down back streets and side streets, past the smoke and the ruined buildings. While we were driving out to East Los Angeles two days after the riots began, slowing down behind a line of traffic on a four-lane road, gunfire erupted. "Get out of here! Move! Now!" We looked around; it was a knot of teenagers firing a rifle, crouched like Wild West bandits. Later that day, the interviewing all finished, we raced back to the hotel to write another story. Stopped by a stoplight, my brother turned his head toward giggles coming from the car in the lane next to us. Two women, attractive. "Where are you all going?" my brother asked. They heard him; they pretended not to. Harry went through a long spiel about his brother — "right here," he said, jerking his thumb at me — "a reporter for the *Boston Globe*, staying at the Hilton. Care to join us?" he asked. They looked at him as if he were insane, and drove on.

We drove on, too. My brother asked me if I would go by and pick up his friend Jeff, give him and Jeff a ride back to South Los Angeles before the curfew that had been imposed. Harry phoned Jeff from a phone booth, told him we were on our way. We rolled up to a curbside. Jeff asked me to open the trunk; he had several large bags with him. I flicked the handle below the seat, the trunk popped open, Jeff loaded it and hopped in the back seat. Jeff was skinny, jittery; a toothpick played in his mouth.

As we rolled along, embers of fire still smoldering in the buildings, the National Guard soldiers marching around, Jeff started reminiscing about Vietnam, his wartime service. "Wil," he said, abruptly leaving Vietnam behind, "you know anyone who wants to buy some wedding dresses?"

I shook my head; I asked him where he had come by some wedding dresses.

"I looted them. From a store window. Right off the damn mannequins. They're in the shopping bags I put in the trunk. You wanna buy one?"

I veered to a curb, parked the car; my heart began beating fast. I'd be stopped, the trunk would be checked, the wedding dresses would be noticed, I'd be arrested, I'd be charged with looting. I'd lose my job. I got out and told Jeff to get out, to take the shopping bags. "I can't have you in this car with me," I said loudly.

My brother defended Jeff, ordered me to get back in the

car, ordered Jeff to get back in the car. I argued, wouldn't move. Jeff shook his head at me. My brother shook his head at me. Eventually I left them both at curbside, with stolen bags of looted wedding dresses, and sped off.

Later that night Jeff and Harry showed up in the lobby of my hotel. They wished to apologize — and they wished to borrow my rental car so Jeff could go see a lady who lived "in the valley" and, he said, might want to buy the wedding dresses. They looked red-eyed; they looked high. I asked them both to leave. We exchanged loud words in the lobby. Heads turned. When they left, I checked out, switched hotels. I slept uneasily that night. I left charred Los Angeles without saying goodbye.

My brothers were both Jack's boys. They had reached for things in life with such flourish and such flair. It had been so easy to believe in them, that they would find treasure in California. I was sad that it had all gone so badly, turned so dark. Harry suffered more. Harry reached mostly for fun, and when the reach became too difficult, he turned desperate, stumbled badly into the darkness. Macaroni, who had already been to darker places than Harry, went to the edge of the cliff smiling, and when he tumbled over, he rose, alone again, smiling again. They were chasing dreams, just as I had done. But dreams cost.

Of my two brothers, it was Macaroni who first decided to swallow the bitter pill of wounded pride. When he was released from San Quentin in May 1992, he bought a ticket home to Columbus. I flew from Boston to meet him. There would be a big family celebration, a picnic on the river, our old family spot, where we had played as children. Shortly after arriving in Columbus, I reached Macaroni by phone. He was actually living out in Grove City, in the middle of farm country, where the corn grows high. He had to lay his head where he could, and he was laying it next to a woman who had hung a picture of him — he had sent it from San Quentin — in her bedroom. As ever, his voice was hale and full of heart. There were so many plans, ideas. He wanted to see me. He had so many things he wanted to tell me, he said. We agreed to meet for a bite to eat, right away. "Meet me at the plaza over on Mt. Vernon Avenue," he said.

14

I STOOD in the parking lot of the Mt. Vernon Avenue plaza, where he had told me to meet him, on a clear summer's day in 1992. I had flown home from Boston. I had not seen him in several years. It was easy to imagine that a couple stints in San Quentin Penitentiary would be hard on any man. So I imagined that Macaroni would look a wreck, disheveled. He eased from a car. He turned, looking for me. When he spotted me, yards away, he smiled. Then came the long loping strides, the broad shoulders twisting. "How do I look?" he asked when he reached me, spreading his arms wide, still a vain man.

He looked remarkably fit, still suave. It had always been so with Macaroni, who was able to lift himself back up from disaster, able to crisscross storms and howling winds and come out standing up, the clothes tucked in just so, the smile still wide. The many lives of a man — pimp, con artist, prisoner, road runner. He had bummed a ride over to the plaza, and after we began our chat, he turned and waved his driver off. He looked at me, head to toe, always taking the measure of a man or woman — how they looked. Whatever his conclusion, he always kept it to himself. "Let's go," he said, walking off already, still looking at me the way a tailor looks at a man in preparation for measuring him for a suit. "Well, well, well," he said.

We eased onto stools in a dark bar. Macaroni couldn't stop talking. Free as a bird, *chirp chirp chirp*. He had plans. He might become a salesman. He might lecture — about crime. He mentioned the Watergate burglars, how they had served prison sentences, got out, and hit the road, mesmerizing audiences. And he mentioned writing a manual about how to foil pickpockets, telling me that millions and millions of dollars are lost annually to pickpockets; picking pockets had once been his modus operandi. He confided, his voice sounding almost puzzled, that he had actually never had a full-time job. A life lived by wits and on the run. He talked about days he described as good old days, when he could float from town to town, before computers, before high technology. He recalled the days when being a criminal was fun; now it was work, drudgery. "How's Boston?" he asked. "Maybe I'll come and try Boston." I got nervous, changed the subject. Every five minutes or so, someone would recognize him. "Hey, Macaroni! When you get in town?" When he got tired of people who recognized him, he stood up and we bolted out the door, heading across the street into the Macon, another dark bar. When we left the Macon and walked out onto Mt. Vernon Avenue, a knot of men hunched beneath a streetlight yelled his name. He turned to face the darkness, yelled out some hi's, and kept going, moving like a man eager to climb on top of something. He cadged some money from me, told me he had business to take care of; I should go on home, he'd catch a ride home. I wondered to myself that night, what becomes of old pimps?

Days later I rose early, along with other family members, for the welcome-home family picnic for Macaroni. Harry had flown home from Los Angeles — I had bought him a plane ticket — and was subdued and in sunglasses. There was still tension between Harry and Macaroni, because of things that had gone wrong in California. They were still unable to forgive each other.

I got excited, tingly, every time we journeyed back to the river. And every time we turned off the paved road onto the scuffed dirt road that led us to our sacred spot, we were all gripped by fear that some other family had claimed our spot. But they never had. It was always there for us, a couple acres of land, clearer than a good picture come to life, trees and grass and small sloping hills. Our town, our river, our piece of land. I do believe that if someone had ever been in our spot, we'd have simply turned the cars around and returned home.

We poured coal into grills, spread blankets, got lazy, looked back down the road now and then. Macaroni said he'd show by eleven o'clock. Noon came and went. Another hour came and went. Then there was the noise of an auto, the engine belching. A noisy car came to a stop on the road, raising dust and gravel, a small two-door thing, a jalopy. Macaroni lumbered out, as slow as a swollen athlete. For a picnic he was overdressed: red silk shorts, matching red silk shirt; a clean smile, a pair of clean sneakers. Denise — we later learned her name — was behind the wheel. Denise wore a pair of hot pants, which I hadn't seen on a woman in a long time, and wild loopy earrings. In that rustic setting, she smelled like a bag of opened cosmetics. She sat on a lawn chair, as proud as a diva, now and then raising her hand and swiping at the smoke that lifted from the grill. She didn't offer to help prepare the food. But she was smiley and chatty, talking to my sisters about nightclubs she had enjoyed a decade earlier that had now closed. Everyone was afraid to ask her what she did for a living, so we made small talk, laughed. She said she loved Macaroni. My mother rolled her eyes.

Macaroni and I went to fetch a trashcan that sat at the bottom of a hill against a tree. During our walk to retrieve it, shoulder to shoulder, for some reason I couldn't resist asking him something I had long wanted to ask. I wanted to know how he had survived life in the penitentiary. Even the name San Quentin sounded like something out of an old Burt Lancaster movie. Hovering at the edges of my question were thoughts about beatings, cellblock conspiracies, rapes. Macaroni said his survival was due to a combination of things. He was older than most of the other inmates, and they looked up to him as a wise old con. And he always was able to snare the best jobs. "Sometimes I'd get a job running errands for the warden. That was a privileged job," he explained. "Or I'd do some cooking for the guards. They liked my cooking. And you know how people just generally like to be around me. I'm a good entertainer."

The afternoon sun settled around all of us, its heat lessened by the thick trees. We listened to music, nibbled on food, offered words of encouragement to Macaroni about life, about starting out anew, about being home. There was much gaiety, and I felt that the women in the family were happy that Macaroni, Harry, and I — Jack's boys — were together again. We loped off down the road toward a basketball court set in an opening, me and Macaroni and Harry joined by cousins and family friends. The games were sweaty affairs, intense, and when Macaroni threw a particularly nasty elbow into my side, I said he was playing "penitentiary ball." He shot me a hard penitentiary look.

Everyone wondered what Macaroni would do. He had no high school diploma, although he rattled some words out one evening, too fast for anyone to believe, about having received a high school general equivalency diploma while in San Quentin. Three weeks out of San Quentin, one week back in Columbus, he had moved in with Denise. She lived twenty miles outside Columbus, in a place called Grove City, a small country town surrounded by fields. Macaroni couldn't stand to be so far away from Columbus itself, dependent on Denise and her car, so he moved out. He laid what few suits he had been able to rustle up since being home across his arm and moved in with Paula, another girlfriend. He carried his personal items in a paper bag.

Paula was tall, hazel-eyed; had been, as they say, around. She worked downtown, as a secretary. She walked with her back straight, as if she had attended finishing school, which she had not. She was starry-eyed and wild about Macaroni. "He's going to talk his way into heaven someday," she told me.

Macaroni found work. A promoter sent him on the road with musical acts, huge concerts held in cities across Ohio and Michigan for teenagers and young adults. Sometimes the multitalent shows could last five hours. Macaroni told everyone it was a job in public relations. Actually, he was selling souvenirs — trinkets, hats, T-shirts, brochures — following the concerts, his hands clasped in front of him like a priest's, rocking on the balls of his feet. He was good at such work, smiling, winking, a natural salesman. But something happened out on the road. Things came up missing. Macaroni was sent home. He didn't want to talk about it, said the job was beneath him anyway, announced fancifully that it was time to get serious about lecturing. It galled him that other criminals were making money off their misdeeds. G. Gordon Liddy, of Watergate fame, was even making dramatic appearances on episodic television! Macaroni thought there was value in his life, in the wrong way it had been lived, in the fact that he had survived. So he started writing down speeches on lined paper, asking me to edit them. He grew more intense about this new endeavor by the day, wanting to gobble up the entire Webster's dictionary, wondering which local college had the best public speaking courses.

When I was back in Columbus one evening to attend a public event with my family — in fact, it was a little something thrown together on my behalf — Macaroni pulled me aside, wanted to introduce me to someone. It was James Jackson, the city's police chief. I had already met him, had no idea Macaroni knew him. We all looked back and forth at one another like guests at a surprise party. There was something that I noticed between Macaroni and the police chief that stayed with me. It was Macaroni's posture, his body language. In front of the police chief, he shrank, softened like putty, was almost childlike. I've now come to imagine that that was how he survived all those years in the penitentiary.

Later that same evening there was a little party at a swank supper club just north of town, with my family, relatives, friends. My brother Harry arrived, his coat thrown over his shoulder like Errol Flynn. He ordered a drink, turned to me, and asked me to slip him a twenty-dollar bill. "Don't let anyone see you do it," he whispered.

I spotted Macaroni on a sofa talking to Patti Doten, one of my first editors at the *Boston Globe*. Over the years she had become a dear friend, like family. That night she was wearing something black and dressy, with quiet jewelry. She was in animated discussion with Macaroni. "Your brother is absolutely charming," she said to me later that evening. I nodded, and down deep began to worry about just what Macaroni had been saying to her. They had been talking about his life, about her life — single woman, two children, fine home in the coastal New England town of Cohasset. A woman of means. I did not have the nerve to tell Patti later that Macaroni had inquired about her dating status, her house, her annual salary. "I like Patti" is how he put it. I told him to stop, to leave her be; I rolled my eyes. I told him he made me feel ashamed. Macaroni had adopted a habit of twirling away from people when they said something he didn't like. He twirled like someone on a pair of ice skates. When I told him he made me feel ashamed, he smiled, twirled away.

Paula soon began to notice things missing around the house — a scarf, a skirt, a blouse. Macaroni hunched his broad shoulders; he didn't know where they were. He twirled. Her son's overcoat; he said he had no idea where it was. But he had drifted back to heroin, had sold the clothing for money to buy drugs. Six months after his 1992 release from San Quentin, Macaroni was back hanging out on Mt. Vernon Avenue, making buys in front of the old Tyler's Drugs, then walking across the street and shooting up behind the closed and dilapidated Manhattan Club. Paula put him out, and this time there were fewer suits laid across his arm, fewer items to put into a paper bag, just loud and painful words, a door slamming shut.

He couldn't resume his pimping career. The young girls laughed at him. The older women had left the profession. He wanted to set a couple girls up in Las Vegas, where prostitution was legal, told them they could wire him his cut. They just laughed. Check scamming and forgery were now more difficult. Some of his old allies were still in prison, some dead; one former pimp was spotted painting houses on the east side. My sister Diane phoned me in Boston. She was worried about Macaroni. I told her that he was a grown man, told her there was nothing I could do.

He was strutting down the street and there they were, as

vivid as police officers. They weren't police officers, just ordinary Joes to whom Macaroni owed money, two sharks. They dragged him to a darkened stairwell, where they beat him with a baseball bat. He yelled something about the money, said he'd get it, needed another day, that's all, but the more he yelled, the more they swung, and they kept swinging. They were young men, in their twenties, muscled and mean. Macaroni was badly bruised. Hurt and with nowhere to go, he moved in with our sister Wonder.

Driving through downtown Columbus one morning, Macaroni made an illegal turn at a corner. A police officer on horseback, out of view, galloped after him. The arrest was made in broad daylight; onlookers gawked. Driving without a license and improper display of license tags. The arrest record, which I am looking at now, shows the date: 2–14–93. Valentine's Day. He did a week in the county jail and was released. Two months later he was arrested at Lazarus department store; theft. Lazarus agreed to drop the charges provided he never set foot inside the store again. He quickly agreed. But he was back two months later, believing that Lazarus was an easy mark, the older clerks were slow of foot, his charm was more irresistible than their alertness. Once again, however, store security was on to him, and when he reached for a bundle of clothing and attempted to flee, they grabbed him.

The courts had had enough and sent Macaroni to the Franklin County workhouse, a military-style building on the city's far west side. On a visit home I journeyed out to the workhouse with Ty, our cousin. Ty was fresh from a sandy foxhole in Desert Storm. We saw Macaroni before he saw us. He was preening in front of a mirror inside an open dorm, combing his hair, wearing workhouse blues and house slippers. The guard on duty had an uneven mustache and an

Appalachian accent and seemed quite cheery. All the other inmates seemed so much younger, seemed like kids, half Macaroni's age. He was unable to keep his hair dyed while locked up, and it had turned a cloudy white. He was pushing fifty. Behind the Plexiglas, twisting in the plastic chair, he seemed, as always, full of good humor, bouncy, animated.

"I'm going to be fine. Trying to get into rehab. I think the judge is going to turn me loose. Don't worry about me. But do me a small favor. Leave a little money, ten bucks if you can, with the deputies on duty out front. My account in here is empty, and I need to buy some things."

I left the money in his account, walked outside into the brittle sunshine, felt like sucking in my freedom, so I did. And I wondered, for the first time ever, if Macaroni had run out of line on any given life, out of rope. I wondered if he was on his way to spending the rest of his life in prison, in little increments — a year here, two years there, then you get sick, old, and old inmates only get older, start to feel chills day and night, close their eyes for good one day and then there's some guard standing over you, poking you in the chest, calling the coroner's office. I got sad; my cousin Ty got sad.

The judge instructed the county to escort Macaroni out to the Maryhaven drug rehabilitation center to be interviewed for possible admission. Diane took him clothing. Maryhaven, northeast of Columbus, is a bucolic place of quiet buildings and wide green lawns. The social workers have been known to catch patients out back, hiding behind trees, smoking dope. (My sister Wonder was booted out for such an infraction.) If Macaroni could get back in front of people, open-minded people, like the people he imagined to be at Maryhaven, he was sure he could sell himself. He had gone through this routine before, out in San Francisco, at the Delancey Street Settlement House. But the Maryhaven social workers did not like Macaroni, smelled something funny, imagined a con artist at work, didn't see much hope, and reported their brutally candid findings back to the judge. Macaroni spent the entire summer at the workhouse, was released and placed on probation.

He wandered around town like an itinerant, in and out of our sister's apartment. He stole when he could, borrowed money from friends — the ones who still called him "Macaroni" with reverence — and never paid them back. Now and then he'd be in the company of women. But mostly the women were desperate, bone thin, gobbling up sweets and drugs. Macaroni still had a touch of discipline: he wouldn't venture outside in the mornings unless he had a clean shirt. He told me this one morning when I had flown home to check up on him, give him money. I found myself lecturing him. Then came the little smile, the little twirl, him wanting to talk about global politics.

Then came a letter from the police department. The ghosts were now swinging from the bridge. It was an old charge, theft; Macaroni had given a false name; the police had figured out the ruse. He was charged, rustled up a lawyer, and was released. The lawyer told him he'd probably be sent back to prison this time, a likely sentence of two years. "I can do two years," Macaroni told me, the voice shaky.

But things were making him more nervous than ever. "I'm starting to get some omens," he said to me. "I think it's time to fold — the life, the women, the drugs, everything." He sounded like a sage. At rope's end, Macaroni was tired of the scams, of fleeing. He began to think of — wouldn't you know? — religion: "I had nowhere else to go."

There was the issue of a church, where to pray. He couldn't go to Shiloh. It was high-class — too seddity. Trinity, our family church, sandwiched between the Bolivar Arms housing project and Mt. Vernon Avenue, the long-winded Reverend Parham still there in the pulpit, was too risky: too many uncles and aunts — Jimmy's brothers, his in-laws — knew Macaroni's background, where he had gone, deeds he had done. The whispers at Trinity would be high; so would the well of suspicion.

Macaroni walked into the Refuge Baptist Church, next to the Macon Bar, across the street from the Mt. Vernon Avenue plaza. There wasn't another church like Refuge in Columbus. Its congregation was eclectic, peppered with reformed criminals, reformed prostitutes, reformed pimps. Reform was a huge religion at Refuge. The church's arms spread wide, welcoming all comers. Its ministers — many of whom had come in from the streets, the cold — were true believers.

Macaroni's friends howled when he mentioned he was going to get into religion. And his family laughed.

Refuge was a small church, its pews polished and gleaming, its pulpit laid out in red velvet, the ceilings high. It was the kind of church where everyone hugged everyone else during services, then again after services. It didn't have much, and yet it gave away much. It was one of those small churches that worked mightily, night and day, squeezing and squeezing its resources, then working tirelessly to replenish them. The Reverend Roderick Pounds had followed R. F. Hairston into the pulpit; Hairston's father, R. F. Hairston, Sr., had founded the church. In the heady days of Mt. Vernon Avenue's prime, it was one of the most popular churches, reaching out to serve the poorer members of the community, hosting Baptist conventions. Pounds was street savvy, surprised by little, hopeful that new and troubled members would reform, not too disheartened if they vanished and took again to the street, because that was life, because some fruit spoiled. In the pulpit he was theatrical, jumping around, howling. But there was no denying that his sermons were riveting.

Macaroni recognized some members in the congregation, men and women from the streets. On his first Sunday, a minister introduced him to the congregation. "We got Macaroni with us in the church today," he said. Many knew that name — Macaroni. The minister was candid, talked about Macaroni's just getting out of jail, being on probation, being flat broke. There were gentle smiles, head-nodding. There was no gasping. Many of these parishioners had risen from troubled waters themselves. They passed a collection plate just for Macaroni. Someone scooped up the money and handed it to him. It was sixty dollars. He was touched.

In the beginning he sat in the pew alone, holding a Bible, looking quizzically at its pages, as if it were written in Chinese. The ladies of the church thought him charming, spoke behind his back about his fine manners. He volunteered to do little jobs around the church; just before Easter he did some repair work in the bathroom. During church dinners he moved swiftly to set up chairs, rearrange tables. They began to call him Brother Gary. Old ladies held their arms out and he escorted them up the stairs like an English gentleman. One evening out on the street, someone who recognized him — from the past — offered to sell him a pound of marijuana for four hundred dollars, told him he could make double that in profits. Macaroni listened to the whole proposition; Brother Gary said no.

He began running little errands for some of the deacons. Now and then they'd slip him a ten-dollar bill. The deacons all the while were taking notes, about his attendance, his seriousness and dedication. The church ministry found him a job cleaning up apartment buildings, carrying a mop and bucket down long hallways. It was the first hourly wage job he had ever had in Columbus. He hated it, said some of the workers were smoking marijuana, waving the joints in his face. He said some of the girls were coming on to him. The church found him another job. He didn't complain about operating an elevator. It was numbing work, but he had to forge ahead. The Reverend Pounds began thinking that Brother Gary was ripe for some church responsibility. He hired him to drive the church van, to pick up members of the congregation on Sunday mornings. Brother Gary was prompt, never missed a morning, flattered the elderly church ladies, drove the van slowly and respectfully across Long Street, down Mt. Vernon Avenue. Sometimes at a stoplight, old friends who had noticed the church insignia on the side of the van would peer inside and spy Macaroni behind the wheel. They couldn't believe it. They stood staring, dumbfounded, motioning wildly for him to roll down the window. He would, listening to their cackling. "Just doing God's work," he'd say, a tight smile on his face.

Then came Helen. She was a divorcée, tall and leggy, with large, gracious eyes. Like most everyone else at Refuge, she wasn't naive about the gritty streets outside the church's door. Helen worked downtown, as a secretary for the state. Her concern about Brother Gary didn't seem unusual; caring was simply the Refuge way, the Refuge signature. She gave him a gift, his very own Bible. And he wrote some words in it, as if to himself: "I was once lost, a sinner by choice. But now I've been found and adopted by Christ. What joy. Thank you, Lord." He started to notice Helen's clothing, the brightly colored dresses. They were careful not to sit together in church, not in front of the whole congregation. But downstairs during Bible study they sat together, going over Saint Matthew and Saint Luke. When they were absolutely alone, he told her everything. Her girlfriends who knew his reputa-

BROTHER GARY, *alias Macaroni, and his wife,* HELEN, *today — stalwart members of Refuge Baptist Church in Columbus. Well, Amen.*

tion, who remembered when Brother Gary had been Macaroni, told her to be careful. But she found something fairly intoxicating about his honesty. There were long discussions about running from responsibility, about time itself, about religion, about men and women. Brother Gary started sounding as mournful as old entertainers sometimes sound.

Helen would not allow a man to move in with her without marriage. She had to think of the church; the minister happened to be her cousin. A man offered to sell Brother Gary a ring for three hundred dollars. Gary didn't ask where the man got the ring. He rounded up all but thirty-five dollars. Helen didn't ask him why he wanted to borrow thirty-five dollars from her. They were sitting in those uncomfortable chairs one evening in the church basement, during the weekly Bible study class, when, during a stretch of silence, the Bible study teacher stood up. "There is someone here who wants to get married," he said. Brother Gary had worked this all out in advance. Everyone looked around, including Helen. Then and there, Brother Gary stood up, asked Helen if she would marry him. She was stunned, looked around, saw joy in the eyes of those who sat around her, and felt Brother Gary's charm around her like warm clothing.

I received a telephone call in Boston. I agreed to be best man, though I couldn't help but feel queasy about Gary's being beloved by a church congregation. "My criminal career has officially come to an end," he said. He called again, days later: they couldn't wait, they were as eager as teens; they eloped, apologized to everyone, and honeymooned at a downtown Columbus hotel.

It was Gary's first marriage, Helen's second. Church members were joyful, believed there was no such thing as stretching faith too far, as believing too deeply. Elvira, my mother, hosted a little wedding party, with trays of food she had brought home from the hotel where she worked. Gary took Elvira to the church and introduced her around. She liked it right away, felt at home. "They're regular people" is how she put it — my mother's highest praise.

When Refuge played host to a large Baptist convention in Columbus, Brother Gary was given the responsibility of driving visiting ministers around the city. He took them downtown, showed them the new mall; he drove them down Mt. Vernon Avenue, chatting along the way, mispronouncing some of the new words he had been studying in the Webster's dictionary, but mispronouncing them so smoothly that no one snickered. He pointed out the few remaining stores on the avenue, sounding like a regular tour guide. At the end of some days, old Baptist ministers — the ones from Texas and Arkansas took a special liking to him — listened to him for hours, to the words about his incarceration and redemption and love for Jesus gushing from his throat. The ministers just sat and listened, breathing as easy as saints in their shiny shoes, nodding, thankful and feeling blessed for having all the proof they needed about the power of the Bible right in front of them.

Gary worked like a man who had been asleep for a hundred years and had to catch up. He learned every nook and cranny in the church, became a regular Mr. Fix-It. On weekdays there he was, gliding around the church, fixing a window one minute, opening the door the next, opening it to let in the desperate and wandering souls from the outside, some of whom recognized him, wondered what he was doing there. He was appointed to the Hospitality Committee, the Prison Ministries Committee.

One Sunday I sat in a pew at Refuge and watched Gary walk up to the microphone. "Well," he said, "we're getting ready to have a new roof put on the church. I'm going to be working on the building funds campaign. So don't be shy. Dig into your pockets. Wil, my brother, is here, right over there, visiting from Boston. He's agreed to make the first financial contribution." It was a lie, but I dug into my wallet.

He was haunted by his upcoming court appearance, a last bit of bad news from the past; two charges, theft and using a false name. Two years maximum, the lawyer reminded him. The Refuge hierarchy did not sit idly by. They wrote letters to Judge Marvin Romanoff, who would be sentencing Gary. The letters spoke of Gary's "good work" at the church, his "positive progress" with church responsibilities. Judges see thousands of pleas every year, made by family members and friends and clergy.

On the morning of his court appearance, the Refuge minis-

ters gathered with Gary. It was never easy, the kind of minis-
tering they did. There were woes every day. Someone needed
food. Someone needed help with an electric bill. A family
from Bolivar Arms faced eviction. Their congregation didn't
tithe as much as the Shiloh congregation or the Trinity congregation. They never made comparisons. They just tried
harder. Sundays often started out quiet — church readings,
announcements, the gospel band playing softly. But by the
end, two hours later, the congregation was jubilant, jumping,
hugging, crying. There were so many skeletons, ghosts, at
their front door. They did not wish to wrestle inwardly with
their emotions. So on the seventh day they let loose. Now, on
the day of Gary's court appearance, standing side by side with
him, his future once again in doubt, the Refuge ministers
prayed. Then they climbed into their cars, made a left out of
the church parking lot, a right onto Mt. Vernon Avenue, and
rode downtown to the courthouse to ask mercy for the reformed pimp who sat among them every Sunday.

"I stand here to humbly request the mercy of the court on
behalf of Gary," the Reverend Pounds said. "A man changes
inside. God, myself, and Refuge Baptist have got Gary now."

The judge lectured Gary about the errors of his ways, the
wrongs he had done. Then he sentenced him to two years.
The ministers in the courtroom winced. But in his next breath
the judge suspended the sentence and placed him on two
years' probation. Maybe the letters had worked. Maybe the
prisons were too crowded. Maybe it was because Gary hadn't
committed any crimes with a weapon. Maybe it was all because of Refuge Baptist Church. Maybe it was because the
judge was in a good mood.

The ghosts were gone now. Now Gary could genuinely get
on with his life, plan a future. He wasted little time. Again
there was talk about lecturing on crime and criminals. He'd

catch the city bus to the public library and sit at a desk and write about his life, the crimes committed, then he'd write little narratives about it all. There were plenty of criminals across America making money in the warm light of day by preaching about what they knew. He wrote a crime pamphlet. It was printed on blazing yellow paper. Under the heading "About the Writer," he wrote: "I was involved in criminal activities from the late 60s to the early 90s. I have been in prison many times, the juvenile diagnostic center and the Boys Industrial School as a youth, Mansfield Reformatory as a young man, San Quentin and Soledad State Pen in California as an adult. There are many different kinds of crimes. I will discuss the ones that I have been directly involved with or closely associated with someone who has."

The subheadings were varied. "Car Burglary" was followed by "Follow and Rob." About "Follow and Rob," he wrote: "This is one of the new crimes that has just come on the scene in the last 2 years. It is simply what it implies, the criminal picks an expensive looking car and follows it. Usually they will follow you to your home but any dark area will do. They are almost always armed. Jewelry, cash, credit cards or anything else of value is what they are after. There have been cases where the criminals will follow you into your garage and hold you hostage while they search your home for valuables." There was a section titled "Pickpocketing." "Pickpocketing is one of the oldest criminal professions still in strong existence today," the expert wrote. "It will continue to go on as long as men have wallets and women have purses. Most pickpockets operate in crowded areas. Racetracks, fairgrounds, concerts and so on. Also crowded streets and bus stops are popular areas."

He wrote letters to county agencies, offering himself out as a consultant on criminal issues. He stood in front of mirrors and practiced speeches. The Refuge ministers encouraged him. The Reverend Pounds wrote a reference letter, which Gary attached to his own letters. "Gary has a way of captivating the imaginations of those around him," Pounds knowledgeably wrote.

Refuge appointed Gary a church trustee. Helen was proud. Sometimes during her lunch break, she'd walk around downtown. "Mrs. Macaroni," she was sometimes called. She didn't like it and had to force a smile. What she liked was that her husband had changed. He carried a briefcase, he carried business cards — "Criminal Consultant," they said.

The Franklin County Juvenile Court indeed hired Gary as a consultant. He spoke with troubled youth, gang members. Once he showed up at a home for troubled youth wearing a sweatshirt, blue jeans, and a pair of combat boots. "This is what I wore in San Quentin Penitentiary," he said. "In San Quentin I didn't know if I was going to live or die from day to day." Some of the kids laughed, but he kept talking. He met the mayor. City council members sent him letters praising his work. His pay was more than he'd ever made legally, $260 per week. It wasn't a permanent job, only temporary. Still, it was richer than irony, Columbus paying one of its former inmates to spread the word about crime and crime prevention. One day I received a note from Gary in the mail. It was a check stub. "My last pay stub," he had scrawled on it. "Get paid every week. God is good to me." He went to churches — "black and white churches," he was careful to tell me — and lectured about crime and crime prevention. Before he'd leave a church, he'd hand out some of his self-published brochures.

The ghosts may have been gone, but not the old temptations. Every time he strolled down Mt. Vernon Avenue, saw someone who knew him from the old days, heard someone whisper to him about money, drugs, a scam, he'd pause. There were those who admired him as Brother Gary. But there were still those who admired him as Macaroni. So sometimes he walked down Mt. Vernon Avenue like a man stranded in the middle of a swinging bridge, and when he'd hear "Macaroni," hear it shouted out in all its long-ago glory, his mind would start tottering. And he'd swear Satan was trying to run him down.

15

I'D BEEN TRAVELING for nearly a decade as a journalist for the *Boston Globe*, living — though hardly complaining about it — like an itinerant, roaming across America, in and out of foreign lands. My visits home to Columbus were sporadic. On those occasions I'd steer the car down Mt. Vernon Avenue. So much seemed to be vanishing, getting away. I'd drive past the parking lot where Sandy's used to stand and smile at the memory of my friend Drac, who had slipped me free hamburgers when I was in junior high. I'd ride past the Garfield Elementary School, where my friends and I used to play basketball in the pitch dark, recognizing one another by voices ricocheting in the dark and the faint neon light that spilled from the nightclubs of the avenue.

In 1994 I returned to Columbus for a year as the James Thurber Fellow at Ohio State University: Woody Hayes's school. It was also Thurber's school, though Thurber never got his degree, left in a snit. (Thurber used to crack jokes about the university's obsession with football. His asides got printed up in the *Dispatch*, the local daily. A lot of readers thought Thurber was weird.) I moved into Thurber's house on Jefferson Avenue, the same house I had pummeled with rocks as a child. The house had gone from Thurber quarters to abandoned property to rooming house. Finally, the local historical society, sniffing the wrecking ball, had restored the place in 1985. They did a fine job. Elvira wanted to know if I had to pay rent to sleep there. I assured her I did not.

There were black-and-white Thurber photos on the walls of the house. Long nose, ghostly features. It is, of course, a widely known incident: Thurber was out back one morning, playing William Tell with his brother. The brother tried to shoot an apple off James's head; missed the apple, but not James's eye. Thurber's shot-up eye got worse over the years, until all vision was gone. But he kept drawing, using a crude device in later years to magnify his vision.

So much had changed in my hometown.

Mt. Vernon Avenue was all echoes now, memories. The Mt. Vernon Avenue plaza was still open, but there was bankruptcy talk every other week, tenants still coming and going, mostly going.

When Ernest Mackey retired from Spicer's furniture store, Louise Johnson took it over. She had worked at the store for years, in the back, out of the way — a bookkeeper. Who knew that she was squirreling away her money, that when the store came up for sale she'd stand up and fork over the cash? But she was shy around customers. When the door swung open, she sometimes jumped, startled. She boarded the place up, went home: it remains boarded up. When Mackey died, George Caesar Berry of the Chesapeake Bar & Grill gave the eulogy. Berry tripped on his wooden leg walking up to the podium. His words were beautiful, brought Mackey's daughters to tears.

William Toler, who had sometimes walked by us as we ate our hamburgers at Sandy's, was the last lawyer left from the avenue's glory days. Toler had come out of the West Virginia coal mines and worked himself through Ohio State University law school. (The state of West Virginia, wanting to keep its own law school segregated, paid his admission fees to Ohio State.) When white landlords had a problem getting rent from black tenants on the avenue back in the forties, they hired Toler. He was their strongman. He'd kick in doors, he'd grab men by their throats, he'd leave with the money. He stood five-foot-four. Toler, who had been awarded medals in World War II, who had an IQ of 141, whose middle name was Adolph, who was devoted to his wife, Toni, was considered something of a genius and one of the best legal minds in Columbus. He didn't believe in God. Now and then, in court, he wheeled and punched an opposing attorney. There were a couple of stays in mental hospitals: he'd call the wife on the phone, crying; she'd go get him. A lot of his clients were pimps, prostitutes — "he was the rock of Gibraltar," says Macaroni. Sometimes clients tried to stiff him on what they owed him. He'd ride up on them, all hours of the night, demand his money, and get it. Once a motley crew arrived at his house, two men and a woman, his clients. They questioned his legal strategy, raised their voices. He punched every one of them, tossed the men around his dark lawn, told his wife to go back inside.

Toler was the little big man of Mt. Vernon Avenue, and he didn't take its demise easily. When all the bars had closed — and how he had loved hustling inside a bar, looking around, shaking hands, patting backs, buying rounds of drinks, handing out his business cards — he opened his own bar. Opened it in 1988; it was called the Diva Den. It was right next to the Pythian Theatre. It had a kind of Casablanca feel to it; it was membership only; he wanted to keep out the riffraff. But then in 1993 Toler got sick, had to lock up the Diva Den, the last touch of class on the avenue. He'd sit home with his wife, brooding, nagging. She didn't mind, had long learned to tolerate him: actually, it was just love. He couldn't sit still to go on vacation. They went once, to Paris. He sat by the pool of the hotel, dressed in his stiff suit, complaining to his wife about his law practice, wondering what was going on on Mt. Vernon Avenue, wondering who back there needed him. She told herself never again.

By 1995, with his illness getting worse, Toler would sit at home at the kitchen table every day, scanning a calendar. He told his wife he was trying to decipher which day would be a good day to die. "He'd say he couldn't die between the fifth and eighth because those were the days of the Mt. Vernon Avenue Homecoming Festival, and he'd say he couldn't die on the tenth because that was one of his best friends' birthday," she recalled. She took him out to the festival that summer. He walked up and down the avenue once, got short of breath, sat in a lawn chair, greeted old friends, watched clouds crawl across the sky, went on home. He died three days later.

Five blocks up the street from Toler's Diva Den sat Carl Brown's market. His shelves were a little bare, but the store still opened seven days a week. And the old grocer still rose every morning and drove to work. He was long removed, of course, from riding down south, buying his produce from those Mississippi and Georgia and Alabama farms. Now he bought from wholesalers right in town; he still swore they were charging too much. His clientele was mostly low-income. The Mt. Vernon Avenue District Improvement Association still existed, and he was still its most powerful figure.

But now its meetings were mostly gabfests where the members complained about the powers that be downtown. Edna Bryce, the florist who used to climb the *Call & Post* steps on Saturday mornings, was forgetful, missing meetings, showing up on days when no meetings were scheduled: it was Alzheimer's. Brown's recent anger was directed at the city's housing authority. They had moved more than a hundred families from low-income housing near his market so they could renovate the apartments. The move hurt his business enormously. My Aunt Creola still shopped religiously at the store. Uncle Lacy, as fastidious as ever, complained of its disarray; there were things he couldn't find on the shelves; he'd mumble his way out the door, go to another store. My sister Diane would go there during the holidays to buy her chitterlings. There were always rumors that Brown was preparing to close the store. Just rumors, he said. "I'll hold on until I go."

I stood outside the grocery store one sunny afternoon jawboning with Carl Brown. He looked as brown — and weighed down — as a buffalo. I counted ten cars in the parking lot. A couple workers were unloading some goods from the back of a truck to take inside the store. Brown said that nothing made him prouder than the kids he had given jobs to over the years. He figured he'd given a few hundred kids jobs. I remember in both junior high and high school, friends rushed from school during ninth period to get over to Carl Brown's, where they held jobs. I never applied. I always wanted to rush and play basketball.

Monroe Junior High and East High were no longer basketball powerhouses. A lot of people said that was the price of integration — better schools, fewer basketball talents. The best basketball players, everyone claimed, were now playing in the suburbs, even for the Catholic schools.

Over at the *Call & Post*, Amos Lynch was still behind the

desk. He still had the scowl and the hard voice that never retreated. He still wore rumpled clothes, and he still cared passionately about the community. He was the driving force behind the city's annual Martin Luther King, Jr., breakfast, the largest integrated affair in the city. In earlier years it had been held on Mt. Vernon Avenue. But it had grown too big; now it was held downtown. I went to the King breakfast the year I was home. Lynch sat on the dais. A gospel choir swayed on a stage. It was the Morehouse College choir, and a couple months before the breakfast, Lynch had realized he didn't have the money — a sponsor — to bring it north to Columbus from Georgia. He went over to the offices of the *Columbus Dispatch*, long a conservative bastion and power in the city. Behind closed doors, he asked the paper if it would sponsor the choir's visit; it said yes. A lot got done behind closed doors. During those King breakfasts, Columbus looked better than ever — remembering, vowing to fight the darkness out there. After the governor spoke, he bent down, whispered something to Amos Lynch. Lynch just nodded.

One Saturday morning, when I knew Lynch wouldn't be in his office, I rode over to the *Call & Post*. I asked a reporter if he could get me inside Lynch's office. I just wanted to see it, to feel it without his presence. Once inside, I kept looking over my shoulder, fearing he'd burst through the door, fearing his voice. I wrote down everything that I found in his office:

A 1947 edition of the *Ohio State News*. (Lynch was fired from that newspaper: he was a cub reporter, too eager, sassed an editor, was shown the front door.)

A CMACAO Man of the Year Award.

A piece of fruit — an orange — lying in a wicker basket.

Sixteen file cabinets.

Five Merit Award plaques from the National Negro Newspaper
Publishers Association — 1952, 1953, 1954, 1955, 1956.

A tiny TV set.

A huge framed photo of the Mt. Vernon Avenue District
Improvement Association.

Four stacks of newspapers, from cities all across America.
(There seemed to be heaps of newspapers from Los Angeles.)

An oil painting of Lynch himself.

A huge photograph of the first Martin Luther King Memorial
Breakfast. (This photo takes up an entire wall.)

A photo of King.

A manual Olympia typewriter, which is old, dustless, and quite
beautiful.

Of course, this was more than just an office. It was a nerve
center, the place where Amos Lynch reached across black and
white Columbus, the place where he tried to keep the city on
guard with his newspaper and responsible for its citizens with
his conscience. Citizen Kane; Citizen Lynch.

In a way, it was amazing what Lynch had done with his little
weekly newspaper. Week to week, always a battle, hustling for
ads, never enough money to hire adequate staff, always caught
between tabloid journalism and advocacy journalism, always
having to abide the young reporters who swore they knew
more than he did about the business. (While I was home, the
IRS kicked in the doors of the *Call & Post*. Some unpaid bills
had been the responsibility of headquarters up in Cleveland.
Amos Lynch found himself without a paper. That lasted one
week. He knew too many people. He found some investors,
hired some hungry journalists, called in some chips from the
old days, went back to work.)

An old battler: in 1963 Lynch sent John Combs to cover the
March on Washington. When Combs arrived in Washington,

the *Call & Post* printers were just walking out on strike. Amos Lynch was sitting on one of the greatest unfolding stories of the time, and he had no printers! He browbeat Combs, told him to return to Columbus immediately following King's speech. Combs got going, as fast as he could, which wasn't very fast. He too fretted that he might have no outlet for one of the great stories. By the time he got off the plane, Lynch was grabbing his copy from his hands and rushing out to West Jefferson, on the outskirts of Columbus, where he rousted a printer from bed and had him print the newspaper. Amos Lynch got things done.

I'm sitting in a small home on the east side of Columbus. A midwestern summer breeze is blowing through the screen door. It has taken some effort, but John Combs has risen up from his bed. There's a dent about the size of a thumbprint on his forehead. It's from the brain surgery. His walker is over in a corner; he says he's getting along all right. There's a piece of paper in his manual typewriter. He had started to write something, then stopped. He wants to write, badly — to tell his life story, about being born on a plantation in Opelika, Alabama, in 1906. "I'm like Ulysses S. Grant, trying to write his memoirs on his deathbed," John Combs says.

There are shoeboxes filled with copies of stories Combs has written over the years. He grunts, reaches for one of the boxes. He pulls out the story about Betty Butler, the lesbian whose execution for murder he witnessed. He swears that that story has the makings of a bestseller. I ask him if there is anything he needs. "If I ever need anything," he tells me, "all I have to do is call Amos. He'll get it for me."

The years were rushing forward now like blown playground leaves.

I knew the voice on the line right away. "You know we just

lost Carl Brown," Amos Lynch said. "How would you like to cover the funeral and write the story up for me?" Somehow the question came out sounding like an order. I was too afraid to say no, anyway.

Carl Brown hadn't been sick, but he was seventy-seven years old. It was the heart. The funeral was held at the Union Grove Baptist Church, around the corner from Brown's store. Like a lot of other people that morning, I parked in the grocery store's parking lot. The lot was full; it had been a long time since Brown's lot had been so full. The church was packed. A host of city dignitaries showed. Amos Lynch sat at the end of one pew, arms crossed. Eddie Saunders, who had been my grandmother's favorite gospel DJ, read a poem: "When You Come to My Last Party, My Lord Will Be Your Host." It sounded homespun; the audience listened with rapt attention. Various ministers offered words. One minister asked all those who had ever worked for Brown, part-time or full-time, winters or summers, to stand. Pew after pew rose, at least three quarters of the congregation. The moment was touching. "Carl Brown put people to work," the minister said. Of course, no one mentioned Singletary's market and those dark days when it seemed Carl Brown might go under. "You want to give something back?" another minister asked. "Go back on Mt. Vernon Avenue today and shop. Go over to Carl Brown's when you leave here and shop."

Outside the church, in the sunshine, I spotted George Pierce taking the photographs. George Pierce didn't take a lot of photographs anymore; the occasion had to be special. The caravan turned left onto Mt. Vernon Avenue, and Carl Brown disappeared beneath the sun.

Waldo Tyler left town a couple years back. He was up in Cleveland, working in the pharmacy business on a gritty side of town. But somebody had to operate a pharmacy on the avenue; somebody had to continue to care. One night, with rain slashing in crooked lines, I sat inside Otto Thomas's pharmacy. Thomas first came out to the avenue in the sixties, after college, to work with the elder Tyler at Tyler's Drugs. He had hung in when old man Tyler died and the younger Tyler took over. But Thomas found it hard to keep quiet when young Waldo went airborne with the rush of the sixties inside him. Words were exchanged, bad feelings etched onto thin air. Now Waldo was gone, and Otto Thomas had a pharmacy all his own to run.

He's a large man, an army vet, talks with a lilting pause. He sounds like a onetime stutterer. I know a stutterer's pause, and I respect it. His smile is gentle and wise. He's been robbed six times, though never hurt. Friends have told him to get a pistol. "I've been in the army. That's the last time I handled a firearm," he says. A lot of nights his wife comes over from the suburbs, where they reside, to pick him up. "My wife's an angel," he says. He knows dope dealers hang out in front of the pharmacy, but old ladies who need medicine come through the front door. "Life is like this: you don't know who you can touch," he says. He tells me he sees kids watching him out of the corner of their eyes. Impressionable kids. He'll run into old friends in other parts of the city. They'll ask him what he's up to. "I say, 'Still at Mt. Vernon and Twentieth. Been twenty years.'"

Toni, the girl I loved in the ninth grade, married Rodney, the boy I envied, not only because she went out with him in junior high, but because he wore his leather coat open in wintertime, as if the cold really didn't matter. (Postscript: Toni and Rodney divorced, then remarried — each other.)

Flan and Olen moved away. Flan became a fireman, moved to Chicago. Still a rock for me to lean on at times. Olen moved to Tampa, married, divorced, moved in with a German woman. Flan and Olen and I planned a reunion not long ago. Flan showed, but not Olen. His girlfriend phoned me, said, "Wil, Olen won't be able to make the trip. I love him very much, but he owes me two thousand dollars."

I tracked down Bob Marsh, my junior high basketball coach, in Auburn, Indiana. He lived off a narrow road surrounded by flat farmland. I thought he'd be ancient; he was only in his late forties, and he looked remarkably fit, still married to Shirley, his wife of twenty-four years. He left coaching, bitterly, arguing with school officials back in Columbus: he told them they weren't being fair to inner-city schools; they told him in so many words that he was getting too big for his britches and he should mind his own business. Down in the basement he had stored a bunch of Monroe Junior High memorabilia. We leafed through some notebooks, shared a lunch, let a winter day's worth of daylight fade to dusk. Then it was time for me to roll on. He had half of a basketball court beside his house, beside the frozen field. There was a net on the rim.

So time had rattled on.

Jimmy, my grandfather, rose one Columbus morning, felt sickly, dressed, put on his fedora, grabbed his cigar, and walked a mile — easy for him — to Doctor's North Hospital. It was stomach cancer. They gave him a week to live. At night, in the hospital bed, he tried to get up, to leave, wanted to walk back home. They had to tie him down. "He's fighting," a doctor told the family. "He's strong." He could hear family voices from the bedside. He kept fighting. Heard every voice except Emily's. She couldn't bear to come, to see him tied down. Elvira, my mother, told me to bring Emily, his wife, to the hospital. She came in a shawl, her long black hair combed out, still lovely. "James," she said, "let go. It's all right." I was balled up in a chair of his hospital room that night, doing night duty. I heard a tussling of the sheets; I ran for a nurse. He had let go.

My grandfather's brothers gathered for the funeral. Jimmy was the oldest, their leader. Jordan Burke, always the strangest of the clan — appearing and disappearing without warning, leaving food on dinner tables, vanishing out a back door — arrived from Alabama. He was in country clothes. His shirt collar was buttoned to the neck. He looked like somebody out of an old Gordon Parks photograph. His corduroy jacket looked too small. His shoes were scuffed but rather elegant. Everyone was delighted to see him. Odd, sometimes, how the strangest can also be the most beloved. Jordan was the only Burke still trying to make a living at farming. He was having a hell of a time; he was hanging on; he talked about getting his crops in the ground. His voice was soft, almost feathery. I wanted badly to slip him some money, out of everyone's eyesight. But he looked too proud to stand for something like that. Jordan had come north by bus, and it was my job to take him back to the bus station. But when I went to pick him up the next morning, he was gone.

George Burke, the Burke who looked most like Jimmy, arrived from Arizona, seventy-five years old and sporting a huge white Afro. Henry and Lacy and Thomas, along with David and Joe, all still lived in Columbus. Together, aging, they continued to look like a powerful bunch of men. Henry, the baby brother, leaned over, kissed Jimmy's casket before it was laid in the ground. Henry seemed to take it the hardest. Elvira was as still as furniture.

Uncle Ira came one day soon after Jimmy died and removed his shotgun from the house. He barely said a word.

All of my grandfather's brothers had gardens. In the city. In their back yards. It was something I didn't realize until I moved back home for a year. Their way, perhaps, of holding on to their Alabama. You leave a place, but it still hangs on your mind; it crawls back, even if only in memory and through picking at dirt, watching okra and tomatoes and collard greens come up out of the ground. You could get lost in my Uncle David's garden. His cornstalks rose to my shoulders. He'd sit in a chair, yelling at me through a screen, telling me which ears to pick, which to leave alone.

My Uncle Lacy, the famous mink hunter, lived a block from Mt. Vernon Avenue, still did his banking on the avenue, wouldn't dream of doing it anyplace else. He'd recently fallen in love with some twenty-eight-year-old, let her move in. "I had the darnedest time getting her out of here," he told me one sunny afternoon, cackling. His pants rose high up on his waist, nearly to his chest. Uncle Lacy's furniture was old, 1940s and 1950s; it was inching up on antique mode. Newspapers were everywhere in his house. A couple of upstairs rooms were filled with toolboxes, slabs of wood. On the day I went to visit, Uncle Lacy prepared lunch. Before I arrived, he told me over the phone he'd prepare lunch, made a big deal out of it. He had a garden; I imagined I'd eat some fried tomatoes, corn on the cob. He served me a wiener and a cupcake; he set the table like a butler. He asked me if I wanted another wiener when I finished. I did not. After lunch Uncle Lacy grabbed a bag, grabbed my arm, led me outside to his garden. He was wearing cloth slippers. Large tomatoes hung from his vines like baseballs. I was amazed. He filled the bag with tomatoes. "Take these to Elvira," he said. "And take a couple for yourself."

Of all the brothers, only Thomas made trips back to Selma. He went every year. He participated in the reenactment of the walk across the Edmund Pettus bridge in Selma. He came back to Columbus wearing a "Selma March" hat.

Emily died four years after Jimmy, died in her sleep in the

home she and Jimmy had bought. When she died I was in the desert in Somalia for my newspaper; I had to rush home. As I said, my grandmother belonged to the Masonic society called Eastern Star. Every Sunday for years she had visited the women in the group; as she got older, there were phone calls. We never saw them. Yet when I looked down the row of a pew at my grandmother's funeral and spotted a group of women I had never seen before, I instinctively knew who they were. In hushed tones they recited details about me and my life, my sisters. My grandmother had shared our lives with them.

Now and then, riding around Columbus, touching up against childhood, I'd take a ride out to the Olentangy River dam: my old dam. I'd stand there, looking at the water gushing, listening to the passionate gurgling, remembering my days standing on those slippery rocks, the fear that gripped me when I fell into the water, the rising up so quickly — into sunshine, light, life.

Our town; my family. The family I've loved, the family that has at times frightened me. It has come to this: we've survived, held on. Harry and Brother Gary and myself: Jack's boys. Elvira, my sisters: her daughters. The darkness hasn't destroyed us, even if, as Emily knew, so much has come to light.

Jack, my father — or, as that beautifully titled Hemingway short story puts it, my old man — goes over to the avenue now and then to do a little shopping, see some friends. The rooming house he lived in when he first arrived in the city after the war has been torn down. My father retired from a lifetime of working on cars in 1992. His second wife had died by the time I returned home. I found myself visiting him often. I had never set foot in my father's house in all those years; I think I felt as if I'd be violating something sacred — his other family, their privacy. Sometimes, though, I'd wonder what the house was like inside. I'd circled it, driven by it, a hundred times or more. Inside it was spare, the floors a dark wood. You could feel the absence of a woman. Things lay about haphazardly.

My father made me feel as welcome as someone who has been away on a long journey. The visits made me feel good, warm. He'd talk about cars — new ones, old ones, stalled ones. He'd go off on long monologues about engines, car batteries, trade-in values on cars, used-car salesmen. "See, it used to be you could trust a used-car salesman. You can't do that anymore. Take this lot right down the street, over on Parsons. They'll give you a pretty good deal on some Chevys over there. Now, the Fords I wouldn't go near. And the foreign cars, well, you don't want to go near them. Parts too hard to find. Lord no, you don't want to go near the foreign cars. Of course, now I haven't had too many problems out of my Lincoln. Took it down to Georgia, let's see, year before last. Ran like a brand new car." He'd talk about the cost of paint jobs, of snow tires, of engine repair.

I don't know anything about cars, don't care much about cars. I'd listen to my father the way I listen to good jazz, in silence. I'd sit on his front porch and see my brothers, Harry and Macaroni, in him more than my own self. I'd see my brothers inside my father the way you see those little ships lodged inside those bottles on shelves in stores. You can't get the little ship out. You don't want to get it out. You know ship and bottle are forever linked. I'm more Elvira's boy; I carry her bony features and darker skin and sharp-bladed shoulders. Sitting with his legs crossed, his pants legs hitched up, my father would have slivers of bare skin showing at his shinbone. The hairs on his shinbone looked wet; they gleamed. As I sat listening to my father, smelling his cigar smoke, I wished I knew more about him.

Once my father and I took a drive together down to Cincinnati to see his sister, my Aunt Bertha. He talked nonstop, like a country store clerk. Somewhere, however, between Springfield and Dayton, the land flat and brown, whizzing by, he grew silent. I felt him looking at me out of the sides of his eyes, his face angled in my direction just so. Something was on his mind. Then he said, "For the longest time I've been trying to figure out how you became this writer. For the life of me, I couldn't figure that out. But now I think I know. See, my daddy — who, by the way, was as tall as you, no, taller even — used to go out by this tree down there in Georgia. He'd sit all by himself. He'd pull a pencil from his coveralls and a sheet of paper from his pants pocket. He'd start writing stuff down. Be out there writing most of a morning. It would be his list of things he wanted to get from the grocery store and the feed store. He'd just write and write. So I guess he was a writer too. That's been passed down to you." I wasn't about to argue with my father's logic.

Before she died, my Aunt Gussie, also my father's sister, told me what had happened in a courtroom one afternoon. My grandmother Frances had left Georgia land to her children before she died. The children, getting on in years, wanted to sell the land, reap the profits. The land would be sold to the Atlanta Electric Company. There was general agreement among everyone, the sole exception being my father, on a small technical point. Jack tried to broker a deal to hold on to a couple acres. People in that room stared hard at my father. He said, "My boy is a writer. Now, I don't know what-all writers do, but I know they need quiet. So I want to keep a couple acres of land for him. He might want to come down here and build himself a cabin or something. Do his writing." He didn't get his way. But the story touched me, touches me still.

Some afternoons, before going to see my father, I'd go visit some farms out in the country, pick us up some fresh tomatoes, some corn on the cob. Jack would rather tinker with an engine than plant some tomatoes. I'd come through his kitchen door hauling food and bringing forth a smile from him. My old man hates eating alone. He dances around a kitchen quite well, an old navy cook who had to keep the grease in the pot as the ship rocked out there in choppy waters off Saipan. We'd sit together and eat, watch the sun fade and dusk roll over us, watch dusk turn into night. Because he couldn't see the cars coming down the street, he'd lean forward a little, listen to the engines. "Now you see, this here Ford that's coming up is a pretty good car, though you don't want to keep it more than five years before turning it in." One evening, feeling lazy, feeling that maybe I could catch my father off guard, I asked him why he had left Macaroni down in Georgia. His head jerked. "I don't remember why." I knew not to ask again. Jack, like Elvira, doesn't look back much.

Through the years my mother learned to be alone, to live alone. There were fewer and fewer knocks at Elvira's door by gentleman callers. My mother was different, when it came to men, from her sister Creola. Elvira was an island. Creola, for all her strength — she knew she was much stronger than her sister — seemed adrift in the world without a man, a husband. Joshua, her first husband, had died in that horrible truck explosion. She simply separated from Charles, her second husband, when she came to live with us in Bolivar Arms. In 1979 she met Clarence Wallace in the kitchen of the Sheraton Hotel, where they both worked. He was a big, blustery man who preferred silence to conversation with his coworkers. He took a fancy to Creola. They began dating. The courtship was brief before their marriage downtown at the courthouse, with my mother standing next to her sister. Creola had grown lonely living in the tiny home she had purchased.

Emily, my grandmother, didn't like Clarence, thought he was too distant. Clarence drove motorcycles, big souped-up machines, wore leather, belonged to a weekend motorcycle club. It was a sight to see Creola in her leather outfit on the back of a motorcycle, wearing bright red lipstick. Creola was in her mid-fifties, cooking by day and zooming around rural Ohio on the weekends. My mother was happy that her sister was happy, but my mother did not like Clarence.

The beatings came when he was drunk. His mood shifted drastically. He came to work at the Sheraton once when he had been drinking. He began yelling at coworkers, making threats. He went into the giant freezer to fetch some meat; the coworkers slammed the door shut, called the police. For some reason the boss gave him another chance. Creola was silent about the beatings. When her bruises were visible, she avoided Emily and Jimmy and Elvira.

Back from a summer motorcycle trip — August 23, 1979 — the drinking began. Creola drank until she was satisfied, then stopped. Clarence drank until he was angry, and he kept drinking. He went from stumbling to making threats to swinging at Creola. He grabbed her arm, twisted it. She felt a bone break; she ran from the house. He yelled for her to come back; he was swinging wildly, at thin air, lumbering after her. The only place for her to go hide was the garage. She kept a handgun in the garage, hidden in a corner, behind bric-a-brac. Standing at the garage doorway, he had a metal pipe in his hand. She was cornered, crouched, pleaded with Clarence not to come any closer, and when he did, raising the pipe, she fired. Two shots.

Creola was taken to the hospital, with bruises and broken bones. Clarence was taken to the county morgue.

It has always been inspiring to watch my family, cornered by misery, come together in times of crisis. Jimmy called his brothers. Then he reached for his hat. Everyone was to meet at the hospital. My father, Jack, picked up my mother. Creola, being wheeled down a hallway, raising her head, spotted Jack before she spotted anyone. "Jack, I didn't mean to kill him." She was nearly screaming. "I just wanted him to stop beating me."

The police came to the hospital. Jimmy and his brothers stood resolute. In the past Jack had gotten into arguments with these Burke men, but all that was dust now. Jack stood resolute too. Some of my grandfather's brothers wanted at Clarence now, even with the man dead, for what he had done to their niece. They cursed the dead man in low voices, rubbed the brims of their hats. The police knew who had shot and killed Clarence. Creola was charged with manslaughter. Every Burke man offered to post bond. They'd use their houses as collateral; they'd go to their bank accounts. Jimmy used his house. This was his daughter. He wouldn't hear of anyone else pulling a dime from his pocket. Elvira was proud of that, proud of her father.

Jimmy and Elvira — Emily was too nervous — rode over to see the lawyer Otto Beatty, Jr. He was Myrna and Otto Senior's son; they owned the Novelty Food Bar, where my mother finished off her Mt. Vernon Avenue nights eating and where I took lunch breaks from the *Call & Post*. Myrna and Otto sent their only son to law school on profits raised from the money made on liver and onions, on fried chicken and lemon pies. The young Otto Beatty said he was going to defend Creola on the grounds that she had been beaten; she had no choice but to shoot her husband, she was trying to defend herself. It did not take him long to find a list of women who would be witnesses to Clarence Wallace's abuse of women.

ELVIRA *and* CREOLA, *holding on.*

I expected, at moments like this, that my mother would break, reach for the bourbon glass, knock back a drink, then another, until all her woes were blurred, until she finally fell away from the world, into sleep. But she did not. My mother steeled herself, and you could tell she was being challenged, standing at her screen door, waiting for my Uncle Henry or my father to come pick her up, take her to visit her distraught sister. Sweet Jesus.

Jimmy kept his brothers aware of the court date. He'd tell them the time, the courthouse, and he'd say it like it was a military operation — full of gruffness. He didn't have to ask them to show up for support; they knew what they had to do.

The testimony from various women was grim — stories about Clarence drinking, hitting them with bottles, sticks, his fists. In the courtroom, Creola explained what had happened.

Her voice quavered. A defense of wife abuse seemed a relatively novel thing in 1979. The jurors listened wide-eyed. Creola was acquitted. The Burke men nodded to one another. Then they went home, Uncle Henry to his wife, Carrie, Jimmy to Emily.

Elvira hadn't taken a nip during the whole trial process. But now it was over, her sister had pulled through. She tiptoed to the cabinet, reached for her bottle. Times like these we didn't really frown at our mother's drinking. At the last minute, a parachute had opened. To us, she had earned her drinks, her safe landing.

Of all the urban gardens in my family, the largest one was tilled by my Aunt Creola. The things she couldn't find at Carl Brown's grocery, she simply grew in her back yard. She'd spend hours canning vegetables for wintertime. In 1980, Aunt Creola remarried. She met Fleming at a bar on Mt. Vernon Avenue. He didn't have a job. He didn't have a bank account. When they rode to Detroit once, she found out he couldn't read. He said he didn't need a map, he knew where he was going; then he started missing exit signs. They drove and drove; she kept quiet. There was curiosity from various corners of the family as to why she wished to marry him. Maybe it was guilt, from shooting Clarence. Maybe she simply chose to make generous allowances for human flaws rather than be alone. She lived happily with Fleming. And he never raised a hand to her.

Aunt Creola would bring bags of vegetables over to Elvira in the late afternoon. Aunt Creola also did most of the cooking for our family reunions. Our most recent was in the summer of 1995. Relatives came from Gary, Indiana, from Detroit, from my mother's Alabama. Aunt Creola cooked mounds of food, set it atop trays, with decorations. Music poured out of large speakers in her back yard. Fleming, shirtless, stayed at the grill, sweat pouring off his back like rain, his small eyes as red as cherries: been drinking. I never saw Aunt Creola take a bite. She just kept refilling her food trays. An hour into the reunion my mother was stumbling. We — her children — tried to look away. We hoped no one would notice. Everyone noticed. Harry told me to take her home. "Don't touch her." That was her sister Creola talking. "Just leave her alone."

A month following that reunion, Aunt Creola suffered a stroke. I wondered if we had driven her too hard in making preparations for our get-together. Family gathered at the hospital: Burke men in fedoras; her children; my sisters; Elvira and Jack pretty much around the clock. The doctors said she'd pull through. There would, they cautioned, be some physical therapy; her speech would be slurred. Too many people were in her hospital room. She worried about who was missing work. Her work ethic was huge. One must not miss work. "You make sure you go to work tomorrow," she said to my mother one night as my mother was walking out the door. The next morning she was dead. The doctors said she had taken a turn for the worse in the night.

My mother played the stalwart during the mourning, during the funeral. Comforting others, making the long-distance phone calls, holding us together, not touching a drop of alcohol. Insurance papers had to be signed. But Fleming, my aunt's husband, vanished. Harry and I drove for hours looking for him. We found him inside the Mt. Vernon Avenue Loveland Bidwiz Social Club. It was just a house with a little sign thrown up over the mailbox. Inside, men sat drinking, smoking dope, playing cards. Harry balled his fist at Fleming until he finally rose and came outside. He was disoriented, kite-high, so we left. We just told Elvira we couldn't find him. Now and then I'd notice my mother in the kitchen, standing at the stove all alone, swimming in silence.

By any measure, she's come a good distance from a small farm in the woods of Alabama.

A few years back I made a trip down to Montgomery, my mother's neck of the woods. I went to interview George Wallace for a story. He was, of course, wheelchair-bound from those bullets during that aborted presidential run, that epochal year when his movement hissed like snakes and he rolled across the land like some modern-day Elmer Gantry. Sitting in his wheelchair, he spoke in a low and hollow voice, like a voice from shadows. He wore a red cardigan that swallowed him; his head turned now and then, as slow as a turtle's. There were pictures on the walls — the governor and world leaders, the governor in his youth, as a boxer. In the boxing photo he looked sinewy, fearless. I didn't expect to see the picture of him in the schoolhouse door, and didn't.

I wanted him to know of my links to Alabama, that my mother was born in the state.

"Is that right?" he asked.

He wanted to know where she lived. I told him Ohio. He wanted to know if she came back to Alabama.

"She's never been back," I answered. Deep down, I think I wanted to make him feel a little guilty.

He grew silent; his head bounced a couple times.

"Will you please tell Mrs. Haygood I'm sorry if I've caused her any pain. Will you please tell her this is a better Alabama than it was long ago. Please. Will you do that for me? I'm not a bad man. Will you please tell Mrs. Haygood to come to Alabama? Bring her to visit the governor. I'd love to meet your mother."

He sounded tragically sad. I felt sorry for him, and wished I had not mentioned my mother.

He pulled a picture of a small girl from his desk; no more than seven or eight years old, in pigtails. He turned the picture over: "From Marion — to Governor Wallace — I love you." "That tells it all," he said, turning the picture back over, pressing the little black girl's picture into my palms. "Tells it all."

My mother was forced to move off Mt. Vernon Avenue. The apartment she lived in was scheduled for renovations. So she moved around town, from apartment to apartment, living alone, and finally back to Emily and Jimmy's house. She moved back after Jimmy died, so Emily would not be alone. Sometimes they'd call each other "sister"; I found it charming. When my grandmother died, Elvira didn't want to let go of the house. I urged her to: too much trouble, too many repairs. But she would not. She doesn't come out and mention it: she keeps the house because a family member might come back through that front door; that's the Emily and Jimmy in her. She had two dogs, both mangy. The deaf one ran off one day, never came back. My mother sadly mused that he might have been hit by a car; in addition to being deaf, the dog had only one eye. Jack, my father, gets lonely, so he comes by often to visit my mother. They sit on the porch talking, about little things, big things, life. And automobiles. Jack brings things for Elvira. A lot of rabbit — my mother is still crazy about rabbit. They talk, of course, about their children.

Harry remains in California, still working at the VA hospital. Barbara, his longtime girlfriend, came home from church one fine Sunday, told Harry she had had a religious experience. She explained to him that she could no longer live with a man and not be married to him. Harry thought she was having one of those bluesy bouts of California introspection. She'd come around, he figured; maybe something as simple as another bout of lovemaking would do it. Three days later he came home and noticed his belongings at curbside. I commiserated with him long distance that night. He lives alone now.

He still hopes to appear in a movie someday, get himself one of those coveted Screen Actor's Guild cards. He feels that Cousin Lou let him down. But he's befriended Milton Berle: Harry works a part-time job as the doorman at the Hollywood apartment complex where Milton Berle lives.

Brother Gary continues to do battle with Macaroni. He's remained free, though, working a job. There was one relapse. Someone spotted the church van outside a drug den. Macaroni was inside, zonked. Afterward, Brother Gary felt ashamed, asked the church's forgiveness. Forgiveness being their calling card, he was forgiven. "God was talking to me," he confessed.

Wonder has seemed to right herself. Geraldine has moved into a senior citizens' home with a man who has one ear and professes his undying love for her.

A Columbus friend once told me that all families are the same. I don't think she meant the character makeup — the different personalities — but rather the manner of affection we give to one another, the things we do, sometimes against our better judgment, to keep a family intact, above water.

For years I had been trying to urge my sister Diane to leave Columbus. I'd tell her that she was shouldering too much responsibility for the sake of the family; I'd tell her the world was large; I'd brag about my own travels and new beginnings. I'd mention faraway cities she might like. She'd listen, nod, and just stay put. Diane's the Jimmy Stewart character in our family version of *It's a Wonderful Life*. If not for her, I might not have left Columbus; Geraldine and Wonder might not be located and dragged to our family house for emergencies. If not for her, Harry and Macaroni, gobbled up by the darkness, might not have been found. I might not have picked up that microphone at her fashion revue rehearsal and magically stopped stuttering.

The men in my family fled. The women stayed put, giving us a place to come home to. I now see there's plenty of bravery in staying put, claiming ground.

Diane and I might well be overly responsible for steering the family ship these days. But it's a blessed chore — though not without its difficulties in getting through storms, of facing storms not yet kicked up. More often than not, I'm at the head of the family vessel. It is not because I should be. Diane should be, for her gifts are the most bountiful. But from the back of the vessel, my sister can watch my back, can judge the water's depth. Diane alone knows that whatever I may bring to our family, I'm still haunted by a little-boy affliction: I still can't swim.

Acknowledgments

SUPPORT AND GENEROSITY came from various corners during the writing of this book. Peter Davison, my editor, tops the roll call. This is our third book together, and on this one — as with the others — his insights were profound, his patience remarkable. I could tell by the way Liz Duvall copy-edited the manuscript — with vigor, shrewdness, and passion — how much she cared, and I'm grateful. Mindy Keskinen, Peter Davison's assistant, took care of the little things, which, more often than not, were hardly little. Esther Newberg, my agent, was a keen and benevolent reader. The *Boston Globe*, where I've had a writing desk for a decade now, was unfailingly supportive: I am indebted to Matt Storin, Helen Donovan, and Greg Moore — and so very much to Tom Mulvoy. The James Thurber Foundation in Columbus provided a much appreciated grant. Phil Bennett, Ben Bradlee, Patti Doten, Mark Feeney, Stan Grossfeld, Paul Hendrickson, Jonathan Kaufman, Sharon Owens, and Mike D'Orso provided the balm that often kept a writer going.